DATE DUE

#47-0108 Peel Off Pressure Sensitive

AMERICA
and her
ALMANACS
by
Robb
Sagendorph

Wit, Wisdom
& Weather
1639—1970

Introduction

The writer is indebted to the librarians and curators of the Libraries and Societies listed under *Bibliography* and *Sources* in the back of this book. He is indebted as well to many readers and friends of *The Old Farmer's Almanac* who have been not only diligent but generous in their help and suggestions. In the past thirty-five years I have devoted myself to the study, as well as the publication, of Almanacs. In combining this practical experience of editing and research with the publication and sale of Almanacs, I have long felt a need, and an opportunity, for this book. Teachers and students will find it a valuable adjunct to their sources of American literature. The general reader will, I trust, find it informative—and in places—amusing.

Helen Shed, Esther Fitts, and Nancy Guild have been most helpful in the typing and retyping the various stages (no less than nine rewrites!) of this manuscript; Judson Hale on revamping and reorganizing the content, C. Robertson Trowbridge on production and distribution. The book was designed by Douglas Alvord and Carl Kirkpatrick.

R. S.

To BEATRIX, whose understanding, patience, and confidence has made possible, not only this book, but lots, lots else.

Contents

SECTION ONE

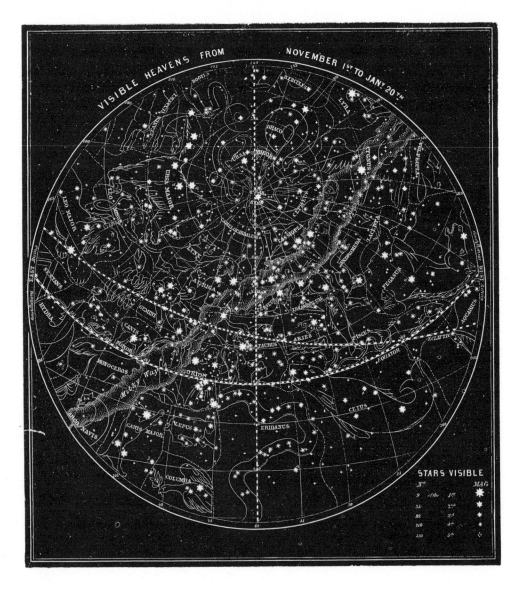

From the beginning

*Many almanacs were
being published long before the discovery
of America. One can safely say that
in most of the countries of the world
the almanac was its first publication.
This was only natural for
mankind has always lived
by the sun and moon and
stars and planets and has
needed some sort of a
calendar of the heavens
as a guide. This
chapter takes
you back to
those days
when . . .*

chapter one

calendar
of the
heavens

The stars in this drawing suggested to the ancients the form of PEGASUS

In all my years of experience in publishing *The Old Farmer's Almanac* and collecting almanacs of all kinds, holding one up before a friend or subscriber or visitor —no matter which one—has never failed to produce a smile. Exactly why this is, I do not know. However, as almanacs are of so ancient an origin, I believe that when 20th century man sees one, the sight tickles something in his funny bones or awakens some pleasant experience from the subconscious—hence, the smile.

Ancient origin? Yes, one must start at least as early as 3000 B.C. with the pyramids of Egypt, Latin America, and the South Seas. The word "Almanack" is apparently of Arabic descent and means a timetable of the skies or, in other words, "calendars of the heavens." When one could see the Pleiades, for example, through the opening at the end of one of the long halls of a pyramid, it would be Spring.

George P. Putnam, in 1856, summarized the origin of almanacs this way.

> The word "Almanac(k)" is of unsettled origin. Most antiquaries have supposed that the "Al," in this word, is derived from the Arabic article, which signifies *the;* but then, some derive the remainder of the word from the Greek word, a lunary circle, or the course of months. Johnson takes it from the Greek, μὴν—a month; others from the Hebrew, *Menach*—to count—or *mana*—a reckoning; others, again, from the Dutch, *Maand,* or German, *Moand*—the moon, or an account of every moon, etc. As the various rites and observances in most religions were regulated by the periods of the moon, none of these derivations are improbable. It is certain that the word Calendar, which is used in connection with our almanacs, was derived from the Greek, *Kaleo*—I call—because a sacrifice was offered at the appearance of the new moon by the proclamation of the priest. It is singular that all should agree to take the first syllable, *Al,* from one language, and the two last from so many different ones. It is probable that Verstigan is more nearly right. He says that it is a Saxon word; that the first of them were kept on carved sticks called *Al-mon-aght*—signifying, in old

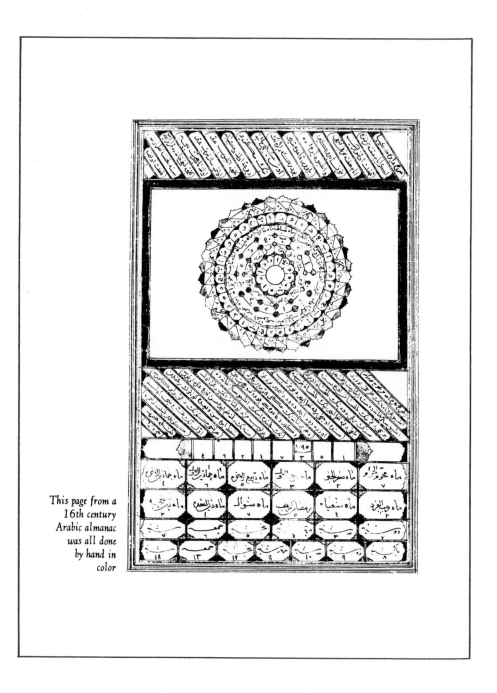

This page from a 16th century Arabic almanac was all done by hand in color

English, or Saxon, *ull-moon-head,* or the regard or observation of all the moons, and hence the word Almanac. This latter seems, at least, to have been the more immediate derivation, and the former more remote. The Egyptians computed time by instruments which were probably not so rustic as the carved sticks, which are represented by the runic almanacs, used by the Danes, Swedes, and Norwegians. These latter were called Reinstocks, Runstocks, Primstanes, Clogs, etc. The Egyptian Obelisks may yet prove to be almanacs or astrological calculations. The Egyptian priests called them "fingers of the sun." The Almanac was canonised as St. Almachius at an early date in the Roman Calendar.

The clog almanacs mentioned by Mr. Putnam were square and, by holding them to the sun, one could determine the date of church and royal feasts. They were introduced at the time of King Athelstans. These were eventually superseded by parchment, then paper. The first printed almanac appeared in 1475 under the imprimatur of Regiomantus.

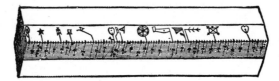

This Saxon clog
almanac was a square
stick about
2" x 2" and
perhaps
12" long

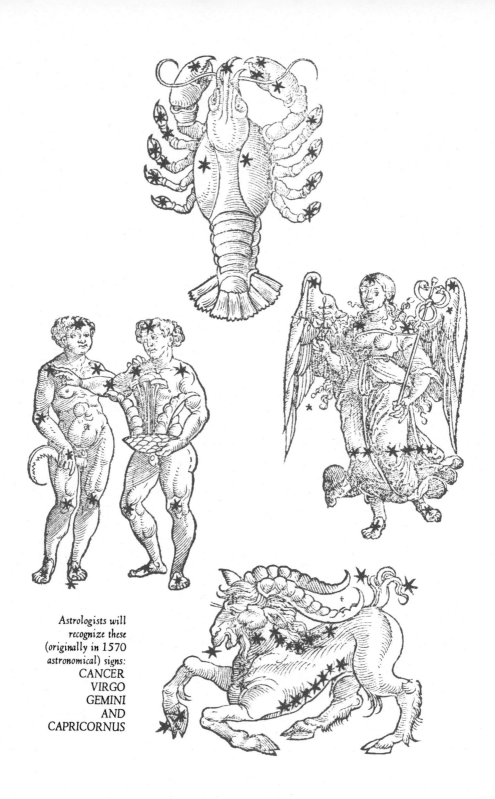

Astrologists will recognize these (originally in 1570 astronomical) signs:
CANCER
VIRGO
GEMINI
AND
CAPRICORNUS

Between 1200 and 1600, however, the beautiful, so-called Books of Hours appeared. In a sense these are religious almanacs, a calendar of Fast, Feast, and Holy Days. The workmanship in these treasures (the Morgan Library in New York has a superb collection) and the brilliance of their illustrations after all the years are matchless. You will not find too many of them outside of museums. I own one which was made in the south of France in the 15th century, and I suppose it, too, should be laid away under glass in a museum. But I like to think it gives more pleasure and instruction out in the open and free to viewers. I carry it to wherever I happen to be speaking, mention it, and invite individuals of the audience to come up afterwards and examine it.

Christine de Pisan
presenting her Book of Hours
to the Queen of France
about 1400 A.D.

15

The number of different almanacs published at various times in America continues to astonish me. One Milton Drake of New York City, for example, worked for some twenty-five years just to list the titles! His bibliography "includes some 14,000 entries and represents the almanac holdings of 558 institutions, 36 State libraries, 38 State University Libraries, 39 State Historical Societies, the Public Libraries of the 10 largest cities, and 37 of the libraries of the 50 largest cities. Also represented are the Library of Congress, American Antiquarian Society, Boston Athenaeum, and many of the great University libraries. More than 40 leading private almanac collections are included. Libraries in all 50 states are included." With Mr. Drake's check list in hand, either through purchase (at $35.00) or from a library, interested readers of this book should be able to find their way to whichever almanacs they wish to see first-hand.

• • •

These are the massive two volumes produced by Milton Drake. Among his other accomplishments is the song "Mares Eat Oates"

To study the old almanacs, of course, is to study *their* sources, too. The English "Book of Days," in two volumes, is something I have found rewarding. Each day is described in connection with its patron saint and everything of importance which happened on that day.

I also found a book similar to the Book of Days listed in an English bookseller's catalog this way:

(PERENNIAL CALENDAR) The Perennial Calendar and Companion to the Almanack; Illustrating the Events of Every Day in the Year, as connected with History, Chronology, Natural History . . . Popular Customs . . . with useful rules of Health, observations of the weather, etc. edited by T. Forster, 8 vo. bds. & lea. 803 pp. uncut. Lond. 1824.

This particular book proved to be not only fascinating to me but it contained the germ of an idea which eventually inspired this book you, gentle reader, are now holding in your hand. It reads as follows: "We could wish that there were such a thing as a history of Calendars and Almanacks, from the earliest recorded period of history to the present time; we believe that the first European Datebook, which assumed the title of Almanac, is the *Almanach Royale de France* of 1579; it includes notices of Postdays, Fairs, and Festivals." T. Forster, Editor, The Perennial Calendar, London, 1824.

There obviously had been no almanac history up to 1824 and there has been none since. But to fulfill this wish adequately would now take many, many volumes. So I've had to content myself with American almanacs —perhaps some other enterprising soul will do as much for England, the continent and other parts of the world.

However, even American almanacs, I have discovered are too large a subject to cover completely in a single volume such as this. Not included in my research, therefore, are a large number of "newspaper Almanacs" such as *The World Almanac, The Reader's Digest Almanac, Information Please Almanac. The World Almanac* is the oldest (founded circa 1868) of these, and *Reader's Digest Almanac* the youngest (founded a few years ago). Distributed nationally, they contain a vast amount of statistical information useful for reference purposes. I call them newspaper almanacs because there are many almanacs of this kind published for local consumption—Chicago Tribune Almanac, Providence Journal Almanac, Philadelphia Inquirer Almanac, etc. The World Almanac came out of the old New York World. Information Please Almanac, however, originated with a popular radio-television program of this name; and Reader's Digest Almanac from a monthly magazine of that name. The New York Times has announced its plan for one. These almanacs will run 200 to 500 pages long, cost close to $2.00 each, and have had, since 1900 anyway, a wide sale. As sources of statistical information they are invaluable. As such, of course, no editor or library would be without one, nor would anyone else who has a fascination for being right or for being bemused by the date when Forefathers' Day is observed, who served as Postmaster General under Buchanan and where the principal tornadoes have occurred since 1900.

Tracing the lineage of that vast number of old American almanacs known collectively as the "farmer's almanacs" has been no easy task. But at least these old Almanacs, once on the road, seldom changed format. One may differ slightly from another, but once an editor had introduced himself and his almanac to the public he pretty much had to stay with the contents and arrangements of his first edition. I learned at an early date why this had to be. After the late Mr. Loring B. Andrews assumed responsibility for the astronomical calculations of *The Old Farmer's Almanac* for me in 1940 (more on Mr. Andrews in my final chapter), I asked him to change the heading of the moon column on the left-hand calendar pages. Such a minor change as this evoked the following letter from a farmer of Nashua, New Hampshire.

Dear Sir:

I have read The Old Farmer's Almanac for the last seventy-five years and I wish the damned fool that changed the heading of the Moon's place column had died before he done it.

Yours respectfully,
F. C. Crawford

Typical farm homestead about 1810. This was at Cranbury, New Jersey on the grounds where Rev. David Brainerd preached to the Indians in 1746

Again, when I found that the right-hand calendar pages which carry the aspects, fasts, feasts, etc. for each day had become too crowded, I occasionally omitted the height of the tides for as many as three days. What a storm of letters that change brought! I had not realised before how very many clam diggers had to know these tide heights, not only for clam digging but for the unbeaching of their boats.

Clam digger on shore of Ipswich Bay, Massachusetts. Photo by Martha Harvey, 1895

This strong conviction that almanacs are not meant to change their format in any way is exemplified, too, in a supposedly true story—one of my favorites—dating back to the 16th century.

The King of France banished all almanacs because one of them had come out in favor of the Dauphin, but when these same almanac editors migrated to Germany, they again ran into trouble.

It seems that certain Prussians (who always were sticklers for science) complained through the German Scientific Society to Frederick the Great that there was too much astrology in the almanacs for the Society's approval! It was proposed that these almanacs be banned and a more scientific one be published in their stead by the Society. To this Frederick is said to have assented.

When the scientific edition appeared the following year an hausfrau asked her husband to bring one home with the groceries. He did, she took one look at it and killed him!

Although she was condemned to die for her crime, an act of Parliament not only pardoned her but decreed she had been justified in her actions. The old almanacs were back in favor once more.

● ● ●

As nearly as I can discover, the distribution of almanacs in Colonial America was largely conducted through country pedlars and bookshops. Often, a printing establishment would have its own bookshop. If it printed an almanac, naturally it would be on sale there. I have no way of knowing how many copies of any given early almanacs—even of The Old Farmer's Almanac—were sold in a year's time. I think there is a rumor of "never less than 50,000" but I could not—nor would anyone else—be able to prove it. I am inclined to believe that since most of the early almanacs were printed on one sheet of paper—eight pages on one side, eight on the other—that a first run comprised from three to five thousand copies. When these were exhausted perhaps two or three more editions would bring the total to ten thousand. Mathew Stickney, in an Essex Institute paper of 1878, states that the Ames Almanac sold 60,000 copies annually. The pedlars did not produce exactly great circulation for the almanacs. Their progress from house to house was slow. They stayed for hours at each house trading off pins, and pens, and thread, pots and pans and brooms, almanacs and Bibles, clocks, or what have you for cash or produce which, carried back to the city, they could sell for cash.

Photographs or drawings of the authentic early peddlers are hard to come by. The locale of this early one is Trumbull, Connecticut. The engraving on the opposite page is "The New England Peddler" by Henry Wolf

E. Johnson
1879

Henry Wolf sc.
1885

A great many of the bookstores, particularly after about 1800, had their own names printed on the front covers of the almanacs which they sold in their shops. This practice sometimes led, for example, in Springfield, Greenfield, and Hartford, to editions which would be localized by extra advertisements and text wrapped 'around the original almanac.

When the early newspapers began to increase their circulations there was more of this kind of thing. However, this was not regarded as helpful by old Nathanael Ames. He was quoted as saying the Boston newspapers couldn't tell the difference between his Almanac and several competitive imitations which spurious Connecticut publishers were distributing in New England. The imitators were receiving the publicity old Mr. Ames felt he deserved. This was how he expressed himself in 1765. "Never let me write again to the printers of Boston newspapers for they are all knaves, liars, villains to serve their interests and when they appear most friendly have most of the Devil in their hearts."

"Advertisements" reprinted directly from 18th century newspapers

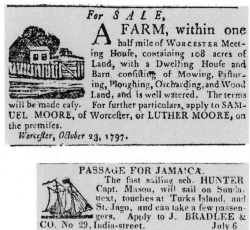

For SALE,
A FARM, within one half mile of WORCESTER Meeting House, containing 108 acres of Land, with a Dwelling House and Barn consisting of Mowing, Pasturing, Ploughing, Orcharding, and Wood Land, and is well watered. The terms will be made easy. For further particulars, apply to SAMUEL MOORE, of Worcester, or LUTHER MOORE, on the premises.
Worcester, October 23, 1797.

PASSAGE FOR JAMAICA.
The fast sailing sch. HUNTER Capt. Mason, will sail on Sunday next, touches at Turks Island, and St. Jago, and can take a few passengers. Apply to J. BRADLEE & CO. No 29, India-street.   July 6

CATTLE AND MEAT MARKET.

[Reported for the Boston Cultivator.]
Brighton, Thursday, Aug. 28.

At Market, 900 Beef Cattle—1200 Stores—17 pairs Working Oxen—84 Cows and Calves—5000 Sheep and Lambs—450 Swine.
PRICES......BEEF CATTLE—Extra, $6 25—First Quality, 6 00—Second, 5 50 @ 5 75—Third, 4 50 @ 4 75.
STORES—Two years old, $12 @ 16—Three years old, 20 @ 26—Yearlings, 8 @ 10.
WORKING OXEN—$70—85—90—100.
COWS AND CALVES—$20—24—26—31—35—40.
SHEEP AND LAMBS—$1 50—2 00—2 50—3 00—3 50.
SWINE—4½c—Retail, 5 @ 6. Fat Hogs, 5.

[Reported for the Boston Cultivator.]

Publicity? What did the old time editors do? My studies indicate that before 1850 there were very few paid advertisements of any kind. There were announcements of horses and cattle for sale, ships wanting cargoes, stage schedules, and land opportunities. But they were more notices than they were advertisements—simply listings of what was available. I do not recall seeing any paid advertisements for almanacs in any of the old newspapers of that era. Once in awhile, however, in a weekly publication like the *New England Farmer* there would be what we today would call unpaid-for reading notices. This one for The Old Farmer's Almanac appeared on December 28, 1842:

THE FARMER'S ALMANAC FOR 1843.

BY ROBERT B. THOMAS.

Once more our trusted and valued chronicler of what has been or is to be, in the risings and settings of the sun, in the waxings and wanings, and the comings up and goings down of the moon, in the ebbings and flowings of tides, &c. &c.,—once more he has sent out his work, and we wish him an extensive sale.

Finally, I must mention that almost all of the early almanacs were edited in towns rather than cities. For most of the almanac makers of the 18th and 19th centuries, the boundaries of the U.S.A. were Quebec, Pittsburgh, and Savannah, Georgia. It would take quite a while for them to get to the Mississippi, still longer the Pacific Coast. Herewith you will note a map of New England, which appeared in the 1831 edition of The Old Farmer's Almanac. Along with it was a notation

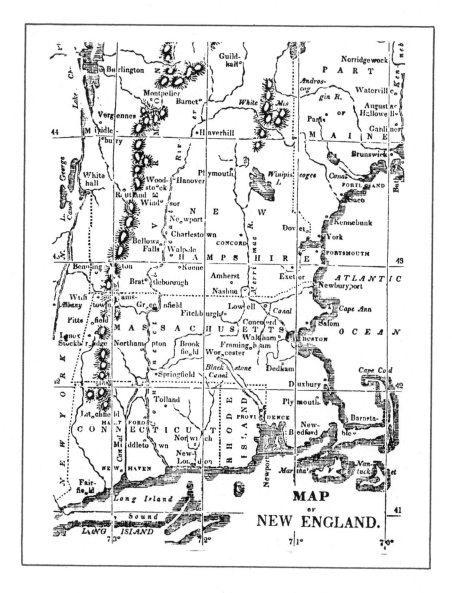

MAP
OF
NEW ENGLAND.

26

that several railroad routes were being proposed, 1) Boston to Albany, 2) Boston to Brattleborough, 3) Boston to Burlington via Concord and Montpelier, and 4) Boston to Providence. In the same issue are tables showing "The principal Towns on the Continent and the Distances from one established Tavern to another." Niagara Falls was as far west as Robert B. Thomas, editor of The Old Farmer's Almanac, thought we went; Montreal and Quebec as far north; and as far south as—guess what—New York. On this map only the seaports of New Haven, Providence, Boston, Portsmouth, and Portland seem to rate small capitals. What the ships had done for the seaports, the railroads would soon be doing for the interior.

But, to begin our story, we must go back to a year when there was only one settlement in the entire state of Connecticut (Wethersfield) and no more than a dozen (including Boston, Plymouth, and Salem) hamlets existed east of the Connecticut River. We must go back to a time when there was no colonial newspaper, when observing the position of various celestial objects was the only way to navigate or, indeed, tell the time of day or night; when news traveled only by word of mouth and most of this concerned the weather, Indians, the Spaniards, the Dissenters and trade.

We must go back to the year 1635....

Webb House
in Wethersfield, Connecticut

A household necessity

*From about 1740,
when Nathanael Ames and
Benjamin Franklin were both going strong,
until about a century later when the
specialty almanacs began to appear,
the farmer's almanacs reigned
supreme. In these years appeared
the strongest and most important
almanacs, and almanac makers
of all. Those looking for
"gold" will find it
during this
period.*

chapter two

the early years

At midnight on August the fourteenth, 1635, the week long sou'wester which by then all New Englanders were beginning to resent, suddenly shifted, by way of the southeast, into a boisterous nor'easter with violent wind and torrential rains. Among other ships grounded in this storm were the *Great Hope,* out of Ipswich, England; the ship *James,* out of Bristol; and from the same then distant port, the *Angel Gabriel.* Another vessel, a Boston pinnace, was caught and destroyed off Cape Ann. Of its sixteen passengers only Anthony Thacher and his wife were to survive. This couple is remembered in the name which he gave to the island of rock which saved their lives; Thacher's Island. The Rev. John Avery, his wife and six children who were also aboard, were not to survive but were memorialized in Whittier's "Swan Song of Parson Avery." William Bradford, the second governor of Plymouth Colony, and Captain William Pierce, a noted mariner of the time, both witnessed this Great Storm of 1635 from the shore.

"But, good gracious," I can almost hear Cap'n Pierce later asking the Governor, "didn't the *James* know she was dangerously near the Isle of Shoals on the night of the Great Storm—and, no matter how bad the blow, why didn't she tack out to sea?"

Any knowledgeable seafarer will admit this was a good question. An equally good answer, had the Captain of the *James* been present, would have been, "But how was I to know? There is no almanac I could consult which deals with these waters."

It has been supposed, but not verified, that Columbus to some extent used the Almanac *Regiomantus,* one of the world's earliest printed (1475) books, in discovering this continent. It is certain there were several almanacs flourishing in England, as well as on the Continent, in the early years of the 17th century and Captain Pierce and Gov. Bradford certainly knew about them.

However, it was not with the astrological and frost predictions in these British almanacs that Captain Pierce would be concerned. With him, as with his fellow sea captains, what really mattered were the New England positions of the stars and the moon and the times of sunrise, sunset, and of course the tides. About the only other salient material needed for an almanac to serve New England well at that time would be the calendar showing the Sabbaths, important religious Fasts and Feasts such as Easter Day; but not Christmas, then considered by the Puritans a frivolous pagan celebration.

The first printing press in New England was established after its trip across the Atlantic to these shores in 1638 by the widow of Rev. Joseph Glover in Cambridge, Massachusetts. It was set up in the home of Henry Dunster, first President of Harvard College. Thus did Mr. Dunster, in marrying the widow Glover, obtain for Harvard what is now, after various changes in ownership, the Harvard University Press. According to Winthrop's *Journal,* the first document printed on this press by Stephen Daye, its operator, was the "Freeman's Oath." This was in 1638. It may be seen at the John Carter Brown Library in Providence, Rhode Island. The next printed document from this press appeared in 1639. It was entitled an *"Almanack Calculated for New England,* by Mr. Pierce, Mariner." No copy of it is extant.

Thus began in the American colonies this branch of American literature to which Professor Tyler in his *History of American Literature* gives this forceful tribute:

> No one who would penetrate to the core of early American literature, and would read in it the secret history of the people in whose minds it took root and from whose minds it grew, may by any means turn away, in lofty literary scorn, from the almanac, most despised, most prolific, most indispensable of books, which every man uses and no man praises: the very quack, clown, pack-horse and pariah of modern literature, yet the one universal book of modern literature, the supreme and only literary necessity even in households where the Bible and the newspaper are still undesired and unattainable luxuries.

It is unfortunate that no copy now exists of this Pierce *Almanack*. Isaiah Thomas, 18th century almanac maker, printer, founder of the American Antiquarian Society, indicates in his *History of Printing* that the Stephen Daye Press printed an almanac yearly from 1639 until the press was taken over by Samuel Green in 1648–9. None of these copies apparently has been preserved either.

Lawrence B. Romaine, well-known Massachusetts bibliophile, indicates that the Pierce almanac was a "one leaf sort of broadside affair." He also points out that before Stephen and Mathew Daye relinquished their press to Samuel Green, they had brought out (1645–9) several 16-page almanacs prepared by Samuel Danforth of Roxbury, Massachusetts, a Harvard tutor.

The only known original in this Danforth series is one for 1646 which may be seen at the Massachusetts Historical Society. Its cover resembles the 1661 cover of an almanac recently acquired by the American Antiquarian Society and reproduced here with the Society's kind permission.

In appearance, size, format, and contents, the Danforth almanacs are representative of those now known as the Cambridge, Boston, or Philomath almanacs of the last half of the 17th century. "Cambridge" because most of them were either printed in Cambridge, Massachusetts, or edited there; "Boston" because some were edited and published in that city; "Philomath" because these colonial editors chose to affix this word, meaning "lover of mathematics," to their names either in full or in the abbreviated form of "Philo." Variations of this affix appear as "T.S. Philomathemat," the Greek "Philomathais," "Philopatr," and "Astrophil." And, occasionally it appeared alone with just the initials of the editor, as with T. S. Philomathemat on one of 1656.

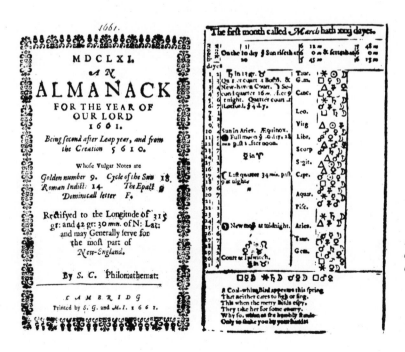

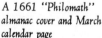

A 1661 "Philomath" almanac cover and March calendar page

There are strong Puritan religious overtones in these early Philomath almanacks. Danforth's first issue, for example, contains a treatise on a comet which Cotton Mather was to praise not only for its scientific value but also for improving the "opinion of a comet's being portentous, endeavoring as it became a devout preacher to awaken mankind by the portent, out of sinful security."

The astronomy in the Philomath almanacs was limited by the scientific knowledge available to students of the heavens in the 17th century. But it was sufficiently advanced to include computation charts showing the time of the sun's ingress into the signs, explanations of the "Observable Circles," as well as other matter such as eclipses, moon phases, etc.

Perhaps the most interesting aspect of the almanac of this period is its usefulness in telling time. Few families owned clocks or watches; indeed, in the entire Massachusetts Bay Colony there were perhaps not more than fifty householders who could boast of having one. Such clocks (with wooden works) as there were served for decoration only. Even sundials, then in common use, were not considered too reliable. But with an almanac in hand and the computation of the star Alioth indicated in its pages, there was little need (at least in clear weather) of watch or clock. Using the terminology of John Ward in his *Farmer's Almanack* of 1823 as one better understood by us than that used in colonial times, this was how one set one's clock or watch.

The time of Alioth's passing over the meridian or when a plumb line apparently cuts both the pole star Sirius and Alioth, is given for the first six months above the pole and for the last six months below it, to five days in every month . . . Sirius and Alioth will be visible coincident with a level East and West line at 5 h. 59 m. before and after Alioth passes the meridian but for common use say six hours: Thus, we may regulate time pieces to a minute, or tell time without them. the pole star is on the meridian 8 minutes later than Alioth . . . Alioth is the first star in the tail of the Great Bear; viz, that next to the square or it is the third star of the seven, commonly called the waggon or plough, toward those two of them which are denominated the pointers.

In addition to such astronomical data, there were notices of artillery meetings, election dates, and court sessions contained in these Philomath almanacs, and some contain the earliest examples of secular and elegiac verse in this country. Here is an example from one of them:

The stout Celestial waggoneer
  Now with the sturdy bullock strives,
And in a flaming swift career
  For thirty days together drives.

No wonder then (with plowing spent)
  He makes our earth so moist and soft,
If all his drops of sweat be sent
  Down from the water-spouts aloft.

Stanza for April, 1656

  The glorious Monarch of the Sky,
    Time's moderator, keeps his court,
  The Scales of Justice hanging by
    The golden Mean; and here resort.

  Pomona bringing mellow fruit
    And Ceres corn upon her back,
  And kind Silvanus spreads this bruit,
    His budget's full of nutts to crack.

September, 1656

Samuel Brackenbury, who may have compiled his first almanac at age eleven, included in his edition of 1667 many astronomical signs and locations. In doing so, as this accompanying verse to his readers indicates, he probably felt that few would understand them.

> *A word of advice to those whom it may concern,*
> *My Friends, you look for Verse, be pleas'd to*
>   *know*
> *You'l miss, Urania would have it so;*
> *Here's how the Sun his course in's Circle goes.*
> *I write Celestial harmonie in prose;*
> *Also your Fancies 'twould be hard to hitt,*
> *You may then judge according to your witt,*
> *The Planets set good faces on the matter,*
> *Then take it how you will, I cannot flatter.*
> *Now use't, and if Erratas you do find,*
> *I give you leave to men them to your mind;*
> *If such there be, it is by oversight,*
> *Believe me, I'd as live it should be right.*
> *Thus right or wrong, pray take it as it is,*
> *But use't aright, and then you'll never miss.*

That astrology was not a "fittin' subject" for these early almanac editors or readers is made clear by Thomas Brattle, Philomathemat, in 1694. "Astrologicall Predictions . . . serve only to Delude and Amuse the Vulgar . . . not fitting to be joyned with Astronomical Certainties."

● ● ●

On May 27, 1674, the General Court of Massachusetts "granted that there may be a printing press elsewhere than at Cambridge." With this permission John Foster opened his printing shop at "The Sign of the Dove" in Boston. On his foot stone may still be seen "Skill was his cash." Some of this skill went into the production of a series of Boston Almanacks, compiled and printed by himself. Some of these issues bear his name in bold letters on the cover, others are signed simply "Astrophil." This man was not only Boston's first printer but also America's earliest known wood engraver. The wood block cut made by him of Richard Mather (appearing herewith in reduced size) is considered America's earliest engraving.

Richard Mather
America's earliest woodcut
made by John Foster,
Boston's first printer
(1675)
Courtesy:
Massachusetts Historical Society's
"John Foster" by
S. A. Green.

It seems perplexing to me that there were not more engravers available for these almanacs and their printers in these years, and that not more than an occasional rough drawing of the sun or moon was used. This lack of illustration runs contrary to the practice of the wide use of illustration on the Continent in Books of Hours, religious and other books with which the

Cambridge and Boston editors must have been familiar. One may only conclude that, even as the Christmas celebration was regarded by these early Puritan fathers as pagan, and astrology (or fun making of any kind) was deemed sacrilegious, so too the adornment of these little almanacs would be considered entirely frivolous. John Foster, Printer, was succeeded by Samuel Sewall, Printer. He was later to become the judge at the famous witchcraft trials. *The Boston Ephemeris,* 1683, bears the inscription "Printed by S. G. for S. S." Samuel Sewall denied the implication and attributed the almanac to Cotton Mather but there is little doubt that Sewall was just as greatly involved in these almanacs, and the Puritan strain running through them, as ever were the Mathers and John Foster.

In fact, in the linking of Judge Samuel Sewall's name with these Boston Almanacks, we soon come hard upon the trail of the witchcraft trials and executions.

It seems inconceivable that the Philomath editors could have avoided knowing, long before their own witchcraft involvement, what was going on in this respect elsewhere. History tells us that up to 1647 European

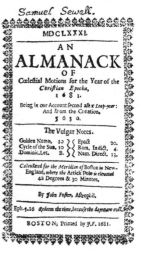

Samuel Sewall,
The infamous
witch trial judge
His Almanac,
(1681)
and himself

Cotton Mather
Theologist, Soul-saver,
Puritan Seer

witchcraft claimed at least 200,000 innocent individuals. We must assume that these Puritan editors and
their friends were well aware of this and that they
were also cognizant of such facts about their own
motherland. Howells, the letter writer, wrote about
them on February 26, 1647: "Within the compass of
two years near upon 300 witches were arraigned, and
the larger part of them executed, in Essex and Suffolk
(England) only. Scotland swarms with them more
and more and persons of good quality are executed
daily."

Elizabeth Sawyer
executed in England
for witchcraft
1621

How does one even begin to explain the personalities of these, our founding fathers, and their actions and thoughts which eventually led to our Constitution, this turning of their backs upon the evils of the witch hunts and hangings abroad and at home? How come that when these evils reached these shores, they in turn, as violent worshippers of a Christian God, were to participate in these atrocities themselves?

One explanation is that in the Puritan belief the Bible was seen as literal truth. The eminent English Judge, Sir Mathew Hale, for example, in giving his charge at the witchcraft trial of Rose Cullender and Anne Duny in England in 1668 had given a legal precedent for our Judge Sewall to follow. In this charge he said that he "made no doubt that there were such Creatures as Witches, for the Scriptures had affirmed it, and the Wisdom of all Nations had provided laws against such persons." Then, too, had not Bishop Hall of England also written that "Satan's prevalency in this Age is most clear, in the marvellous number of Witches abiding in all places?"

In any event, Sewall relented. He prayed in church every day of the remaining years of his life for forgiveness. We, in turn, might just as well dismiss the omissions of the Philomath editors by pointing out that almanacs really are not concerned with world affairs (few have ever carried anything about our wars). Their business is with the heavens—the timetabling of events universal.

● ● ●

The chronology of the Philomath Almanacs carries these well into the first quarter of the 18th century. The rising tides, however, of toleration which were to submerge the Puritan hierarchy and its neurotic, abnormal interpretation of the Bible shortly after the witchcraft trials (1692) had certainly begun to come in as early as 1685.

Mathew Hopkins
The Witchfinder
(about 1620)

It would take a closer student of that period than I to date exactly the year when the bells rang in the new, more tolerant generation of our forefathers and rang out the old. But we do know that in the year 1685 William Bradford established in Philadelphia the first printing press outside the New England colonies. Whether or not this may be attributed to relaxed vigilance in the colonies as well as in the mother country at ·this time, or just circumstance, somebody else will have to decide. In any event, Bradford was to become, as these pages will later reveal, an important figure in Middle Colonial almanac publication.

The arrival, however, of Benjamin Harris in Boston in 1686 (and his having become the proprietor of the London Coffee House there) does hold real reformation significance. It marks the beginning of a different American almanac style, format, and content. Harris had formerly been a printer in London, where he had brought out many tracts of a religious or political nature. For his trouble, he eventually was fined five hundred pounds in 1681 and condemned to stand in the pillory. This apparently ruined his business and we hear no more of him until he arrived in Boston.

I would like to have known Benjamin Harris. Were I as good a biographer as Catherine Drinker Bowen, I would most certainly include his name on my list of future biographies. For one thing, he had the perspective or sense of humor so much needed in this transition from the old Puritan philosophy to the new more liberal way of thinking. The history of printing reveals that presses in the colonies were not to throw off the yoke of censure by governor and council until the Revolution. "Licensed by authority," or "Imprimateur, Edw. Randolph Secr." graphically stamped on many of Harris's imprints, clearly reveal he was not taking any more chances on fines or the pillory. Yet somehow

A	In ADAM's Fall / We sinned all.	N	NOAH did view / The old world & new
B	Heaven to find, / The Bible Mind.	O	Young OBADIAS, / DAVID, JOSIAS / All were pious.
C	Christ crucify'd / For sinners dy'd.	P	PETER deny'd / His Lord and cry'd.
D	The Deluge drown'd / The Earth around.	Q	Queen ESTHER sues / And saves the Jews.
E	ELIJAH hid / By Ravens fed.	R	Young pious RUTH / Left all for Truth.
F	The judgment made / FELIX afraid.	S	Young SAM'L dear / The Lord did fear.

Benjamin Harris' New England Primer

he was satisfying the demands of many readers whose views were not exactly coinciding with those of the authorities. It was Harris, for example, who was the first to popularize the immortal New England Primer (a catechism of which the hierarchy would assuredly approve) and, he was the first to publish the Tulley almanacs (a series to which the hierarchy would refer as "heathenish" and "not Christian.")

One reason why Harris may have been unsuccessful in pleasing both sides may be seen in the fact that the first advertisement in the Colonies for the favored *The New England Primer* appeared in (1690) a Boston Almanack from the Harris press. The approach of Mr. Harris to the censor may have been that, if the censor would allow almanacs to go forth, these would be the means of sustaining, through such advertisements, public interest in Mather's attempts at revival of the then dying Puritanism.

Be that as it may, the fact remains that one John Tulley, a liberal "outlander" from Saybrook, Connecticut, was to prepare his almanac material "on sheetes of large papour" furnished to him by Harris, and was able to complete an issue each year from 1687 through and including 1702, presumably aided and abetted by Harris.

The complete set of the Tulley almanacs, now safely on file at the American Antiquarian Society, reveals some startling changes from the almanac formats and contents of the Philomath almanacs with which the preceding century was concerned. For example, the year is begun with January as the first month rather than with March, which for years had been the old Puritan custom. Again, Tulley introduced into his calendar pages the Feast, Fast, and Saint's days which Mather, Sewall, or Brattle never would have tolerated: Valentine's, New Year's, Easter, Shrove Sunday, etc.

Finally, this man, John Tulley, a liberal outlander from Saybrook, Connecticut, has the honor of having introduced for the first time in Colonial history, an American almanac weather forecast. In the accompanying illustration of his January page for 1693, one notes opposite the three days of January 18, 19, and 20—

> *Snow or cold rain*
> *about this time*
> *Clear and cold*

Such phraseology is not entirely different from the same or similar wording used in the thousands and millions of

American almanac weather forecasts which were to appear after Tulley's death in 1702, and which continue to appear in the farmer's almanacs of today.

• • •

JANUARY hath 21 Daves.

First quar. 4 day 44 min. paſt 7 morn.
Full Moon 11 day 27 min. paſt 11 night.
Laſt quar. 18 day 6 min. paſt 6 night.
New Moon 26 day 8 min. paſt 1 morn.

M.	W.	Spr. Tides & Weather. ♄ ☉s. ☉pl. ☽ pl.		Full Sea
1	♉	☽ in wet ſign ☐ ♄ ☽	7 25 5 22 VS 21 Piſces ♂	03 12
2	2	perhaps Snow	7 25 5 23 23 Aries	04 00
4	3	Fair and ☽ Apoge	7 24 5 24 24	04 48
3	4	Freezing	7 23 5 25 25	05 36
5	5		7 22 5 26 26 Taur	06 24
6	6		7 21 5 27 27	07 12
7	7		7 21 5 28 29 Gemi	08 00
8	♉	Cloudy cold 8 ♄ ☽	7 20 5 29 30	08 48
9	2	and Windy	7 19 5 00 ♒ 31 Canc.	09 36
10	3		7 18 5 01 32	10 24
11	4	☽ Eclipſed Viſible	7 17 5 02 33	11 12
12	5	Snow or Rain ☽ ☍	7 16 5 03 33 Leo	12 00
13	6	Clear and Cold	7 15 5 04 34	12 48
14	7		7 14 5 05 35 Virg.	01 36
15	♉	Cloudy ☐ ♄ ☽	7 13 5 06 36	02 24
16	2	dry and windy	7 12 5 07 37 Libra	03 12
17	3	☽ Perige	7 11 5 08 38	04 00
18	4	Snow or cold rain	7 10 5 09 39 Scorp	04 48
19	5	about this time	7 09 5 10 40	05 36
20	6	Clear and cold	7 08 5 11 42 Sagit.	06 24
21	7		7 07 5 12 43	07 12
22	♉	Cloudy ♂ ♄ ☽	7 06 5 13 44	08 00
23	2		7 05 5 14 45 Capr.	08 48
24	3	Winds bringing	7 04 5 15 46	09 36
25	4	Snow or Sleet ☽ ☍	7 03 5 16 47 Aqua	10 24
26	5	the Weather	7 02 5 17 47	11 12
27	6	fit for the	7 00 5 18 48 Piſces	12 00
28	7	Seaſon	6 59 6 19 49	12 48
29	♉	Snow like ☐ ♄ ☽	6 57 6 20 49	01 36
30	2		6 56 6 21 50 Aries	02 24
31	3		6 54 6 22 50	03 12

45

The Man of Signs, along with weather forecasts, and feast days, was nothing new to the Continent or to England. From at least as early as the XIIth century he was a common entry in most almanacs. However, to a society which held the mention of Christmas Day as pagan and punishable, one can well imagine how such a society would react to this (usually disemboweled) figment of the astrologer's imagination. The "Man" proposes to show how twelve different parts of the human body are controlled by twelve corresponding parts of the heavens through which the sun (or really the earth) and moon travel. If, for example, one is born under the "sign" of Pisces which is that segment of the heavens in which one sees the Moon between February 19 and March 20 each year, then that individual will benefit by anything which has to do with feet (running, climbing, etc.) but may suffer from diseases of the feet. This is indeed pagan belief. Yet here before our very eyes are passages from the pen of John Tulley which flaunt almost everything the old Puritans had held sacred.

Even more fearless on Tulley's part was the introduction into his almanacs of the famous old "Man of the Signs." In doing this Tulley (and Harris) literally waved the flag of independence under the very nose of Mather's dying bull. Variations from the Tulley "Man of the Signs" appear here.

Tulley's, 1693

Man of Signs used by Abe Weatherwise 1784

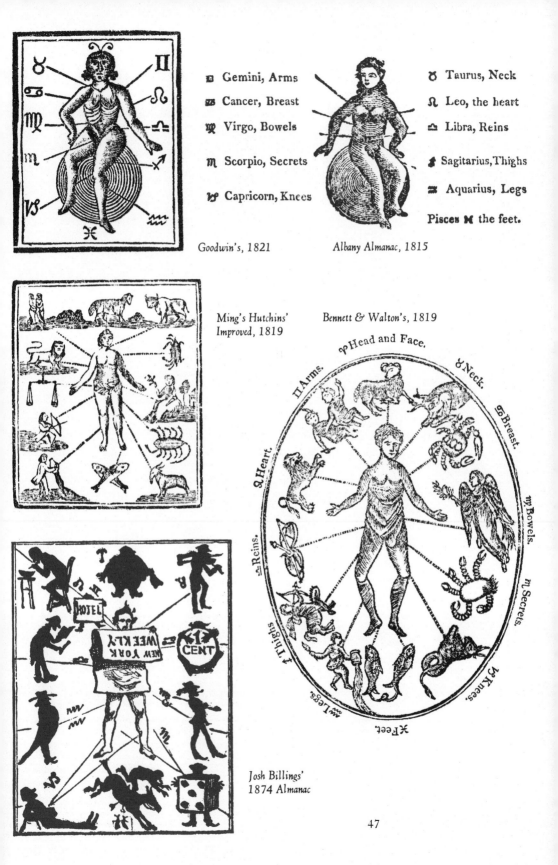

Gemini, Arms
Cancer, Breast
Virgo, Bowels
Scorpio, Secrets
Capricorn, Knees

Taurus, Neck
Leo, the heart
Libra, Reins
Sagitarius, Thighs
Aquarius, Legs
Pisces the feet.

Goodwin's, 1821

Albany Almanac, 1815

Ming's Hutchins'
Improved, 1819

Bennett & Walton's, 1819

Head and Face.
Arms.
Neck.
Breast.
Heart.
Bowels.
Reins.
Secrets.
Thighs
Knees.
Legs.
Feet.

Josh Billings'
1874 Almanac

47

John Tulley's farewell Almanack of 1702 bears a note on its front cover the year he "dyed while he was finishing this Almanack; and so leaves it as his *Legacy* to his Country-men." Such a legacy was more than an expression of rebellion against the old Puritan philosophy. It led, for example, to the publication of America's earliest book advertisements. One of these was an "Antidote against all Manner of Gripings, called Aqua-Antitorminalis." Here are the beginnings, also, of the appearance in print of the theories and sayings of native seamen and farmers schooled not so much by books as by observation:

The obscuring of the smaller stars is a certain sign of tempest approaching, the oft changing of the winds is always a forerunner of a storm. There is no surer sign of rain than two different currents of clouds, especially if the under-currents appear in hot weather, they shew that a thunder storm is gathering.

On wet and dry seasons the following rules are laid down:— "When there has been no storm before or after the vernal equinox, the ensuing summer is generally dry, at least five times in five."

When a storm arises on the 25th, 26th, or 27th of March, and not before, in any point, the succeeding summer is wet four times in five.

If there should be a storm at southwest, or west southwest, on the 19th, 20th, 21st, or 22nd, the succeeding summer is generally wet, five times in six. It rains less in March than in November, in the proportion of seven to twelve.

When it rains plentifully in May, it generally rains but little in September; and the contrary.

Out of 41 years there will in general be 22 dry springs, six wet, and 13 variable ones; also 20 wet summers, 16 dry, and five variable ones, and probably 11 dry autumns, 11 wet, and 19 variable ones.

When the Swallows fly high after their prey we think ourselves sure of a serene sky; but when they fly low and brush the surface of the water with their wings, we judge that rain is not far off.

When the Gnats collect themselves before the setting of the sun, and form a sort of vortex, in the shape of a column, it announces fine weather.

The Earth, after a very long and abundant rain, is sometimes seen to be almost dry, and the roads quite free from dirt. This is a sign that the rain has not altogether ceased; and denotes a continual efflux of electric matter, which, being renewed carries with it, in the form of vapour, all the moisture that falls on the earth.

There is sometimes a great deal of dirt after a very moderate rain; this is a sign of fine weather; because it indicates that evaporation has ceased.

Tulley's inclusion of such popular and widely held sayings led readers to scribbling their own observations, comments, propitious dates for harvest, when to take the cow to the bull, planting dates, epigrams, and anagrams in the margins of their almanacs.

Now the people of our land will crouch unto one
That will swagger although he be but of the sixes
But they will crow over a man that's gentle
Though he be of the large thirteen.

Or, there might be some reader's favorite religious maxims such as these found in one even before Tulley had died:

God is a God of order,
The Divell is king of confusion,
God is the God of union,
The Divell is master of Division.

The author's personal copy of the 1693 Tulley Almanac reveals the price the scribbler paid for a bushel of corn and for a peck of onions. For one calf skin he received all of "two shillings . . . cash."

Later almanac makers noted and assimilated the practical and poetical notes of these readers and they added to them pithy proverbs, wit, riddles, entertainment, and instruction. But to John Tulley, unoriginal as his almanacs may have seemed to his English contemporaries, one must grant the origin of the farmer's almanac as this country eventually came to know it.

• • •

Tulley's immediate successor as a farmer's almanac publisher was Samuel Clough and his *The New England Almanack,* which ran successfully from 1700 to 1708. Among his prophecies are such amusing colloquialisms as "Misling Weather with some dripling showers," printed opposite April 26th. By this time, however, colonial society was taking longer strides than the almanac makers could match.

Longfellow's "Wayside Inn" at South Sudbury, Massachusetts, had become well established as the "Red Horse Tavern." *Publick Occurrences,* the first newspaper on this continent, had already made its brief appearance and by 1704 the Boston News Letter had taken its place. The whaling industry had become not only profitable but widespread. Traffic in rum had become a thriving business. Public schools were available to all. Captain Kidd had been gibbeted, Detroit had been founded and settled, and there were already more negroes enslaved by colonists (75,000) than almost four times the combined populations of Boston (12,000) and New York (7,000).

Along with this burgeoning growth of the seacoast cities and their industries, in New England at least there was an almost steady warfare with the native Indians. On

February 29th, 1704, the town of Deerfield, Massachusetts, was razed and most of its population massacred. Four years later Haverhill, Massachusetts suffered the same fate.

These were no easy times for the almanac makers or anybody else. The Dark Day of October 21, 1716, for example, when "one could not recognize another four seats away, nor read a word in a psalm book" was an occasion of great excitement, a supernatural occurrence which would never be explained to them.

In December 1716, snow fell to the depth of five feet. With most of it still on the ground, a great storm in February of the following year completely buried one-story houses, chimneys and all. Cattle were found dead in the snow weeks afterwards still "standing and with all the appearance of life." The mail between Salem, Massachusetts, and Portsmouth, New Hampshire, a distance of but forty miles, took nine days one way and eight days to return.

The first appearance to New Englanders of the Aurora Borealis on May 15, 1719, and the great storm of February 24, 1722–23 was also an occasion great-great-great-grandpa lived through with such intensity that his later tales of these events to his descendants were surely unbelievable. Despite all this turmoil and ferment—natural, supernatural and man-made—which would have provided excellent grist for the almanac maker's mill, none of any importance appeared to rival Samuel Clough during the first quarter of the 18th century.

Edward Holyoke, later to become President of Harvard, tried his hand at one. Thomas Robie, Harvard's noted librarian, tried another. Nathaniel Whittemore of Lexington, Massachusetts, and Nathan Bowen of Marblehead also produced little annual editions. However, these editors and publishers were caught up in the controversy over whose astronomical theories were correct—those of Copernicus or of Ptolemy, and they were also hampered by a trying business climate. Perhaps it is too much to expect the times to have produced more than it did.

The first real step towards the establishment of the almanac as "an household necessity alongside the Bible" was made by Nathanael Ames of Dedham, Massachusetts, in the year 1725 when he first issued his *Astronomical Diary and Almanack* for the year 1726. This was to have a continuous run under his direction until

The eighth page of Dr. Nathaniel Ames' first (1726) Almanac

TO THE READER.

Courteous Reader,

I Have here adventured to present you with an Almanack for the Ensuing Year. It being my first made Publick by the Press; should it find Acceptance, I have my End and shall receive sufficient Encouragement to Undertake somewhat more for your benefit. Thus Reader for your sake I have exposed my self to the dangerous & sharp Teeth of envious Detractors, which is a great Hazard : specially in this polish'd Age, among so many fine & curious Wits, who scarcely can approve of any thing, tho never so Judiciously Composed. There has been no pains, nor care, wanting to render these Calculations as free from Errors as possible, yet if any fault committed by my Pen or Press pass Uncorrected, Excuse it ; in so doing you will not only do your self a Kindness, but also oblige him, who is a Friend to all that are Mathematically inclined, and a real Lover of the most sublime study of Astronomy,   **N. Ames.**

Bridgwater, Octob. 12th. 1725.

*REad then and Learn but don't all faults Object,
Since they can only judge that can Correct ;
To whom my Works appeal, and if I find,
The Sons of Art to favour them inclin'd ;
With their Propitious smiles, it shall suffice,
To counterpoize the Frowns of Enemies.*

TWice in a Century (Old *Indians* say.)
Our Land abounds with *Bears* & *Beasts* of Prey;
Whereof some do embrace ProudNeptunesWaves
And with the Scaly Tribe swim to theirGraves :
Others Retreat towards the Frigid Zone,
And dwell in Desert yet to us unkhown ;
They'll come, no more from whence they do Re
Until a Jubilee of Years Expire.   (tire,

[*Dele Sup.* C. Boston, *the First Tuesday* in May.]

52

his death in 1764 when his son, Nathaniel Ames, Jr., continued it until 1795.

Students of this run of Ames' Almanacks will find *The Essays, Humor, and Poems of Nathaniel Ames* edited in 1891 by Samuel Briggs an amusing and valuable source book. The meticulous may be troubled at first by the spelling of this name, Nathaniel. Both Professor Kittredge of Harvard and the Columbia Encyclopedia use the "iel" ending. The actual cover, however, of the 1749 edition uses "ael" while that for 1757 has the "iel." Goodspeed's Bookshop, quoting prices for Ames' editions in its Catalog 506 offers these as Nathan*ael*'s.

Before Ames had published his 8th annual edition, Benjamin Franklin, by then a resident of Philadelphia, brought out in 1732 his first edition (for 1733) of the famous *Poor Richard, an Almanack, by Richard Saunders.* Although the two almanacs were to run concurrently for at least a quarter of a century, and the two editors presumably were personal friends, geography, slow communications and differences in editorial approach kept them competitively separated.

Dr. Nathanael Ames was not only a practising physician in good standing but a serious student of astronomy as well. To his profession and his avocation he was also to add, by the purchase of the *Sign of the Sun* at Dedham in 1750, the role of tavern keeper.

Ames' Tavern
Dedham, Massachusetts

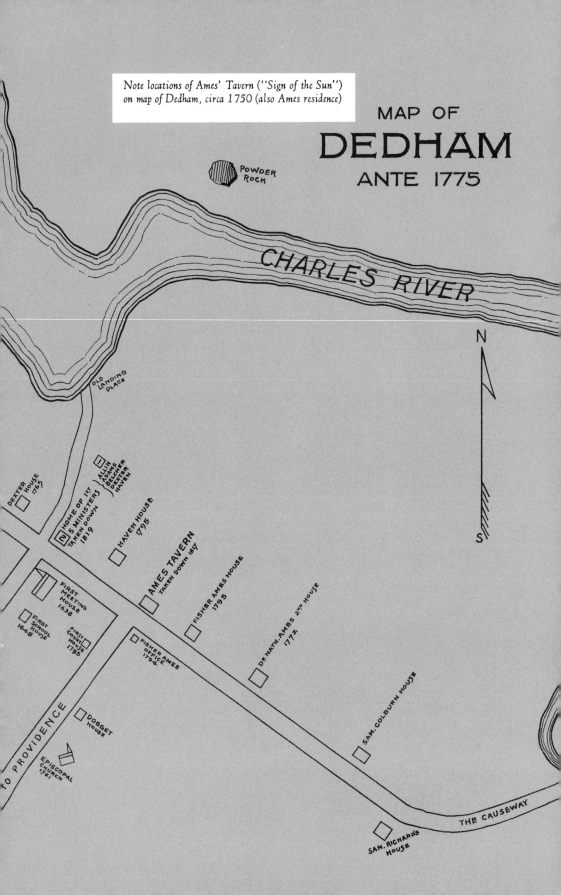

Note locations of Ames' Tavern ("Sign of the Sun")
on map of Dedham, circa 1750 (also Ames residence)

MAP OF
DEDHAM
ANTE 1775

POWDER ROCK

CHARLES RIVER

N

S

OLD LANDING PLACE

DEXTER HOUSE 1767

HOME OF 1ST 5 MINISTERS TAKEN DOWN 1819

ALLIN
ADAMS
BELCHER
DEXTER
HAVEN

HAVEN HOUSE 1795

AMES TAVERN TAKEN DOWN 1817

FIRST MEETING HOUSE 1638

FIRST SCHOOL HOUSE 1648

FIRST COURT HOUSE 1795

FISHER AMES HOUSE 1795

DR. NATH. AMES 2ND HOUSE 1772

FISHER AMES OFFICE 1794

SAM. COLBURN HOUSE

TO PROVIDENCE

DOGGET HOUSE

EPISCOPAL CHURCH 1761

THE CAUSEWAY

SAM. RICHARD'S HOUSE

It was fortunate that the good doctor was something of a wit, for in those days neither medicine nor astronomy was entirely divorced from the pseudo-science of astrology. As Professor Kittredge points out in his *The Old Farmer and His Almanack* (University Press 1904), Dr. Ames knew, on the one hand, how Paracelsus had decreed that "no physician ought to write a prescription without consulting the stars," and realized, on the other that this same astrology was but "superstitious ornament." Thus one finds in his almanack of 1729 Ames' own confession of editorial compromise beneath the first appearance of his ugly, unoriginal figure of the Man of the Signs.

> *The Blackmoore may as easily change his Skin,*
> *And men forsake the ways they'r brought up in;*
> *Therefore I've set the Old Anatomy,*
> *Hoping to please my Country men thereby,*
> *But where's the Man that's born and lives among,*
> *. . . . . Can please a Fickle throng?*

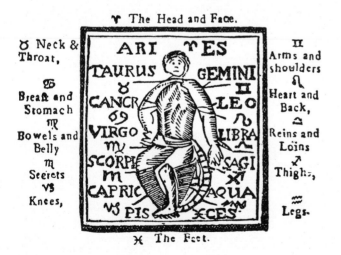

The last appearance of the Man of the Signs in the Ames Almanacks was in 1734.

In orienting one's self to the times and thinking of the first half of the colonial 18th century, reading these Ames' editions is a rewarding exercise.

Lawrence Roth, for example, in his *The Colonial Printer* points out that the Library of Congress' copy of the second issue of Ames' Almanack for the year 1757 was printed by Fowle in Portsmouth, New Hampshire. In this same edition we also learn that the Granite State's first press was established in 1756—the very one upon which the almanac was printed that November. Another historical tidbit is found in Ames' Almanack for 1729 printed in Boston by B. Green, which lists the prices paid for rags for use in making paper by the founders of the first paper mill north of New Jersey at Milton, Massachusetts in that same year. The second issue of Ames' 1730 edition mentions that it is printed on the first paper made there.

Space enthusiasts may well ponder on the 1748 and 1749 Ames' notes to his readers. After explaining how the planets are accommodated for inhabitants, and that they are actually inhabited; that rational creatures there sing the "Praises of their Creator who has bestowed His goodness on them in as bountiful and magnificent a

Cover of Ames' 1749 Almanac in which he explains his ideas of life on other planets

An ASTRONOMICAL DIARY,
OR, AN

ALMANACK

For the Year of our LORD CHRIST,

1 7 4 9.

Being the firft Year after. Biffextile or LEAP-YEAR.

And in the Twenty-fecond Year of the Reign of our moft gracious Sovereign King GEORGE II.

Wherein are contained the Lunations, Eclipfe of the Luminaries, Afpects, Sun and Moon's Rifing and Setting, Time of High-Water, Courts, Spring Tides, Judgment of the Weather, &c.

Calculated for the Meridian of Bofton, in NEW-ENGLAND, Lat. 42 Deg. 25. Min. North

By **Nathanael Ames.**

NO Hero's Ghofts, with Garments roll'd in Blood,
   Majeftick ftalk ; the golden Age's renew'd :
No hollow Drums in *Flanders* beat ; the Breath
Of brazen Trumpets ring no Peels of Death.
The milder Stars their peaceful Beams afford :
And founding Hammer beats the wounding Sword.
To Plow-Shears now ; *Mars* muft to *Ceres* yield,
And exhil'd PEACE returns, and takes the Field.

BOSTON in NEW-ENGLAND:
Printed by **J. Draper,** for the Bookfellers.

Price Eighteen Pence *Single, &* Twelve Shillings a *Dozen.*

manner as on us," he proceeds through various arguments to the conclusion that "had we Commerce with 'em, had we the little Spanish Ganzas [One of the birds which, in a romance by Godwin, bore Domingo Gansales to the moon.] to carry us to Jupiter, one of the portly, tall Inhabitants of that great World would excite our Respect; but if he was angry he would make an hundred and fifty of the pygmy inhabitants of our small world tremble at his looks."

In applying the different astrological theorems (Robert B. Thomas would never have dignified any part of this pseudo science with such terminology), one finds the early almanac editors neither too shy, nor, to be sure, overly bold. Benjamin Franklin in the first edition of Poor Richard ($50,000 Rosenbach) explained his formula for forecasting the weather by observing when Venus was seen to disappear behind a cloud. When this happened, wrote the old master in his preface, rain was sure to follow.

In a 1756 Ames edition, opposite the 24th and running through the 27th of December appears: "Now Sol in Capricornus appoints fierce Rheumatisms to rack the Joynts."

All through the Ames almanacs one notes how their editor quotes the aspects (that is, the angles which the planets make with each other) as the basis for all sorts of other events such as wars, peace treaties, and pestilences.*

---

*Almanac editors as far back as 3000 B.C. were adept at naming the days of the year which would be lucky or unlucky. In fact, Dr. C. W. Roback, President of the Astrological College of Sweden, observed in 1854 that "In Adam the knowledge of Astrology appears to have existed by inspiration." Perhaps Dr. Ames had this knowledge "by inspiration" also! Without giving the reader any key at all to his reasoning he does face up boldly to the days, lucky and the luckless.

Sept. 3 and 4, 1749: *Now some are Losers, some Gainers.* Sept. 17 and 18: *Now comes a lucky day for hunters.* Sept. 24, 25, 26, 27, 28: *Some luckless Undertaking is now afoot, and many complaints among children.*

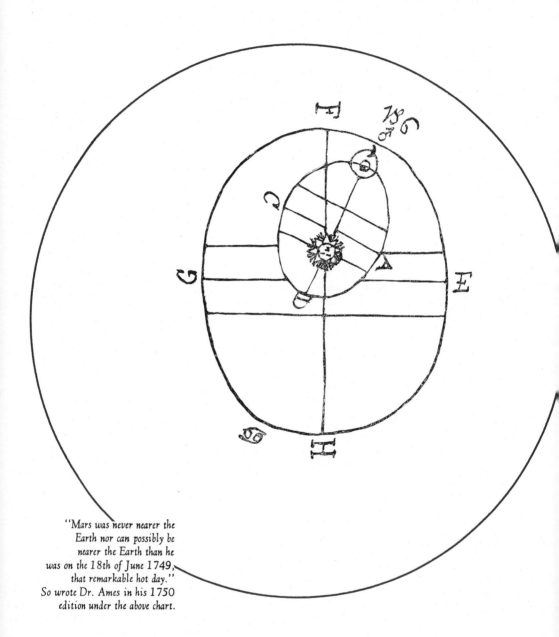

"Mars was never nearer the
Earth nor can possibly be
nearer the Earth than he
was on the 18th of June 1749,
that remarkable hot day."
So wrote Dr. Ames in his 1750
edition under the above chart.

It would be unfair to leave Dr. Ames alone with these astrological antics. While these are predominant in his earlier issues, one must remember the format of these early almanacs. They comprise only 16 pages, including the covers, and were printed on a single sheet of paper and then folded. Some twelve of these pages were devoted to the monthly calendars with their weather forecasts, sunrise and sunset tables, place of the moon in the zodiac, lucky and unlucky days. Another page or two were devoted to such necessities as a foreword, stage coach routes, eclipses, and explanations on how to use the calendar pages. After using one page for the cover, Dr. Ames was left with only two pages, each about 3½" by 5", for all his other editorial matter.

As one vast source of this material, he had his familiarity with Addison, Thomson, Pope, Dryden, and Milton to draw upon. For another, as a doctor he could not only call upon his latest information with regard to cures, but also upon the folklore with which many of his patients must have been imbued. In addition, there were the rural, national, and world affairs of his era with which we know he was familiar. Moreover, there was no Puritan "sword of the censor" to restrict him as it had Tulley and Harris.

The first signs we notice on Ames' part of departing from a straight astrological brew are in his poetry and proverbs. The latter, which were to be the real meat of the Franklin almanacs, do not seem to have caught editor Ames' fancy as strongly as they might have. In his edition for 1735, it is not until May that we find one:

> *Three things breed Jealousy—*
> *A mighty State, a rich Treasure,*
> *And a fair Wife.*

July of the same almanac has:

*Lyons are known by their
Claws, Cocks by their Combs,
And envious Men by their
Manners.*

September:

*Hatred is blind
    as well as Love.*

November:

*Let thieves beware of
Burglary, lest we dissect
their bodies and set up
their Bones for Skeletons.*

1739, February:

*Adversity makes
a Man wise.*

July:

*Zeal has no ears
but Slander has
a great many.*

December:

*A Cloak
for matters of Religion
is easily found.*

1749, January:

*If there was less debating
and more acting 'twould be better.*

March:

*A man without Work,
Money, or Credit
Stands but a poor Chance.*

August:

*Would you be well this
month beware of cold raw
Fruit and Evening Air.*

October:

*He that lives by Fraud
is in danger of dying
a Knave.*

December:

*Ladies, take heed,
Lay down your Fans
And, handle well
Your warming Pan.*

Proverbs and maxims, if they are to be effective, should be profound and oracular. They are as arrows designed to hit the bull's eye in a reader's mind. One must conclude that those used by Dr. Ames rarely hit this mark and, consequently, would not have been missed had they been left out altogether.

In the space remaining to him on his calendar pages, Dr. Ames turned to poetry. Although he was wont to quote Dryden and other English poets, it would be an understatement to say that he was not averse to writing some of these verses himself. So humble was his own private opinion of his poetic ability, however, that finally, in his 35th almanac to which he was able to add "half a sheet," he ran half a page of verse on his Eclipses. If this verse were as meaningless to his readers as it seems to us today, it certainly qualifies as "18th century modern."

There is no denying, however, that there is a Wordsworthian quality to his pen, when, from his study window, he takes a good look at his environs. In fact, the continuing verses in his edition of 1735 seem to give us more of the character of this editor as a friend or acquaintance than all else he has left for us. There is a

JANUARY:
'Tis Cold my Friends: The dull and tedious Nights
Old Batchellers and Widowers invites
To Marry, now in hast.—Women be
Fram'd with the same Parts of the Mind as we,
They are the best of Goods or worst of Evils,
Resembling bright Seraphims or—.

FEBRUARY:
As youthful Lovers with those Hours away,
That are between their Mistresses and they,
So many wish for the Auspicious Spring,
Whose Smiling Birth shall many Blessings bring,
When Nature's Face by Sol shall be renewed,

MARCH:
The *Winged Travellers, that soar Elate,
With Pleasure gliding through the liquid Air,
Guided by Instinct or some secret Fate,
Unto their Northern Rendevous Repair.
Their Captain (foremost) leads the Feather'd throng,
And knows what Ports to light at all along.
*Wild Geese

APRIL:
Now Amsters Breath dissolves the Winters Snow
Which on the barren Hills so long has lain,
Which makes the Silver murmering Riv'lets flow,
And Fertilizes every Sunny Plain.
The Plants sprought forth, the Grass again is green,
The Fields will quickly yield a pleasant Scene.

MAY:
Arcadian Muses now inspire the Swains,
With Songs of Love, While on the grassy plains
Their Sheep and Goats do graze, and wanton Lambs
and Kids, run Frisking round their bleating Dams.
The Fields (like the Elyzian Fields above)
Are fill'd with Harmony, with Mirth and Love.

JUNE:
Those abject Men whose greatest Talent lies,
In prying into Others Qualities,
Who strive their Neighbours Vertues to conceal,
And magnify their Faults with Art and Skill,
Are like the Crow and other Birds of Prey,
Who search out Moorish Ground where Carrions lay.

JULY:
Orion King, who in the Winter Reigns,
And binds the barren Earth with Frosty Chains,
Brightest of all the Train that Set and Rise,
With our bright Prince of Day, ascends the Skies,
So Drunk with Heat their Stomachs overflow,
And vomit Lightnings round the World below.

AUGUST:
Those Magazines where Thunder Makers dwell,
Under the Ground, in Natures private Cell.
Sometimes take Fire, and kindle into Flame,
Which rends huge Caves and arched Vaults in twain
All things give way to the Expansion great
Which makes the trembling Earth's Foundations shak

SEPTEMBER:
The Sun grows careful of his lavish's Heat,
And to the Southern Clime does now Retreat
Under the Earth, lengthening the Nightly shade,
Which makes the Summers verdant Beauty fade.
Autumnal Insects with a mournful Crake,
Do Chippering strive to Sing, but Discord make.

OCTOBER:
Immortal Scandals fly on Eagles Wings,
Whilst vertuous Actions die and scare are Nam'd
Men that have done most noble, worthy Things,
For one miss deed perpetually are Blam'd
Ignoble Souls would spit their poisonous Gall,
Thinking to Raise themselves by others Fall

NOVEMBER:
When Man's grown Ripe he presently decays,
All things do fluctuate and nothing stays,
Time alters all, this present Tear's grown Old,
And Winter threatens us with pinching Cold.
Our Comforts past will but increase our Sorrow,
If we are unprovided for To-Morrow.

DECEMBER:
Dame Tellus lies bereav'd of all her Charms,
Coldly Embrac'd in Winters Icy Armes,
Bound fast with frosty Chains, cover'd in Snow,
Expos'd to all tempestuous Winds that Blow:
But Sol shall come and Re-ascend his Throne,
And make his Power to cruel Boreas known.

swing to these verses (shown at left) of man in his seasons.

Although it is difficult to catch the elder Ames at his serious best, there are places in his almanacs when his position as an eminent physician does show through. In his edition for 1755, for example, he cautions his readers not to "Breathe the Air of *Cities,* where breathless winds imbibe Effluvia from the Sick and Dying, from the Dead, from Docks and Dung-hills: where thousands of Lungs with Exhalations foul, sate the Air with strange Corruption, and make that vital Element a nauseous Mass . . ."

Again, with regard to Diet, he notes that his contemporaries seem to live upon smoked and dried fish and meat despite the fact that to the stomach "Wood is scarcely more rebellious." But he rejects for "those whose Fibres are unstrung, the infirm and the delicate, the very young and the very old, all luscious Food."

> Your languid stomachs, your elastic tubes are not sufficiently braced and the Machinery of Nature (in you) is not strong enough to Grind such vicious Fluid, but rather chuse Meat that is young and such as gain their Food with Exercise from Grass, from Grain, from flowery Herbs.

Finally, it is Exercise or Labour which cures all.

> 'Twas Toil that taught the Romans how to conquer; they went from the Field to the Senate-House; and from the Plough they led their Legions on to War . . .—Then you of firmest Clay, *New England's* hardiest sons, let Agriculture exercise your Limbs. You, with the Spirit of the *Romans,* conquered *Louisburg:* Manure this Land which your Forefathers planted with Herculean labours.

After exercise the old doctor recommends a bath but, for those who are unable to work in the fields he suggests, not a bath but "Friction with a Brush."

Perhaps the most significant encounter found in all of Dr. Ames' writings is with the small pox. It established him at the very end of his days, and despite his failings for astrology and bad verse, as honest in the acceptance of greater authorities than himself.

"The disarming of Small Pox," he writes in his Kind Reader foreword of 1761, "of its malignity and danger is a matter of great importance. Some at this day affirm they have found this great secret: If what I have wrote on this subject might stir up the Ingenious to make due inquiry into this affair, and refute or confirm the pretensions of these gentlemen, it will answer some good purpose."

On the last two pages of this edition he explains why he believes that small pox is contagious and that to avoid catching it, one must keep out of its way. As to its cure, he believed that mercury was the "best medicine to prevent the Dangers arising from the Small Pox." He added that some practitioners also believed that a preparation of calomel with an admixture of mercury and other medicines was also effective, but cautioned his readers that such cures in the hands of "quacks" could be worse than the disease itself.

In any house where this disease had been present, Ames recommended that the feather beds and blankets be taken up and laid across the backs of chairs, the contents of the rooms be taken from the closets and bureaus, and fires made in each room of "four or more pounds of Brimstone mixed with wood ashes in iron pots."

A few years later, in the Winter of 1763–4 and Spring of 1764, both of Dr. Ames' sons came down with this malady. He sent them to a Boston hospital in the care of a Dr. Mather, whom he congratulated on having adopted the methods of Boerhave (Mercury) and Lydenham.

I have just payed away a large sum since my sons entered the Hospital: and it is now perfectly low water with me but be so kind as to send me your Bill and also the Bill for Nursing and all other demands and I will Discharge them as soon as possible.

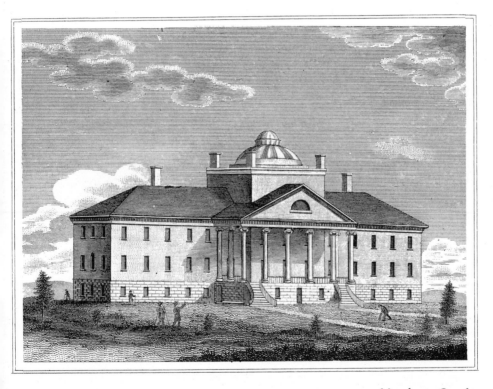

Massachusetts General Hospital, 1764

Dr. Nathanael Ames died in this same year of 1764. As I have already mentioned, his son, Nathaniel, Jr., took over the continuation of the Ames' almanacs, the last of which was to appear for the year 1795. Although the son seems to have carried on pretty much in his father's footsteps, one does note a greater emphasis on husbandry in his editions.

Nathaniel, Jr.'s edition of 1773 devoted pages 2, 3, and most of 4 to New England vineyards and the varieties of wines which might be made therefrom. After discussing the vines which seemed to have provided the best wines in England and on the Continent, he proceeded to actual instructions for planting them in New England.

> Set them about the distance Indian Corn is usually planted. In September shorten the shoots according to their strength and in the following Summer the strongest of them will begin to shew Fruit. . . . Pole them as we do Beans . . . in such manner that the grapes may grow near the Ground . . . the nearer to the ground . . . the sweeter and riper they will be and the stronger the vine. . . . Mountain wine will sell for much more than that growing in the valley, and the same observation holds good for cyder . . . if notwithstanding care, weeding, and pruning, the vines are not inclined to bear large bunches of grapes, lay ox's blood or carrion about their roots in November . . . or human dung that has lain until it has lost its odour.

However entertaining these Ames' almanacs are, we must turn now to the good doctor's fellow almanac-maker and personal friend, Benjamin Franklin.

chapter three

BENJAMIN FRANKLIN and POOR RICHARD

*Old time font tray
used for
sorting type*

Four years after Nathaniel Ames published his first almanack in Dedham, Massachusetts, in 1726, Benjamin Franklin in Philadelphia became the owner of his own printing press. By then, at age 23, Franklin had already sown most of his wild oats behind him. The boy Franklin had matured early in life. Between the ages of thirteen and seventeen, as an apprentice to his brother James in the latter's Boston printing establishment, he had acquired sufficient education and writing ability to attempt to twist the tail not only of Cotton Mather, but also of the Boston hierarchy in general. He took the public stand, for example, (one he was later to regret,) that Mather was wrong in urging smallpox inoculation. As we have seen, this was no time of freedom of the press. Brother James had found that out and paid for it with a term in prison. Even while James and his second newspaper in the American colonies were walking the tightrope over the abyss of banishment and worse, the two Franklin brothers had the nerve to shake the rope. They printed this paraphrase from *Hudibras* directed straight at the deans of Boston's morals:

RELIGIOUS KNAVE: OF ALL KNAVES THE WORST

A most strict Sabbatarian, an exact observer not of the day only, but of the evening before and the day after it; at church conspicuously devout and attentive, even ridiculously so, with his distorted countenance and awkward gesticulation. But try and nail him to a bargain! He will dissemble and lie, sniffle and whiffle, overreach and defraud, cut down a laborer's wages, and keep the bargain in a letter while violating its spirit.

"Don't tell me," he cries, "a bargain is a bargain. You should have looked to that before. I can't help it now."

If there is any one key to the personality of Benjamin Franklin we believe it is found in one of the last para-

Portrait of
Benjamin Franklin
by
David Martin
1767
Owned by
H. W. Biddle (1906)
Philadelphia

graphs he wrote for his brother's paper before he packed his bag and set sail for New York. In it he expresses his reaction to the strong hand of his father who had bound him to James; to his brother James whom he did not like and for whom he did not like to work; and to the Boston Puritans to whom life was without humor.

> Pieces of pleasantry and mirth have a secret charm in them to allay the heats and tumults of our spirits and to make a man forget his restless resentments. They have a strange power in them to hush disorders of the soul and reduce us to a serene and placid mind.

Thus we see how Benjamin Franklin, oppressed, and in danger of losing his freedom, turned at this early age upon his tormentors with his humor. It was the walking stick on which he leaned all his life even to his final day when, upon being asked to turn himself over in bed to allay his pain, he remarked: "A dying man can do nothing easily."

In New York he applied for work to one William Bradford. Bradford, Pennsylvania's first printer (1685) but exiled to New York "upon the quarrel (1724) with George Keith" referred him to his son Andrew still carrying on the family business in Philadelphia. With Andrew his luck was no better. However, he did find employment with a competitor "lately set up, one Keimer." It is important to notice that Benjamin Franklin, with his lively interest in all things printed, would have become familiar at this time with the *Kalendarium Pennsilvaniense* or *American Messenger* by Samuel Atkins. This was an almanac printed by William Bradford in 1685 for the year 1686. It is now regarded as the first almanac to be published in the Middle Colonies. Franklin, too, must have closely followed the welfare and contents of another Bradford Press imprint; "An Almanack and Ephemerides" by Daniel Leeds. Edited and published from 1687 until his death in 1720, it had been continued into Franklin's time by Daniel's son, Titan Leeds.

Franklin makes no mention of Leeds or Ames or of any almanac at all (except his own) in his Autobiography. But it is hardly disputable that he knew the two men and their almanacs. Furthermore, it is well to remember that this name Titan Leeds, in the manner in which Franklin was to put it to his own use in later years, marks an amusing episode in American almanac history.

Before one learns how this was and is, one must travel

to England where Franklin was in residence for some months in 1726, as a result of a "fool's errand."

Here again printing became his trade, and the reading of literature his constant occupation. He became well acquainted not only with the classic literature of England and the Continent but also with various almanacs and their histories on that side of the water. He would have read how it had been that those two almanac editors had predicted the great London fire of 1616, and because people believed they had then set the fire, paid for it with their lives. This knowledge, added to his own experiences with the Boston authorities and Bradford's trouble with Governor Keith in Pennsylvania, influenced him in favor of using a pseudonym, rather than his own name, as editor of the almanac he would later establish as his own. Franklin, too, would have become conversant with the prophesies of almanack maker, Lilly,* and with the weather indications contained in Murphy's annual issues which brought their owner, through some years of continuing success, a fortune only to lose the fortune for him in one year of downright failure.

Gulliver's Travels, Jonathan Swift's great masterpiece, first appeared when Franklin arrived in London. Franklin must have read it eagerly and, too, been attracted to that great satirist's duel of words with John Partridge. The latter was a popular almanac editor of that time. However, Swift condidered him but a "quack astrologer," and even went so far, in that country where libel has always been avoided as the plague, as to predict in the public press that Partridge would die on "March 29, 1708 about eleven at night with a raging fever." That this prediction did not come true is seen in

---

* William Lilly, 1602–81, English astrologer whose autobiography was published in 1715.

this rare letter from John Partridge dated April 2, 1708 to his old friend Isaac Manley, then Postmaster of Ireland, at his house in Dublin.

> "OLD FRIEND,   *Lond. April 2,* 1708.
>
> "I DON'T doubt but you are imposed on in Ireland also by a pack of rogues about my being dead; the principal author of it is one in Newgate, lately in the pillory for a libel against the State. There is no such man as Isaac Bickerstaff; it is a sham name, but his true name is Pettie; he is always either in a cellar, a garret, or a gaile, and therefore you may by that judge what kind of reputation this fellow hath to be credited in the world. In a word, he is a poor scandalous necessitous creature, and would do as much by his own father, if living, to get a crown; but enough of such a rascall.
>
> I thank God, I am very well in health; and at the time he had doomed me to death, I was not in the least out of order. The truth is, it was a high flight at a venture, hit or miss; he knows nothing of astrology, but hath a good stock of impudence and lying.—Pray, Sir, excuse this trouble, for no man can better tell you I am well than myself; and this is to undeceive your credulous friends that may yet believe the death of
>
> Your real humble servant
>
> JOHN PARTRIGE."

The name to which Partridge refers in this letter as having made this now famous prediction is Isaac Bickerstaff, the name Swift used as his pseudonym in this and other instances. That Partridge ascribes it to one "Pettie" may be explained as Partridge's way of assassinating Swift's character without fear of libel. Benjamin West of Rhode Island was later to use this same Bickerstaff pseudonym as the author of several American almanacks.

But what do we find in Volume One, Number One, of the almanac which Benjamin Franklin was to edit, pub-

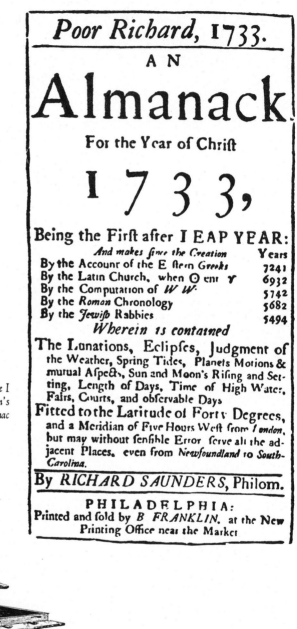

Cover of Volume I
No. 1 of Franklin's
own Almanac

Benjamin Franklin's
Printing Press

Poor Richard, 1733.

A N

Almanack

For the Year of Chrift

1733,

Being the Firft after LEAP YEAR:

And makes fince the Creation	Years
By the Account of the Eaftern Greeks	7241
By the Latin Church, when ☉ ent ♈	6932
By the Computation of *W. W.*	5742
By the *Roman* Chronology	5682
By the *Jewifh* Rabbies	5494

Wherein is contained

The Lunations, Eclipfes, Judgment of the Weather, Spring Tides, Planets Motions & mutual Afpects, Sun and Moon's Rifing and Setting, Length of Days, Time of High Water, Fairs, Courts, and obfervable Days

Fitted to the Latitude of Forty Degrees, and a Meridian of Five Hours Weft from *London*, but may without fenfible Error ferve all the adjacent Places, even from *Newfoundland* to *South-Carolina*.

By *RICHARD SAUNDERS*, Philom.

PHILADELPHIA:
Printed and fold by *B. FRANKLIN*, at the New Printing Office near the Market

lish, and print at Philadelphia in the year 1732 for the year 1733? It is his memorable prediction of the death of almanack maker Titan Leeds on "October 17, 1733 at 3:29 P.M." Leeds, as we have already pointed out, was at that time the editor of the almanac printed by Franklin's rival (Bradford) press. Thus, despite the fact that some have maintained the fiction that Franklin's *Poor Richard's Almanack by Richard Saunders* was modeled upon the Ames' editions, it would seem more likely that Franklin used established precedents with which he'd become acquainted in England.

Titan Leeds lived on not only to deny any intention of dying on that date and at that hour but also to enjoy good health for at least as long as 1740 when Franklin, in his *Poor Richard's* for 1740, noted that Mr. Leeds did die at midnight, October 4, 1739 and that the William Bradford Company, printers, had been carrying on Leeds' almanac for him ever since. Franklin gave as his authority for this statement a letter he had received from Titan Leeds out of the spirit world confirming that his death took place within five minutes and fifty-three seconds of the appointed time.

There is only one true original of the first Franklin almanac around now in existence. It is at the Rosenbach Foundation in Philadelphia. Much sought after, this run of the Franklin Almanacs from 1733 to 1756 has been photostated, reprinted, mimicked, and copied to a point where its immortality is virtually assured. The apparent reason for the popularity of these almanacs is not revealed, curiously enough, until after its long run has finished. For it is not until 1757 in a *Poor Richard Improved* edition for 1758 that one finds Franklin affixing his collected "Poor Richard" proverbs as the harangue of a wise old man attending an auction. This edition was eventually to have world-wide sale and popularity. One can conclude without too much fear of contradiction that the Franklin proverbs in his *Poor Richard's Almanack by Richard Saunders* are what made it popular and lasting.

Benjamin Franklin's own conclusion in this regard appears in his one and only mention of his Almanac in his *Autobiography*, (Houghton Mifflin Company, 1906).

In 1732 I first publish'd my Almanack, under the name of *Richard Saunders;* it was continu'd by me about twenty-five years, commonly call'd Poor Richard's Almanack. I endeavor'd to make it both entertaining and useful, and it accordingly came to be in such demand, that I reap'd considerable profit from it, vending annually near ten thousand. And observing that it was generally read, scarce any neighborhood in the province being without it, I consider'd it as a proper vehicle for conveying instruction among the common people, who bought scarcely any other books; I therefore filled all the little spaces that occurr'd between the remarkable days in the calendar with proverbial sentences, chiefly such as inculcated industry and frugality, as the means of procuring wealth, and thereby securing virtue; it being more difficult for a man in want, to act always honestly, as, to use here one of those proverbs, it is hard for an empty sack to stand upright.

These proverbs, which contained the wisdom of many ages and nation, I assembled and form'd into a connected discourse prefix'd to the Almanack of 1758 as the harangue of an old man to the people attending an auction. The bringing of these scatter'd counsels into a focus enabled them to make greater impression. The piece being universally approved, was copied in all the newspapers on the Continent; reprinted in Britain on a broadside to stack up in houses; two translations were made of it in French and great numbers bought by the clergy and gentry to distribute gratis among their poor parishioners and tenants. In Pennsylvania, as it discouraged useless expense in foreign superfluities, some thought it had its share of influence in producing that growing plenty of money which was observable for several years after its publication.

II Mon. **April hath xxx days.**

Kind Katharine to her husband kiſs'd theſe words,
' Mine own ſweet *Will*, how dearly I love thee!
If true (quoth Will) the World no ſuch affords.
And that its true I durſt his warrant be;
For ne'er heard I of Woman good or ill,
But always loved beſt, her own ſweet Will.

1	G	All Fools.	1	29	5	32	7	*Great Talkers,*
2	2	*Wet weather, or*	2	♈	5	31	7	*little Doers.*
3	3	7 * ſet 9 0	2h	29	5	30	7	New ☽ 3 day,
4	4		3	♉	5	29	7	at 4 morn.
5	5	*Cloudy and likely*	4	29	5	27	7	☽ ſets 9 29 aft.
6	6	*for rain.*	5	♊	5	26	7	*A rich rogue, is*
7	7		6	18	5	24	7	*like a fat hog, who*
8	G	2 Sund. p. Eaſter	6h	♋	5	23	7	*never does good til*
9	2	☉ enters ♉	7	26	5	22	7	*as dead as a log.*
10	3	7 * ſet 8 50	8	♌	5	21	7	Firſt Quarter.
11	4	Days 13 h. 20 m.	9	22	5	20	7	☽ ſets 1 46 mo.
12	5	*Wind or Thunder,*	10	♍	5	19	7	*Relation without*
13	6	☍ ☉ ♃	10	16	5	18	7	*friendſhip, friend-*
14	7	☌ ♄ ♀	11	28	5	17	7	*ſhip without pow-*
15	G	3 Sund. p. Eaſter	12	♎	5	16	7	*er, power without*
16	2	7 * ſet 8 21	1	22	5	15	7	☽ ſets 4 7 mor.
17	3	*and rain.*	2	♏	5	14	7	Full ● at 10 at
18	4	*Beware of meat*	2h	16	5	13	7	night.
19	5	*twice boil'd, & an*	3	28	5	12	7	*will, will witho.*
20	6	*old foe reconcil'd.*	4	♐	5	11	7	*effect, effect with*
21	7	Days inc. 4 h. 26	5	22	5	10	7	☽ riſ. 11 aftern.
22	G	4 Sund. p. Eaſter	6	♑	5	8	7	*out profit, & pro-*
23	2	S George ☍ ♃ ♀	6h	16	5	7	7	*fit without ver-*
24	3	Troy burnt	7	29	5	6	7	*tue, are not*
25	4	St. Mark, Evang.	8	♒	5	5	7	Laſt Quarter.
26	5	*Cloudy with high*	9	24	5	4	7	*worth a farto.*
27	6	*winds, and perhaps*	10	♓	5	3	7	☽ riſ. 1 31 mor.
28	7	7 * ſet 7 47	11	22	5	2	7	
29	G	Rogation Sunday	12	♈	5	0	7	Days 14 hours
30	2	☌ ☉ ♀ *rain.*	12	22	5	59	S	7 * ſet 7 34

Specimen page from "Poor Richard's" showing how proverbs were indicated

In view of the importance of these proverbs, we can hardly omit here the reprinting of a sampling of this heretofore mentioned edition of 1758. If these seem too heavy a load, bear in mind that Dr. Franklin also lives in these. He really believed in them and took great pains in his daily life to impress upon his neighbors that he did.

Courteous Reader

I have heard, that nothing gives an author so great pleasure, as to find his works respectfully quoted by others. Judge, then, how much I must have been gratified by an incident I am going to relate to you. I stopped my horse, lately, where a great number of people were collected at an auction of merchants' goods. The hour of the sale not being come, they were conversing on the badness of the times; and one of the company called to a plain, clean old man, with white locks, "Pray, father Abraham, what think you of the times? Will not those heavy taxes quite ruin the country? how shall we be ever able to pay them? what would you advise us to do?"—Father Abraham stood up, and replied. "If you would have my advice, I will give it you in short; for *a word to the wise is enough,* as Poor Richard says." They joined in desiring him to speak his mind, and gathering around him, he proceeded as follows:

"Friends, says he, the taxes are, indeed, very heavy; and, if those laid on by the government were the only ones we had to pay, we might more easily discharge them; but we have many others, and much more grievous to some of us. We are taxed twice as much by our idleness, three times as much, by our folly; and from these taxes the commissioners cannot ease or deliver us, by allowing any abatement. However, let us hearken to good advice, and something may be done for us; *God helps them that help themselves*, as Poor Richard says.

It would be thought a hard government that should tax its people one tenth part of their time, to be employed in its service; but idleness taxes many of us much more: sloth, by bringing on diseases, absolutely shortens life. *Sloth, like rust, consumes faster than labor wears*, while the *used key is always bright*, as Poor Richard says.—*But dost thou love life, then do not squander time, for that is the stuff life is made of*, as Poor Richard says.—How much more than is necessary do we spend in sleep; forgetting that *the sleeping fox catches no poultry*, and that *there will be sleeping enough in the grave*, as Poor Richard says.

If time be of all things the most precious, wasting time must be, as Poor Richard says, *the greatest prodigality;* since, as he elsewhere tells us, *Lost time is never found again;* and *what we call time enough always proves little enough;* Let us then up and be doing, and doing to the purpose; so by diligence shall we do more with less perplexity. *Sloth makes all things difficult, but industry all easy;* and and *he that riseth late, must trot all day,* and shall scarce overtake his business at night while *laziness travels so slowly, that Poverty soon overtakes him. Drive thy business, let not that drive thee:* and *early to bed, and early to rise, makes a man healthy, wealthy, and wise*, as Poor Richard says.

... Methinks I hear some of you say, "Must a man afford himself no leisure?" I will tell thee, my friend, what Poor Richard says; *Employ thy time well if thou meanest to gain leisure; and since thou art not sure of a minute, throw not away an hour.*

Leisure is the time for doing something useful; this leisure the diligent man will obtain, but the lazy man never; for, *a life of leisure and a life of laziness are two things. Many, without labour, would live by their wits only, but they break for want of stock,* whereas industry gives comfort, plenty and respect. *Fly pleasures, and they will will follow you. The diligent woman has a large shift; and now I have a sheep and a cow, every body bids me good morrow.*

Franklin reading at
night by candlelight

. . . So much for industry, my friends, and attention to one's own business; but to these we must add frugality, if we would make our industry more certainly successful. A man may, if he knows not how to save as he gets, *keep his nose all his life to the grindstone, and die not worth a groat at last. A fat kitchen makes a poor will;* and

Many estates are spent in getting,
Since women for tea forsook spinning and knitting,
And men for punch forsook hewing and splitting.

If you would be wealthy, *think of saving as well as*

getting. The Indies have not made Spain rich, because her outgoes are greater than her incomes.

Franklin carrying his loaves of French bread home for lunch

Away then with your expensive follies, and you will not then have so much cause to complain of hard times, heavy taxes, and chargeable families; for

Women and wine, game and deceit,
Make the wealth small, and the want great.

At present, perhaps, you may think yourselves in thriving circumstances, and that you can bear a little extravagance without injury; but

For age and want, save while you may;
No morning sun lasts a whole day.

Gain may be temporary and uncertain, but ever, while you live, expense is constant and certain; and, *It is easier to build two chimnies, than to keep one in fuel,* as Poor Richard says: so, *Rather go to bed supperless, than to rise in debt.*

Get what you can, and what you get hold,
'Tis the stone that will turn all your lead into gold.

And when you have got the Philosopher's stone, sure you will no longer complain of bad times, or the difficulty of paying taxes.

Franklin with
brother James

. . . And now to conclude, *Experience keeps a dear school, but fools will learn in no other,* as Poor Richard says, and scarce in that; for it is true, *We may give advice, but we cannot give conduct.* However, remember this, *They that will not be councelled cannot be helped;* and farther, that *If you will not hear reason, she will surely rap your knuckles,* as Poor Richard says.

Thus the old gentleman ended his harangue. The people heard it, and approved the doctrine, and immediately practised the contrary, just as if it had been a common sermon; for the auction opened, and they began to buy extravagantly. I found the good man had thoroughly studied my Almanacks, and digested all I had dropped on these topics during the course of 25 years. The frequent mention he made of me must have tired any one else; but my vanity was wonderfully delighted with it, though I was conscious that not a tenth part of the wisdom was my own, which he had ascribed to me; but rather the gleanings that I have made of the sense of all ages and nations. However, I resolved to be the better for the echo of it; and, though I had at first determined to buy stuff for a new coat, I went away, resolved to wear my old one a little longer. Reader, if thou wilt do the same, thy profit will be as great as mine. I am, as ever—thine to serve thee,

Richard Saunders.

Franklin
arrives in London

In *Harper's New Monthly Magazine* for the year 1876 there appeared a series of articles on American humor and caricature. In one of these articles we find:

Poor Richard's was the great comic almanac of the country for twenty-five years, and it was Franklin who infused the element of burlesque into American journalism. He would not advertise a stolen prayer book without inserting a joke to give the advertisement wings: "The person who took it is desired to open it and read the Eighth Commandment, and afterward return it into the same pew again; upon which no further notice will be taken."

Franklin's first, middle, and last loves actually were in the areas of humor. He knew his *Hudibras* by heart, was a personal friend and correspondent of the great Hogarth. It is believed that had not Franklin been called into so many different positions of political importance, he would easily be ranked now with such great American humorists as Josh Billings, Mark Twain, and Thomas Nast.

Although he drew heavily upon Dean Swift, Bacon, Rabelais, La Rochefoucauld, Steele, Defoe, and others, he combined these drafts with his own wide scientific knowledge, political understanding, knack of phrase, and sense of humor right up to his death in 1790.

As an almanac maker, he was a success from the beginning. His first edition enjoyed at least three more printings before even the month of January, 1733, had ended. Some of his humor would not be considered exactly polite by many twentieth century readers. However, there are many other bits to chuckle over. For instance, how a "turbo"—or what we know as a "twister"—storm may be stopped by vinegar; and such tongue curlers as "Ecnephias," Franklin's term for a windstorm from the clouds.

In studying some of the issues of *Poor Richard,* it is difficult to classify them as the writers in *Harper's* did, as entirely "comic." They contain, one easily agrees, a great deal of humor—especially that relating to the predicted death of Titan Leeds; the measurement of longitude with barley corns; and the explanation of how weather predictions are to be made. The strength of Franklin's humor, however, is not because it is comical. It lies chiefly, we find again and again, in the fact that his humorous sayings make sense.

• • •

In attempting to bring alive here through their works these early almanack editors and publishers, I have found them at times something more than just the puppets of their own printed pages. I like to think again of Dr. Franklin, for example, pushing his own wheelbarrow full of paper to his printing plant. And too of James Franklin, his brother publishing The "Poor Robin" Almanac in Newport, Rhode Island for the year 1728, this being the second earliest piece of printed matter in that state. I am amused with James Tulley

when he angrily reports to Benjamin Harris that the
almanack sheets Harris has sent him have been ruined
by the rain. Dr. Nathaniel Ames, running his own
stage coach tavern in Dedham, appears before me
often, as a jovial host away from his books and study,
an excellent judge of good meals, wine, and tavern talk.
Judge Sewall, and Mather, the presidents of Harvard,
working at their Philomath editions, amuse me too
when I see them quarrelling over how much more useful
their editions are to mankind for telling time than the
inaccurate clocks of their generation. With all these
men there was a great deal of hard work for survival
and comfort, education, religion, and good government,
before they could so much as pen a line of an annual almanack. But pen all of the lines of all these almanacks
they did. That other nine-tenths of their living one must
imagine between the lines.

Franklin delivering
his own paper from stage coach
to his shop in
Philadelphia

chapter four

THE REVOLUTION
and beyond

The Midnight Ride of Paul Revere

By 1750, some almanack editors were beginning to establish themselves as useful recorders of history. In the period between 1750 and 1790, the most striking example of this kind of on-the-spot reporting is found in *The North American Almanack,* and *Gentleman's and Lady's Diary for the Year of our Lord Christ 1776* by Samuel Stearns, Student in Physick and Astronomy, Printed by Isaiah Thomas in Worcester; (and sold by B. Edes, in Watertown; and S. & E. Hall, in Cambridge).

We will come to know Editor Stearns (1741–1809) as well as printer Isaiah Thomas better before this chapter has ended. For now, however, the account in this 1776 almanack of the "Commencement of Hostilities between Great Britain and America" cries out for attention. It is likely that Stearns did the report himself but he calls it a letter from the Rev. M. William Gordon of Roxbury, Massachusetts, to a gentleman in England.

> . . . At length the (British) General was fixed on sending a detachment to Concord to destroy the (American) stores . . . about ten of his officers, on the 18th of April, passed over Charlestown Ferry, armed with swords and pistols and placed themselves on different parts of the road in the night . . . to prevent . . . the country's being alarmed which made the (American) Bostonians jealous . . . so that expresses were forwarded to alarm the country . . .

> On the first of the night . . . the (British) detachment . . . of 800 or better repaired to the boats, and got into them just as the moon rose, crossed the water, landed on the Cambridge side. They made a quick march of it to Lexington and got there by half an hour after four.

> Here I must pause to acquaint you that in the morning of the nineteenth, before we had breakfasted, between eight and nine the whole neighborhood was in an alarm; the minute men . . . were collecting together; we had an account that the (British) regulars had killed six of our men at Lexington . . . another (British) detachment was coming out of Boston. I concluded that this (British) brigade was intended to support the grenadiers and light infantry . . . The brigade under Lord Percy marched out, playing by way of con-

tempt, *Yankee Doodle;* they were afterwards told, they had been made to dance to it . . . I concluded that I would ride to Concord, enquire for myself.

Before Major Pitcairn arrived at Lexington signal guns had been fired . . . and the alarm men had repaired to the (Lexington) Common . . . about one hundred and thirty . . . the night being chilly . . . were dismissed to appear again at the beat of the drum . . . Upon information being received . . . that the troops were not far off . . . the remains of the company were collected together . . . in a confused state . . .

The simple truth I take to be this . . . The (American) Lexington Company upon seeing the (Bri-

The skirmish at Lexington between the British and the Yankees

tish) troops and being of themselves so unequal a
match, were deliberating what they should do,
when several of them dispersing of their own
heads, the Captain ordered the rest to disperse ...
Before the order was given, three ... of the regular (British) officers ... seeing the (American)
company ... cry'd out "You damned rebels lay
down your arms." Major Pitcairn ... perceiving
that they did not actually lay down their arms ...
gave the command to fire, then fired his own pistol,
and so set the whole affair a-going. There were
killed at Lexington eight persons ... Eight hundred of the best British troops in America thus
nobly vanquished a company of non-resisting Yankees while dispersing ...

Samuel Stearns

I have omitted here, for reasons of space, some of the fascinating detail in "Rev. Gordon's" letter. I see its author, Samuel Stearns, clearly; bright blue eyes, beady as bullets . . . obsessed almost to a point of greed with the gathering of facts and never mind the fancy. He has to be almanac editor Samuel Stearns himself. It is more than unlikely that a letter of this kind, so uncomplimentary to the British, would have been mailed to England and returned to Stearns for publication. It is more likely that it was written by someone who hounded Lexington's Town Clerk, to have insisted his witnesses give the truth on the Bible, to have traveled on horseback with his companion from Dorchester to Lexington and Concord and back again on patrolled roads at the risk of his neck: the inquisitive reporter-doctor-editor Samuel Stearns.

Back at his desk, I see him fired with enthusiasm. Perhaps when editing this almanac he had been interrupted, as his printer, Isaiah Thomas had been by the battle at Bunker's Hill. Perhaps not. But this was the year of his 1776 almanac in which, for all time, he would set the record straight.

He must have been a busy man during that summer of 1775 as he labored to complete this historic edition for its November publication date.* For, as his eventual summary of the issue indicates, he labored over a number of diversified subjects:

The Lunations, Eclipses, Tides, Feast and Fast Days, Friends' Meetings, Courts in the Four New England Governments, the Seven Stars, Sun, Moon, Clock equations, Roads and Stages, the Battle of Lexington [which we have just now seen], Tories, Whigs, Drunkenness, Soldier Health, the Dysentery, and a short history of the charters of the colonies.

He edited a number of different almanacs between 1770 and 1794—some of them under the pen name (at New London, Connecticut) of Freebetter.

Stearns of course, did get his copy to Isaiah Thomas in time and lived to spend the years from 1785–88 in a Worcester jail for being a Tory sympathizer and a supposed counterfeiter. While there he edited an almanac or two for Mr. Thomas as well as his own. Prior to this period, he had gone to New York not only to

---

* Samuel Stearns was not the only editor and writer battling deadlines in those exciting days. Daniel George, for example, the crippled editor of the *Portland Gazette,* wrote and published at Draper and Phillips, "next door but one to the Sign of the Lamb Tavern," Newbury Street, Boston, his continued narrative of the Battle of Lexington and Concord. He included, as well, a now-much-sought-after drawing of General Warren.

join the Tory cause but to publish (1783) what seems now to be the first true *United States Nautical Almanac*. Later we find him plying his almanack trade in Bennington, Vermont, and in 1789, back again at his old Boston stand with his publication of *The Universal Calendar and the North American Almanack*. By then he had become on his title page, "Professor of the Mathematics, Natural Philosophy, and Physic." Edes and Son, No. 7 State Street, Boston, had replaced Isaiah Thomas as his publisher and printer. In 1801 he published his American Herbal at Walpole, New Hampshire. Until his death in 1810 in Brattleboro, Vermont, he was to spend even more years in jail for indebtedness. Take it all in all, Professor Stearns cannot be said to be as happy as he was interesting.

● ● ●

Isaiah Thomas was born in Boston on the 19th of January, 1749, and apprenticed at the unbelievably early age of six to Zechariah Fowle, a printer. He also worked as a printer in Portsmouth, New Hampshire; Halifax, Nova Scotia, and in Charleston, South Carolina. Back in Boston, to become Fowle's partner in 1770 and by 1772 appeared on the almanac horizon with his *Massachusetts Calendar*. By this time it had become the usual practice of many printers to provide, as a printing service, the twelve or sixteen inside calendar pages complete. Various editors and publishers purchased these for use with their other material. Thomas furnished these so-called "sheet almanacs."

As he was neither an astronomer, nor qualified to make up the tables required for these sheets, it is probable that he persuaded one or another of his professional friends to do it for him. One of these was assuredly Benjamin West of Rehoboth, Massachusetts and

Providence, Rhode Island,* (also known as Isaac Bickerstaff), to whom Thomas gives full credit for the years 1775 through 1786. Others were the redoubtable Samuel Stearns and Daniel George. As these friends were in some years also publishing their own almanacs concurrently with Thomas, I would assume that, just as the Benjamin Harris-Tulley relationship was virtually a joint venture, Thomas also ran joint ventures in almanac publishing with one or more of these men.

Essentially, however, Thomas was a printer and, as such, interested in almanacs only as a sideline or feeders for his hungry presses. One of these presses was also in the newspaper business as Franklin's had been in earlier days. From it, in 1770, for example, came the Whig paper called the *Massachusetts Spy,* a real thorn in the Loyalist side.

When Thomas saw how things were going in Boston a few days before the British invasion of Concord, he took up his presses and type and fled to Worcester, Massachusetts. With them carefully protected there, he returned to join the Minute Men at Lexington and Concord.

After Thomas returned to Worcester, he became America's leading printer. His imprints from there would include some four hundred books, of which at least one hundred were juveniles. In addition there was the newspaper, several magazines, and almanacs. Following his retirement in 1802 he devoted himself to the writing of *The History of Printing in America* which he published in two volumes in 1810. His other major retirement interest was founding, in 1812, The American Antiquarian Society in Worcester.

---

* The first almanac in Rhode Island was printed in 1728 by James Franklin, brother of Benjamin, and known as "Poor Robin's Almanac.

This day published,

And to be sold, by the Thousand, Grofs, or Dozen,
By I. THOMAS, *at the* WORCESTER BOOKSTORE,
and by THOMAS & ANDREWS, *in* BOSTON ;
Sold, also, by E. LARKIN, D. WEST, S. HALL, B. LAR-
KIN, J. BOYLE, J. WEST, W. SPOTSWOOD, J. NAN-
CREDE, W. PELHAM, and at the BOSTON BOOKSTORE,
in *Boston* ; by F. STEBBINS, *Springfield* ; S. BUTLER,
Northampton ; T. DICKMAN, *Greenfield* ; CUSHING and
CARLTON, *Salem* ; J. MYCALL, *Newburyport* ; and oth-
er Bookfellers in this ftate ; by D. CARLISLE, in *Wal-
pole*, Newhampfhire ;— COMINS, in *Windfor* ; I. BEERS,
Newhaven ; THOMAS, ANDREWS, & PENNIMAN, in *Al-
bany* ; and by the Bookfellers in *Rhodeifland* and *Vermont*,
ISAIAH THOMAS's
*Maffachufetts, Connecticut, Rhodeifland, New-
hampfhire & Vermont*
ALMANACK,
With an EPHEMERIS, for the year of our Lord
1 7 9 8.
Being the Second after Biffextile or Leap Year, and Twen-
ty Second of the Independence of United Columbia.
From Creation, according to the Scriptures, 5760.
CONTAINING

In Thomas, then, we have primarily a city-bred individual of strong character and substance. We see him not so much as the Student of Physick, or Philomath, or Astronomer, as were Ames or Stearns and others, but as a business leader, participant in numerous banquets (Masonic and otherwise) in the City of Boston, and friend of the wealthy and accomplished who might contribute antiquities to his Museum.

In all of his long and worthy career, I find only one instance which does not seem to be fully in character with the way I picture Thomas today: austere, gruff, uncompromising, stern, extremely able, and shrewd. This was his association with David Carlisle, editor of *The Farmer's Weekly Museum,* in Walpole, New Hampshire.

In April 1793, according to the *History of Walpole,* Isaiah Thomas became involved there with his former apprentice, Carlisle, to the extent of furnishing not

only a printing plant but also a bookstore of some size
beneath it. Neither Carlisle, his successor, Dennie, nor
even Dennie's successor, Alexander Thomas, was fully
ever able to swing it and the property had a way of
landing back in Thomas' lap. But with all its troubles,
The Farmer's Museum, published at Walpole with
the Thomas backing, became one of America's leading
journals—through not only the humor and hilarity of
its contents, but indeed through its personnel as well.
Thus we must conclude Isaiah had a side which could
chuckle, too.

His almanac career, however, does not seem to flourish in any significant way until he and his come-lately rival, Robert B. Thomas, are running together on the almanac treadmill in the 1790s. In the meanwhile, the rest of the country did not stand still and Nathanael Low's, *An Astronomical Diary; Or, ALMANACK* had long since (1762) begun its long run in Boston.

As his issues progress from 1762 towards the Revolution, we find Nathanael Low of somewhat different character than his predecessors with whom we have thus far become acquainted. Like Dr. Ames, he is a physician, but he does not own a tavern or have other interests to broaden his vision. He is down by the sea in Ipswich, Massachusetts, but unlike Thomas or Tulley, does not go in for joint ventures with his printers or publishers. He is Mr. Low throughout, and no mistake about that, but, as with all headstrong individuals, it is the world that is wrong and not Mr. Low. Thus we find him apologizing in his edition of 1767 for failing to bring out his edition of 1766 with the excuse that the business conditions of that year had made it impossible.

"Candid Reader:" quoth Mr. Low, in this fore-word for 1767, "I have again ventured to make my publick appearance before you . . .; the intermission of last year notwithstanding . . . The perplexed state of public affairs, was the chief occasion of my not publishing an Almanack for last year."

The
Boston
Massacre

Still and all, the Ames Almanack had put in its appearance for that year and one would assume that the times were no harder for Dr. Ames than they were for Dr. Low. Perhaps Ames was his trouble! But one does find this plea in Low's almanac of 1771:

> . . . let us abstain from the Use of foreign Tea. There is no one article imported so fatal to the Cause of Liberty as this; in regard that the duty on Tea, includes the greatest part of the Revenue arising from the Act complained of.—The Law of Self Preservation does also enjoin us totally to discard it.—Were the Ladies of New England truly sensible how much their health is endangered, and consequently their CHARMS by a constant use of this destructive plant, I am persuaded they would need no other motive to induce them speedily to reject it.

Aside from the political motif here (with which we are certain Dr. Ames would have been in agreement), we wonder if Mr. Low is also taking sides against competitor Ames who, a few years earlier, had come out in praise of this same drink?

Perhaps some of Low's troubles arose from the fact that, of all the almanac and newspaper editors of his day, he probably was more outspoken in behalf of American Liberty than any of them. Note, for example, these two comments appearing in his February and March calendar pages of 1771:

CHRISTOPHER SEIDER, first Martyr to American Liberty Massacred by an infamous informer, 22nd day, 1770
    and
An horrid infernal Massacre most inhumanly and barbarously committed by the British troops, on the Inhabitants of Boston, 5th Day, 1770.

In addition to weather forecasts and tables of stages which appear in the early issues of Low one also finds his "Exact Table to bring Old Tenor into Lawful Money." Low, his ear apparently closer to the ground on current business difficulties than most, had a way of expounding seriously upon these matters. Although he was able to bring himself to introduce fables, humorous verse, and other matter (such as stories about tarantulas) into his almanacs, he apparently was unable as Franklin was, to turn the spit far enough over so that these serious issues ever really cooked through.

In following Low's trail down through the years, one finds it well cut—but with a number of diversions left along its sides. There is the engraving of Oliver Cromwell, for example, on his cover for 1774, one of the earliest of almanac illustrations. There are innumerable Rules of Health, long forewords (six pages in 1784), best times for the cutting of hair, much on farming, inflation, and this:

> *Receipt to Keep one's self warm a whole winter*
> *with a single Billet of wood:*
>  Take a Billet of Wood of a competent size, fling it out of the Garret window into the Yard, and then run downstairs as hard as ever you can drive; and when you have got it, run up again with the same Measure of Speed; and thus keep throwing down and Fetching up till the Exercise shall have sufficiently heated you. This renew as often as the occasion shall require.

• • •

However, in spending too much time with Low we are likely to forget that, by 1776, Boston was no longer either the Hub of the Universe, or New England the outer periphery of the world. We have, as the "country people" would have said, "fit" the Battles of Lexington, Concord, and Bunker Hill, and with Low's issue of 1777 (see his page 3 herewith) we accompany him to the new "seat of war" and what our almanac friends are up to in that part of the country.

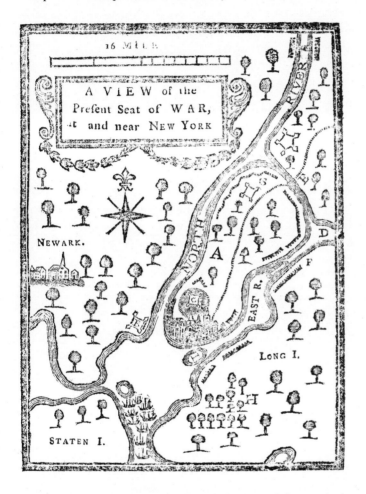

With the war centered in New York and beyond the Hudson, there began a vexatious lack of unity among the Colonies. The struggle, but for the tenacity, wisdom, and courage of George Washington, and the help of God, might very well have brought this young America not only to its knees but to bondage. We cannot here probe as deeply into the reasons for this disunity as we should like. We can, however, at least recognize, (despite being Boston born) that all of the almanack makers of those perilous times did not happen to live in Boston. In fact, there were quite a few good ones who did not.

In New Haven, for example, there was Roger Sherman. I may be wrong in placing Sherman in New Haven. After all, he was born in Newton, Massachusetts 1721, served in Washington as U.S. Representative as well as Senator (1789–93) and published his *Astronomical Diary* in Boston for the year 1760. Here we find a good account of the French & Indian wars then raging, whose final outcome in 1783 brought Canada and Louisiana under French dominion. However, with his *Connecticut Diary* (1750–61) and his roles as Mayor of New Haven and Treasurer of Yale College, this prominent and worthy signer of the Declaration of Independence is difficult to move away from his Connecticut locale.

Johnson's *Pennsylvania and New Jersey Almanac,* calculated by Joshua Sharp, with William Penn on its cover, appeared in 1808 but the first Pennsylvania almanac "Kalendarium Pennsilvaniense" was printed in 1685.

The first printing shop in Delaware was opened in 1761 by James Adams. In his employ was the apprentice, Isaac Collins (1746–1817), who helped Adams to print the *Wilmington Almanack* for 1762. In 1770, by then in business for himself we find Collins as a printer in Burlington, New Jersey and introducing to the state his *Burlington Almanack*. Over the years his editors for this Almanack were Timothy Trueman, William Waring, and Abraham Shoemaker— all probably pen names as were Richard Saunders for Franklin's *Poor Richard; Poor Will* for William Andrews, and *Poor Robin* for William Winstanley (not to be confused with Franklin's "Poor Robin" Rhode Island Almanac). Collins is far from an almanac "great." However, as the second in the colonies to print a good edition of the St. James version of the Holy Bible in 1793, he will not soon be forgotten.

Another string of almanacs was *Hutchins Improved,* edited by a Yale Professor, John Nathan Hutchins, and printed by Hugh Gaine of New York City.* A unique copy (1913) of what may have been Hutchins' first edition (1753), the first book printed by bookseller Hugh Gaine, is on file in the Chicago Public Library. This Hutchins-Gaine joint venture sporadically stretches over the rest of the 18th century and into the 5th year of the next.

As New York city was occupied by the British during the Revolution, it is not likely that turncoat Hugh Gaine, with his "Printing office at the Bible in Hanover Square," would have looked favorably upon any efforts

---

* The first genuine New York almanac is "An Almanac for 1697" by John Clapp, who kept a "house of entertainment about two miles without the City of New York at the place called the Bowry." Opposite the June 24th date in that edition he gives notice that in commemoration of the feast of St. John Baptist, a feast will be held for all Johns at John Clapp's in the Bowry "where any gentleman whose Christian name is John may find a hearty Wellcome to joyn in consort with other Johns."

by Hutchins to agitate the Revolution in those parts. In fact, except for the reprinting of the new Constitution in 1787 and again in 1797, I find no mention (in my limited file of copies at least) of the Revolution in this series of almanacs until the following, which appears in their last edition of 1815.

YANKEE STRATAGEM

During the revolutionary war, two brothers, from one of the eastern ports, were commanders of privateers; they cruised together and were eminently successful, doing much damage to the enemy, and making much money for themselves. One evening, being in the latitude of the shoals of Nantucket, but many miles to the eastward of them, they spied a large British vessel, having the appearance of a merchantman, and made towards her; but to their astonishment, she proved to be a frigate disguised. A very light breeze prevailing, they hauled off in different directions—one only could be pursued, and the frigate gained rapidly on him. Finding he could not run away, the commanding officer had recourse to strategem. On a sudden he hauled down every sail and all hands on deck were employed with setting poles as if shoving the vessel off a bank! The people on board the frigate were amazed at the supposed danger they had run, and to save themselves from being grounded, immediately clawed off, and left the more knowing Yankee to "make himself scarce" as the night rendered it prudent for him to hoist sail in a sea, two hundred fathoms deep.

A further reminder of the bitter struggle of those days between those who would join these United States into one large Union, and those who would not, is a quotation from the Hutchins' edition of 1796 entitled "A Comparison of the Conduct of the Ancient Jews, and of the Anti-Federalists in the United States of America." It is extracted from the works of the "late Dr. B. Franklin." Hutchins reveals how a zealous advocate of our new Constitution had stated that "the repugnance of a great part of mankind to good government was such that if an angel from heaven was to bring down a constitution found there for our use, it would nevertheless meet with violent opposition." He then points out that Franklin had proceeded to explain that this actually had been the case when the Supreme Being had delivered to Moses, His chosen servant, a Constitution and Code of Laws to be administered by Moses, Aaron, and his sons. Benjamin Franklin further revealed that one Corah, wishing to supplant Aaron, so stirred up the populace that no less than 250 of the principal men "of renown—famous in the congregation" cried out for the stoning and destruction of their divinely appointed ministers—and their constitution. Just so, Franklin maintained, the American constitution was also divinely inspired—it had to be for the salvation of so many people—and, by inference, the opposition to it was equally guilty of selfish motives.

However, apart from these two references, both of them appearing in almanacs far removed from Revolutionary times, the Hutchins-Gaine editions did introduce a trend that Low and others were later to adopt. This was the inclusion of editorial matter which was of entertainment value. One good example of this is the Hutchins (1779) *Druid Prediction of the Fate of Charles the First;* another is Hutchins' (1792) account of *A True and Wonderful Appearance of three ANGELS,* (clothed in white raiment) to one Ebenezer Adams of Medford, near Boston, on the 4th of February, 1761, at night.

> The one who stood in the middle named the 2nd Chapter of Colossians and 4th verse, and then uttered these words—"When Christ who is our Life shall appear, then shall ye also appear with him in Glory.". . . from which words (the angel) preached to me for an hour.

In this account of the visitation of the angels, sandwiched between "A Receipt to Cure Inflammation of the Bowels" and one "For the Piles," no room is left for doubt that Mr. Hutchins at least did not wish his readers hamstrung altogether by the grip of discouragement and despair.

The full story of New York's early booksellers, such as Hugh Gaine, is not easily told in a few short paragraphs or pages. However, one cannot study these Hutchins-Gaine almanacs without realising that Hugh Gaine must have made good use of his store of books. From his medical shelf come cure after cure, from "Travel" come anecdotes of the Orient and the South Seas, and from "Curiosa and Erotica" some such items as his "An Old Man may Marry a Young Maid this Month." (1773) Some of these are not exactly dinner conversation topics for 20th-century polite company. As with Low in Boston, Gaine's business problems were not easy. We leave him now still unaware of the year to come of which he was to write in his almanack in July, 1797 "The present year has presented a scene of ruin to the commercial part of America, more dreadful than any known before."

• • •

In the meanwhile, a great star of the almanac world had arisen over Philadelphia in the person of David Rittenhouse (1732–96). Of this great man, Thomas Jefferson had these words of praise:

We have supposed Mr. Rittenhouse second to no astronomer living; that in genius he must be the first because self taught. As an artist he has exhibited as great a proof of mechanical genius as the world has ever produced. He has not indeed made a world; but he has, by initiation, approached nearer to its Maker than any man, who has lived from creation to this day.

David Rittenhouse

Jefferson is referring here to the planetaria which Rittenhouse had built in 1767 for Princeton University and for the University of Pennsylvania. Rittenhouse also had his own observatory and America's first transit telescope through which he observed the transit of Venus in 1769. As a patriot he parallels Sherman of New Haven, having served as a member of the Pennsylvania Assembly in 1776 and as Treasurer of his state, 1777–89.

If he published any almanacs of his own, I have no record of them. But I would assume that among the many almanacs which had sprung up since *Poor Richard's* in the Pennsylvania, New Jersey, Delaware, and Virginia areas during these years, Rittenhouse calculations would have been widely used. At least one almanac, *Bailey's Rittenhouse,* was continuing to use his name in the year 1817. Of the others, scattered about and issued only sporadically not only in the Middle Colonies but also in Rhode Island and Connecticut, only three seem of importance here; namely, those of Nathan Daboll, Isaac Bickerstaff, and Abraham Weatherwise.

• • •

In 1772, Nathan Daboll (1750–1818) of New London, Connecticut, brought out *The Connecticut Almanac* for the year 1773. Although the title has changed, and its current issue is a far cry from the early ones, this almanac has an enviable record of publication and family participation. For at least one hundred twenty years some member of the Daboll family continued the calculations for this almanac.

This is the order of family sequence:
1. Nathan (Master Nathan) Daboll
2. Nathan (Squire Nathan) son of Nathan
3. David Austin, Sr. (brother of Celadon Leeds Daboll) son of Nathan II

4. David Austin, Jr. (son-in-law of Celadon and son of David A. Sr.
5. Loren E. (brother of David Austin, Jr.)
6. C. Ernest Daboll (grandson of David Austin, Sr. and son-in-law of Celadon Leeds Daboll)

It is now (1969) published as a section of The Old Farmer's Almanac in Dublin, New Hampshire.

*Squire and
Mrs. Nathan Daboll*

Some years ago, some correspondence I had with William Stuart Ayers of Leonia, New Jersey, revealed that Ayers was a classmate and close friend of Frederic Allyn Daboll. As I had been unable up to that time to obtain any replies to my queries to the Daboll family about their almanac, I urged Mr. Ayers to find out for me what he could. Some weeks later Mr. Ayers was kind enough to forward me the following letter Frederic Allyn Daboll had written him in these regards. It is dated August 14, 1941 at New London, Connecticut.

W. S.:

About the Daboll Almanac—

It began in 1792 and has been issued each year since. Copies of two issues (during the Revolutionary War) are lost but the rest of the complete file however, has been presented to the New London Historical Society by my Uncle. Three men (the last of them the grandfather whom I recall well, and who established the business of Civil Engineering now continued by my Uncle Loren E. D. here,) did the computations for the Almanac for *128 years.* A rather remarkable record!—It is to be understood of course, that prior to the 1870s, or thereabouts, there was no "Nautical Almanac"* (published by U.S. Gov't.) available to mariners along New England's coast, and no reliable tide-tables, or "southings" and other star records which are valuable in navigation. Since New London was a leading sailing port of register

---

* Established in 1912. It will be noticed that the "Daboll" almanacs from 1774 through 1792 are by one Edmund Freebetter. J. C. L. Clark in his *Famous Dr. Stearns* points out that this pseudonym was not one used by Daboll. Secondly, Clark makes a good case for the fact this name did belong to Dr. Samuel Stearns, of whom we have written earlier in this chapter.

in the early days, Nathan Daboll decided to collect
information for the use of her Captains, and chose
to base his reckonings on the *Meridian of N. L.,*
—instead of on Greenwich.—In the great days of
whaling, it is said that there was a Daboll Almanac or two on *every whaler* as well as merchantman out of Salem, Boston, New Bedford,
and New London. Nathan's son was "Prof. of
Math." at Wesleyan College (Middletown,
Conn.) along in the 1820s. He established a
"School of Navigation" too, here and for 25
years there was scarcely a whaling captain or
"mate" from New Bedford to New Haven who
did not study with "Master Nathan" for three to
four months for advancement in his profession.
I've seen a "list of Captains" in the "Whaling
Fleet for Greenland" where practically every
man had taken the Daboll "Course for Navigating
Officers." Ernest, who publishes the Almanac and

*In the great
days of whaling,
there was a
Daboll Almanac
or two on
every whaler*

makes all the calculations, I suppose picks up $400 or $500 for his work and keeps the thing going— for sentimental reasons.—Circulation in Conn., R.I., and Mass. is about 3400 now.—Issue is 5 to 6 thousand—"A Relic."—

F. A. D.

• • •

After Daboll, is the name of importance Isaac Bicker-staff. Earlier, I mentioned how it was that Jonathan Swift had used (1708) this pseudonym in his scurrilous prediction of the death of the English almanac editor, John Partridge. You may remember, also, how Benjamin Franklin adopted Swift's device for his own prediction of the death of his rival Titan Leeds in Philadelphia. But perhaps it is asking too much to recall that I have also mentioned that one Benjamin West of Boston had calculated several almanacs for Isaiah Thomas in Worcester. To add to this confusion, I am now pointing out that this Benjamin West is not the painter (1738–1820) but the American mathematician and almanac maker (1730–1818) born in Rehoboth, Massachusetts, who also made use of this pseudonym, Isaac Bickerstaff.

It is not clear just why Benjamin West chose to use this pseudonym for his *Bickerstaff's Boston Almanack* in 1768, 1779, and 1783–93. Perhaps one reason was because he also published *The New England Almanack* at Providence, Rhode Island, annually from 1765 through 1781; *The North American Calendar; or Rhode Island Almanack* from 1781 to 1787, and *The Rhode Island Almanack* from Newport from 1804–1806. West also observed the same transit of Venus that Rittenhouse did in 1769 and wrote a paper on it. Fate plays strange tricks on the best of men. Although a distinguished Professor at Brown University, West is best remembered today for the fact that in his

Boston Bickerstaff's appear the first Calendar page illustrations to be seen in any of the American almanacs. The illustrations below are from his 1784 Calendar pages. There is one for each month and the edition winds up with a 3″ by 3″ caricature of "The Monkey Who had seen the World."

It is possible that there were others using the Bickerstaff pseudonym in West's time for we note that in 1779 he was overheard saying that he probably would not continue using it thereafter because "there were too many imitators who had brought the name into disrepute." Four years later, however, he was back with it again.

• • •

Portrait of
George Washington by
Paul Revere in Weatherwise
Almanack 1781

General Washington surveyed
in pleasing attitudes by Wisdom
and Valour while Britannia
deplores her loss of America.

Finally, there is our old friend Abraham Weatherwise whose Boston edition of 1781 carries in it this fine woodcut engraving of George Washington by Paul Revere as well as the Washington "Victory" statue.

Some may very well wonder who this Abraham Weatherwise was, is, or might have been. There is much of the apocryphal in his history. One reason is that in the continuing forewords of his editions of 1781, 1782, and 1783 in which he describes his habitation and accounts of his adventures, he is not exactly serious. From these the story has arisen that he lived on the edge of a Boston dump in a shack built from loose boards.

> Know ye then, my beloved Readers and Customers, (that) at this very time I live in a poor, little, sorry house of clay, the timber or chief support whereof, is much gone to decay, by reason of age, and very good judges give the opinion, that it cannot be repaired, chiefly owing to the damages formerly received by taking in too much Wet: But be that as it will, it stands upon the waste, as other cottages do; and what is still worse, I am liable to be turned out at a minute's warning.

As there were spaces between the boards in his roof, he maintained that, for his profession of weather forecaster, he had not only a clear view of the heavens but closer contact with the weather than any of his rivals. For sustenance he depended largely upon fees from Boston's strolling unmarried couples who, upon occasion, visited him at his South Boston "villa" to be graced with his prediction of which future date would best serve for their wedding.

It has also been held, probably with as much truth, that when Robert B. Thomas, founder of The (Old)

Farmer's Almanac in 1792, was looking around for a weather forecaster that he hired "Old Abe" for that purpose and the old boy has remained in just that preferred position to this very day. If this be true, at this writing, he is alive and well and going strong at nearly one hundred ninety years of age!

More factual, perhaps, is the Goodspeed Bookshop's statement that Weatherwise's Almanack for 1787, calculated for the meridian of Portland, Maine, was the first almanac to be published in that state. It was printed by Thomas B. Wait, of the firm of Titcomb and Wait (Maine's first printers), on Middle Street and makes two almanacs for Old Abe in that same year. Weatherwise's *Town and Country Almanac* for 1787 is by the same editor but for Boston and "Printed for and sold by J. Norman, near the Boston Stone." The name Abraham Weatherwise was also used by Christopher Sower, a German of Philadelphia as early as 1739. In 1759, 1762, and 1769 there are almanacs edited by Abraham Weatherwise in Philadelphia, Boston, and Providence.

I would not debate with anyone the question of whether Abraham Weatherwise is all pseudonym, or partly so, or not at all. Hixson's Life of Isaac Collins (1746–1808) states the name is a pseudonym, but leaves it open to anyone's guess about who used it. Nevertheless, Abe Weatherwise—as I see him in his long white beard and ill-fitting clothes—ushered in the healthiest and most interesting period of almanac making.

Charlestown, Massachusetts
Meeting House

LITH OF E W

chapter five

The FARMER'S ALMANACS

Despite the great depression of 1797, the War of 1812, and the cold summer of 1816, there had come into existence by 1820 literally hundreds of so-called "farmer's almanacs." Indeed, by 1816 some 500 different titles were being published. A number of the almanac makers that we have already discussed—such as Nathanael Ames, Isaiah Thomas, Nathanael Low, John Hutchins and "Abraham Weatherwise"—edited and/or published "farmer's almanacs." This name was being used then much as we would use the name "dictionary," and one was distinguished from another only by the name of the editor. By the early 1800's, however, none had circulations as high as 100,000 copies. Most were computed for strictly localized areas —such as Robinson's for Maine, Leavitt's for New

Hampshire, the two Thomas's for New England, Munsell's for New York. Each one, however, was designed to be helpful in all aspects of the life of their readers who were, in those rural days of America, farmers or small merchants or professional men.

The strongest, most popular, and most durable of these farmer's almanacs turned out to be *The Farmer's Almanac* founded by Robert B. Thomas in 1792 and published in pretty much the same format during every year since.

"Robert B." was born in what is now West Boylston, Massachusetts, in 1766. He was always bemused by the fact that he resided in four incorporated towns, two district parishes, and one precinct. His Welsh father had quite a library and the boy eventually became a school teacher. However, he drifted forthwith —as most New Englanders do—to Boston. There he worked for a while in a bookshop, and progressed into his own business of selling books. In 1790 he took a course in mathematics under Carleton Osgood, himself an almanac editor from Nottingham, New Hampshire. He persuaded Osgood to do his computations for a Robert B. Thomas almanac. So there he was in business. Needless to say, Robert B. Thomas was much more than a bookseller. The Sterling, Massachusetts town hall bears his name and his sturdy, unflinching character and sound advice not only stood the test of his 56 years of editing, but still shines from the present day pages of his almanac.

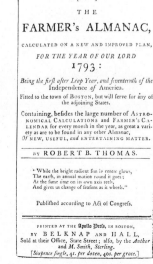

Cover of Vol. I, No. I
of the (Old) Farmer's Almanac,
The (Old) was added in 1832
to distinguish it from
competitors.

After 1832 the word "Old" was inserted in its title to insure its identity. In 1904, Professor George Lyman Kittredge of Harvard University authored a fine, comprehensive book, called *The Old Farmer and his Almanack*. This was about the man Thomas and his almanac. It was copyrighted by Horace Ware, then editor and publisher of the annual editions of the almanac, and published by the Harvard University Press. In 1957 I edited (for Ives, Washburn Company) an anthology of this almanac. There have been innumerable television programs, magazine and newspaper features about it. Since I assumed the editing and publishing responsibility for this Almanack in 1939, I have endeavored to keep its format and content close to the founder's original.

Robert B. Thomas
1766-1846
and Mrs. Robert B. Thomas
1774-1855
Founders of the Old Farmer's Almanac
in 1792

Other farmer's almanac editors of some note, some of whom I have touched upon elsewhere in this book are, Daniel Robinson, Dudley Leavitt, Isaiah Thomas, Nathanael Ames, and Joel Munsell. There were many others besides these but perhaps the short profiles of these which follow may typify the rest.

Joel Munsell, like Isaiah Thomas, in addition to being an almanac maker, was also a printer and antiquarian. He was born in Northfield, Massachusetts, April 4, 1808 and died in Albany, New York, January 15, 1880. He began work as a printer's apprentice in Greenfield, Massachusetts. By the age of 18, he had settled down as a journeyman printer in Albany where he spent most of his life publishing books of history, Webster's Albany Almanac and many others. Unlike his father, a merry soul, Joel took life almost too seriously.

Nathanael Ames was born in Bridgewater, Massachusetts in 1708. He moved to Dedham, seven years after he had founded in 1725 his Astronomical Diary and Almanac. He was a physician, an astronomer, and a physicist as well as tavern keeper. He died in Dedham in 1764. His son carried the almanac on until 1795 when it was then continued by his son, Nathanael the third. All three men were certainly cut from the same cloth and by now it is hard to tell one from the other.

Isaiah Thomas, 1749–1831, was in the almanac and printing business long before Robert B. came along. It is said that before Robert B. decided to publish his own he went to Isaiah and tried to purchase the calendar sheets for it. However, Isaiah, although he furnished them for others would not do it for the man who was eventually to become the more successful almanac maker of the two. He had to move from Boston, being a patriot, in 1775, and set himself up in Worcester. He eventually founded the American Antiquarian Society, spent some years in residence in Walpole, New Hampshire, and was a serious minded top-rung man on the Boston social and business ladder.

Leavitt's Farmer's Almanac ceased publication at Concord, New Hampshire in 1941 after 145 years of continuous existence. Its editor and founder, Dudley Leavitt, began publication in 1797 and stayed with it until 1852—a record of 55 years, one year less than the outstanding record of Robert B. Thomas. Master Leavitt was born in Gilmanton, New Hampshire and later moved to Meredith. For many years a hard laboring man on the farm, he also attended diligently to his schooling. Through this effort, he became a distinguished astronomer. What better combination can we ask for an almanac editor?

Dudley Leavitt, professor astronomer, and editor Leavitt's Farmer's Almanac

Bannaker's Almanack for 1796 had a typographical error on its front cover — the nightmare of every editor. In his own name, the second "A" should have been an "E". *Banneker's Almanack,* published 1792–1802 for Maryland, Pennsylvania, Delaware, Virginia, Kentucky, and North and South Carolina, was by Benjamin Banneker, born in Baltimore of African parents. Through friendship with George Ellicott, whose Almanac George Washington used, Banneker borrowed astronomy books and studied the stars from Ellicott's observatory at night. In submitting his first edition to Thomas Jefferson he asked that the whites "put your souls in our souls' stead."

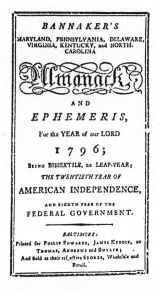

Finally, in this group of profiles there is Daniel Robinson, a direct descendant of a Pilgrim settler who died aboard ship on the way to this country. He came to Maine in 1812 from New York state where he had been a teacher. He got the hang of astronomy for his Maine Farmer's Almanac, founded in 1819 (and still in business) from his father and edited the almanac until his death in 1866. Although a strict Puritan he maintained a rare and genial sense of humor.

• • •

It has not been difficult to maintain The Old Farmers Almanac as it was 150 years ago. Old Robert B. in his fifty-six year tenure as editor left a clear stamp of his character and intentions on his pages.

"As to my judgment of the weather," he wrote in the Preface to his first edition, "I need say but little; for you will in one year's time without any assistance of mine, very easily discover how near I have come to the truth."

Were we two to meet, by some miracle in this world or the next, the first question I would ask Mr. Thomas would be about the origin of the story told for the past 150 years about him and his famous forecast for July 13.

It is said that in March, 1815, Mr. Thomas was ill and in bed with the influenza. A Boston printer's devil was sent to his bedside with the request that he furnish copy for his July, 1816 weather forecast. He was so ill that he sent the boy away with the instructions to the printer that he should put in "anything at all . . . just leave me alone . . ." Consequently, the printer did just that and for July 13th the forecast read "Rain, hail, and snow."

When Mr. Thomas had recovered and eventually saw the proofs, the sheets on which this forecast appeared had already been printed. He ordered the sheets rerun. However, a few had by then escaped. When it actually did rain, hail, and snow on July 13, 1816 these few original sheets with this forecast on them were sufficient to establish Mr. Thomas (and his "partner," Abe Weatherwise—see previous chapter) as not only the best forecasters of those times but also to put most of his competitors out of business. Like the one about George Washington and the cherry tree, this story still persists. The scoffers who would proclaim it as apocryphal are undoubtedly right, but are not believed. Having come to know Mr. Thomas as well as I do, I would not expect any direct answer from him on it.

Almost as controversial as almanac weather forecasting are the pages and pages the old-time farmer's almanac editors filled with strange admixtures of zodiacal signs and phases of the moon for the determination of the best times to plant, to cut brush, to wean the calf—and even when to pull that tooth.

Foulkes, an editor opposed to this sort of thing, in his edition of 1832 was careful to include in his "Notes to the Reader" the following statement:

> The moon's supposed influence on the human body is entirely omitted, as one of those uncertainties which is incapable of demonstration, and which furnishes a play to the imagination, in which there is no rational dependence.

Robert B. Thomas, and others, were much of the same mind about how seriously the old wives' tales and advices with regard to the effects of the moon should be taken. One finds more often than one would suppose flat denials that the moon has any effect whatsoever. However, such denials apparently were never able to eradicate the beliefs that many almanac readers had, and still have, in this respect.

Among the strongest of these beliefs were (and are) those held, for instance, that all vegetable and flowers, the blossoms or fruits of which are to appear above the ground, should be planted in the "light of the moon" and those from which the harvest is made below the ground (such as beets and potatoes) are to be planted in the "dark of the moon." The "light" begins with the first night of the new moon and continues through the night when the moon is at its full. The "dark" is from the night after the full through the night before the new.

Other superstitions, one finds, concern the most advantageous times, according to the moon's phase and place in the Zodiac, for cutting brush, trees and fence posts; weaning calves, and all kinds of farm activities. About the only logical conclusion one can derive from the creeds of these lunarians is that if these people are willing to go to all the trouble of looking up and deciding which time and which Zodiacal place is best for their purposes, they must be conscientious and careful individuals in the care of their gardens and farms. If they are that careful, it is fairly easy to conclude that they will have good gardens, fences, firewood, and farms—regardless of whether or not the moon is in its right place!

• • •

If we put to one side these parts of the farmer's almanacs which grasp at the straws of astrology, moon phase weather forecasting, and lunar superstitions, we shall notice there are even more predictions in these almanacs of a solid, scientific nature. These are the tables of the annual eclipses, arrival of comets, telling time by the stars, explanations with regard to the Harvest Moon, and how to correct one's compass for magnetic needle variations. Leavitt, as well as the *Physician's Almanac* of 1817 had sunspot count theories to explain the cold summer of 1816. Godfrey in 1834 had a full-fledged Philosophy of Storms (discussed in Chapter VII). Andrew Beers in 1810 had his theories about finding the exact moment of the Equinox. Houghton in 1806 even told how it was that the ancients believed eclipses would foretell such great events as a schism in the church, or the advent of the plague.

Anson Allen, in *The New England Almanac* of 1833, describes "The wonderful comet which appeared in the years A.D. 1456–1531–1607–1682–1759 and may be expected to appear again this year or next; and every 75th or 76th year thereafter." Edmund Halley, an Englishman, had successfully predicted its earlier appearances, and in 1910 (two years late this time) the present generation knew it by his name.

Nathan Wild, in his 1836 Almanack took enough time away from his major astronomical calculations to set down for his readers the exact mean variation of the compass to the West of North for the years 1812 to 1834 at Chesterfield, New Hampshire. This mean increased from 6°26′ in 1812 to 7°35′ in 1834. Concord, New Hampshire, had a greater variation by about one degree. In the years since then this same variation has increased at approximately the same rate. In looking up old deeds and boundaries, these compass variations are conceivably of great interest and usefulness to landowners as well as to surveyors. In his edition of 1771, Ames gives these for Boston, Penobscot, and for Falmouth. In the determination of a boundary line in the Town of Stoddard, New Hampshire the writer was confronted with working from a very old deed. As the compass variation in that area had, by 1960 become considerable and these deeds had apparently been transcribed in terms of the magnetic North instead of true, some knowledge of what the variation had been in the years of the old deed helped considerably in finding out what the true boundary lines were.

Little wonder then that a farmer's almanac maker of whatever name, clever enough to forecast the times of sunrise and sunset, times of the moon phases, eclipses, evening stars, and comets would also gain a certain amount of credence in his weather and planting tables.

In one widely known instance an almanac reference to the moon cleared a man suspected of murder. This occurred in the trial of William Armstrong, Abraham Lincoln's first big victory in court. During the trial, Lincoln pointed out that the prosecutor erred when he said his client murdered Armstrong in the "light of the moon." Holding an almanac aloft for the jury to see, Lincoln pointed out that on that evening of August 28, 1857, the "moon was riding low" and, for this reason, his client had no light of any kind. Robert B. Thomas's *Old Farmer's Almanac* is the only almanac for 1857 which states that on August 28th the moon was "riding low."

It was this confidence, built slowly over the years by such conscientious editors as Robert B. Thomas (1766–1846), Leavitt (1772–1851), Robinson (1774–1864), Daboll (1750–1818), and Munsell (1808–1880), which was the mandate to all editors to include in their editions all sorts of other advice—some of it good, some bad, and some intentionally humorous.

• • •

In 1807 for such a simple product as toothpowder one did not go, as we do today, to a drug store and purchase the latest variety in its fancy package at the "advertised" price. Instead you turned to *Hutchins'* or some other farmer's almanac of that year and learned that all you needed to do was place a lump of charcoal a second time into the fire until it was red hot. Upon cooling, you blew off all external ashes; the remainder you pounded to a powder, poured into a phial, and kept from the atmosphere. Every morning, and after every meal, some of the powder you placed upon a soft brush and used, with warm water, on the teeth. Such a powder would "correct the factor which arises from decayed teeth and at the same time whiten them as far as possible."

Should Farmer John heat his rooms with closed stoves or by open fires? Isaiah Thomas, in 1793, was of the opinion that the open fireplaces of New and Old England caused one-third more pulmonary diseases and deaths than were experienced by the Pennsylvania Dutch who used, exclusively, the closed-in stoves. Thomas explained that it was far less injurious to one's health to remain in a stove-heated room of eighty degrees or more—even at the risk of the contrast when one went out of that room into below-zero weather—than it was to subject one's self to the draughty exposures of a fireplace-heated room in which one side of the room (where the fire was) would be close to one hundred degrees, and the other side down to forty or fifty degrees.

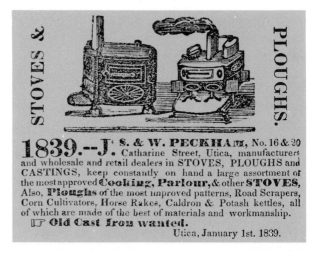

STOVES & PLOUGHS.

1839.--J. S. & W. PECKHAM, No. 16 & 20 Catharine Street, Utica, manufacturers and wholesale and retail dealers in STOVES, PLOUGHS and CASTINGS, keep constantly on hand a large assortment of the most approved Cooking, Parlour, & other STOVES, Also, Ploughs of the most improved patterns, Road Scrapers, Corn Cultivators, Horse Rakes, Caldron & Potash kettles, all of which are made of the best of materials and workmanship. ☞ Old Cast Iron wanted.
Utica, January 1st. 1839.

To take spots off all kinds of colored cloths was done this way in 1796: Half a pound of honey, the yolk of a fresh egg, and a nut of ammoniac salt were mixed together; some of the mixture was placed on the spot; the spot was then washed with clear water and would disappear. Ink spots came out with lemon or sorrel juice, or white soap diluted in vinegar. Iron rust was removed from linens with immersion in hot water followed by rubbing with sorrel juice and salt. Such linen, afterwards washed in the lye of wood ashes, would be found entirely free of the rust spots.

Houghton's Genuine Almanac of 1811 states that the bark of the butternut tree will dye cloth in twelve distinct colors—one for each of the months in which the bark may be collected. In fact, this almanac tells of a New Jersey farmer's wife who had discovered a method of using this bark so that cloth, well colored with its dye in January, would assume a new distinct color as it entered upon each succeeding month of the year. Infusing the root of the arum plant in water, and dyeing the cloth for her husband's coat a handsome gray, she put it away in a closet. Some months later when she went for the cloth to make it into a coat, she was surprised to see it had turned into a bright blue. She insisted that her husband had exchanged her cloth for one of this color, which he denied. However, he was greatly pleased with a blue coat and looked forward to wearing it on muster day in June. When that day came, and he had prepared himself in all his regimentals, he sent upstairs for the coat. Alas, by this time it had become a handsome olive color! Chagrined, he borrowed another. But all was not lost, for in August, when his grandmother died, the coat had again changed color—this time to a fine crow black for her funeral.

A book in itself could be written about these homely household hints found in the old farmer's almanacs —most of them so simple and inexpensive one wonders why more are not used today.

• • •

One does not, however, have this same feeling as one browses through the multiplicity of cures these farmer's almanac editors offered for their "patients." We smile when we learn from a Low Almanack of 1797 how the "changes that have taken place within a Century" have contributed to the "introduction of a numerous class of nervous ailments, in a great measure unknown to our ancestors." With progress has arrived "the hysterics, a disease peculiar to women." And in these hundred years, from 1700 to 1800, a great measure of the ills suffered by mankind are being caused by "first, the present general use of tea (and may I add coffee which is still worse) . . . The second place may be perhaps allowed to excess in spirituous liquors."

Mr. Low does not have the answers for female hysterics but a fragment from his day, the title of which I am unable to identify, does have just the thing for convulsions in children. "Scrape peony roots fresh digged. Apply what you have scraped off to the soles of the feet. It helps immediately."

The almanacs of John Nathan Hutchins and Hugh Gaine gave to cures more space, more consistently, than did the other almanacs of those years. Just in case our own paraphrases of these might seem unbelievable, a few quotations from their pages are shown.

To Prevent Marks of the Small Pox, or Take them away when pitted.
Take the lungs of a Calf, parboil them, and press out all the moisture, then mix it with a double quantity of Barrow's Grease, and two ounces of the Juice of Celandine, and one of Wormwood. Boil these up into a thin Ointment, and anoint the face.

To Kill Bugs

Take a quantity of fresh tar, and mix it with the juice of Wild Cucumber, let it stand two or three days and stir it four or five times a day, then anoint your Bedstead with it.

To Prevent Tooth-Ache

Wash the mouth every morning with cold water, rub the teeth well with the Fingers or a small Brush that no Slime or Tartar may gather on the teeth, And if any appearance of a Scorburich Humor should appear on the gums, then wash the mouth with thy own water, rubbing the gums well.

Preservation of Sight

For Those whose Eyes begin to grow dim with age, wash the outside of the eye every morning with that person's own water, continuing the same for some weeks. By following this method some aged people have preserved their sight so as to read without spectacles till they were seventy years of age and more.

Medicine for the Plague, Small Pox, Measles, and Fevers

Wine and Peruvian bark united with the greatest caution to shun infected places.

Corns on the Feet

Roast a clove of Garlic on a live coal in hot ashes, apply it to the corn, and fasten it with a piece of cloth, the moment of going to bed.

Dr. Rush's Directions for the Treatment of Yellow Fever

As soon as affected, lose ten or twelve ounces of blood from the arm, and repeat same quantity once or twice a day until . . . normal pulse returns.

Take one of the purging powders (fifteen grains of Jalop and ten of Calomel) every 6 hours, in syrup or molasses until you have 4 or 5 large black colored stools. . . .

The bowels should be opened two or three times every day by means of castor oil. . . .

Drink plentifully of toast and water, tamarinds or apple water,—tea or Barley water.

Strength may be restored by a diet of chicken, veal, mutton broth, beef tea, boiled white meats, tea, coffee, chocolate, bread, milk, and fruits of the Season.

Consumption, or Cough

Take a Gill of Mustard Seed, with Burdock Root and Horse Radish, of each a handfull scraped fine. Steep them in half a gallon of wine; take about a Gill, twice each day, two hours before or after eating.

Inflammation of the Bowels

Take away 10 ounces of Blood and repeat the bleeding according to the urgency of the complaint; give a clyster every day, till the patient has two or three stools, and to appease the pain and stop excessive vomiting, give 10 drops of laudanum in a little broth every six hours.

For the Yellow Jaundice

Take an ounce of Castile Soap, slice it thin, put it in a Pint of Small Beer cold, let it boil gently half away, scum it once, then strain through a small sieve, warm it, and drink it all in a morning fasting. Take a small lump of sugar after it, and fast two or three hours. The Party may walk about his business and eat his accustomed meals. If at any time he drink wine, let it be white wine.

For the Piles
Take the powder of earth worms, wash them well in white wine, but so they may not die in the wine; then dry the worms no further than they may be conveniently reduced to a powder. Incorporate exactly as much Hen's Grease with the powder and make into an ointment.

An Excellent Family Receipt
Take one ounce of Green Copperas, fried until white, and reduced to a fine powder. Add one ounce each of Powder of Senna, Jalloproot, and Cream of Tartar, half an ounce of Ginger, twelve drops of Chymical Oil of Cloves, and enough Syrup of Orange peel to make a paste.

(This medium was said to be of "singular good service," for whooping cough, convulsion fits, teething, worms, dropsy, jaundice, stomach ache, head aches, listlessness, colds, and shortness of breath.)

Cold Sores and Ulcers
Take one spoonful of burnt Allum and a like quantity of common salt, dissolve both in a pint of water and wash the affected place, if the Patient can stand it, two or three times a day.

Another Cure for Sores
Take White Oak Leaves that have hung on trees all winter, boil them, and lay them on the Sore like a Poltice.

In getting on we note that old Robert B. Thomas eventually had to submit in a Worcester hospital to the Venner inoculation which his own almanac had recommended as a small pox remedy. Afterwards he related that he felt the disease itself would have been far less injurious to the health and spirits of his wife and himself than was the inoculation.

• • •

One reason I am so fond of these early almanacs is that despite all of their curious cures, predictions, and other instances of what I call preaching from pulpits in which they did not belong, their editors never for one minute lost sight of their strong faith in the Creator. There is always a strand of religion in the cloth of their editions. Eventually, no matter how hard the small pox, or yellow fever, or other epidemic may be pushing them and their readers—against which they know their cures will be of little or no avail—they will return, as in the classic example which follows, with an assurance that faith, God and the Bible mean everything.

This interesting account of the London Plague is from an eyewitness. It is faithfully—and at great length—reported in *Peter Brynberg's Wilmington, Delaware, Almanack* of 1810.

This plague began with the introduction of some goods imported from Holland, brought thither from the Levant. In the house where these goods were opened (in January), four persons died almost immediately. From January 20th to 24th, some 474 people succumbed. By the middle of August over a thousand a day were being carried away, and burials were being made in pits instead of graves. London residents, more than desperate, came to the confessions of their sins in the streets; some of them, crazed with fear and fever, rushed naked into the Thames to die there from exposure and drowning. From the middle of August to the middle of September, no less than sixteen hundred died, "one day with another." As death came to rage in every corner—3,000 in one night,, 100,000 more taken ill—people became frantic, they abandoned their fears, all was

lost, "vain was the help of man." They abandoned all precautions, assembled together in churches again to pray, and went about their business unafraid—because tomorrow, each felt, would be that day when, hopelessly, she or he would be no more. When the psychological tide had thus turned (to the amazement of all) things began to get better. Physicians were surprised to find their patients better. "In a few days everybody was recovering."

"Nor was this by any medicine found out," writes this eyewitness, "or any new method of cure discovered, but it was evidently from the secret invisible hand of Him, that had at first sent this disease, as a Judgement upon us."

"Blessed be God," was then heard in the streets, "and let us give thanks to Him for it is all His doings; human help and skill was at an end."

"In a few days everybody was recovering."

For his own survival, the reporter of the foregoing acknowledged his faith in the verses of the 91st Psalm which began: "I will say of the Lord, He is my refuge, and my fortress . . ."

I should like to dwell longer on these religious and moral overtones. But perhaps one more excerpt, exemplifying the morality of these almanacs tells the whole story. It is from *The Clergyman's Almanack* of 1815:

> The indiscriminate reading of Novels and Romances is to young females of the most dangerous tendency . . . it agitates their fancy to delerium of pleasure never to be realized . . . and opens to their view the Elysium fields which exist only in the imagination . . . fields which will involve them in wretchedness and inconsolable sorrow. Such reading converts them into a bundle of acutely feeling nerves and makes them "ready to expire of a rose in aromatic pain". . . . The most profligate villain, bent on the infernal purpose of seducing a woman, could not wish a symptom more favorable to his purpose than a strong imagination inflamed with the rhapsodies of artful and corrupting novels.

•   •   •

In assimilating the contents of these hundreds of farmer's almanacs one may be attracted to their forecasts, cures, illustrations, verse, historical dates, or any one of the ten or fifteen different components which went into the making of a typical issue. In this, however, one never loses sight of the fact that basically the little books, as we mentioned in the beginning of this chapter, were there to be helpful to the day-to-day welfare of the reader.

One must balance, for example, the cures and remedies with an equal content of the recipes and rules of health which the almanacs offered as guides for the days and nights when disease or fear or unusual weather or some other emergency was not threatening the farmer and his family.

There were, for example, the "Rules for Long Life" in the very first edition by Robert B. Thomas:

1. It is certain that a good constitution must necessarily be the foundation of a long life.
2. That there be in a well organized body a mind sound and gay, yet sage withal.
3. One should eat to live, and not eat to satiety.
4. Act, in everything, with moderation, to keep the body in a reasonable activity.

5. Live chastely if you wish to live long.
6. Abstain from eating different meats, and drinking several sorts of drinks at the same repast.
7. Chew perfectly what you eat.
8. At meals eat, alternately, moist things after dry, fat after lean, sweet after sour, and cold after hot, to the end that one may be corrective of the other.
9. After having drank more than once, eat dry bread or biscuit.
10. Never use yourself to any violent exercise, only in order to give a colour; but never to make you sweat.
11. In an extraordinary sweat, you should not, by any means, be uncovered.
12. After coming out of bed, you should never go look out of the window.
13. You should eat very little of new fruit at a time.

To be sure, these were not original with old Robert B. He picked them up from a "learned Monsieur Comiers." However, he did qualify them with the advice that one should also be descended on at least one side of the family from long-lived parents; be of a contented disposition; have a symmetry of body proportions; have large veins, a deep voice, and skin not too white and smooth. Finally, one must be "a long and sound sleeper."

As for the recipes to which the farmer's wife might turn while her husband was busy with the cattle or crops, the *Pocket Almanack* of 1844 gives us some idea of what these were like.

RECIPES FOR THE LADIES

Sponge Cake—Five eggs, half a pound of sugar, and a quarter of a pound of flour. (Another) Five eggs, three tea cups of flour, two of sugar, and a little cinnamon.

Pound Cake—One pound of sugar, one pound of butter, one pound of flour, nine eggs, and one nutmeg.

Election Cake—Five pounds of flour, two pounds of sugar, three quarters of a pound of butter—yeast; mix it with milk and water.

Marlborough Pudding—One pound of butter and one pound of sugar, rubbed together, one dozen of sour apples—chopped fine, nine eggs—well beat, and one nutmeg finely grated; bake with side crust the same as custard.

Loaf Cake—Four pounds of flour, 2 pound sugar, 1 cup of molasses, three quarters pound of butter, 2 pound raisins, a spoonful of saleratus, and 1 pint of yeast; add cinnamon and cloves—or, clove and nutmeg.

Hard Gingerbread—Two lbs. flour, two pounds sugar, three quarters of a pound butter, nine eggs, and six ounces of ginger.

Cup Cake—Five cups flour, three of sugar, one of butter, one of milk, one glass of brandy, three eggs—spice to your own taste.

Loaf Cake—Five pounds of flour, two of sugar, three quarters of a pound of lard, and the same of butter, one pint of yeast, eight eggs, one quart of milk; roll the sugar in flour; add raisins and spice after the first rising.

Apple Pudding—Take one pint of scalded milk, half a pint indian meal, a tea cup full molasses, a teaspoon salt, and six sweet apples will afford an excellent rich jelly. This is one of the most luxurious yet simple puddings to make.

Composition Cake—One pound of flour, one of sugar, half pound of butter, seven eggs, half a pint of cream, and a gill of brandy: the butter and sugar to be well rubbed together.

Tea Cake—Three cups of sugar, three eggs, one cup of butter, a small quantity of saleratus—and make quite as stiff as pound cake.

Bread Pudding—One pound of bread or biscuit, soaked in one quart of milk, run through a sieve or cullender; add seven eggs, three quarters of pound of sugar, one quarter nutmeg, cinnamon, one gill of rose water, one pound of raisins, half a pint of milk, bake three quarters of an hour in middling hot oven.

Wonders—Two pounds of flour, three quarters of a pound of sugar, half a pound of butter and nine eggs, a little mace and rose water; fried in lard.

Jumbles—Three pounds of flour, two of sugar, two of butter, eight eggs, with a little carroway seed; add a little milk; if the eggs are not sufficient.

If interested in the complete round of what the farm families sat down to three times a day, Sundays and holidays, one does not stop here with these few desserts. One can go on and on among the old farmer's almanacs into the roasts, yeast, bread, cider, wines, sauces, vinegar from honey, and calves foot jelly.

Also of interest to some may be the gradual evolution, as the farm almanacs present it, of farm machinery. There would be the tripod with the ring in its apex through which was threaded a chain or rope by means of which strong men and oxen hoisted foundation or wall stones into place.

There was Phinney's Improved Roller as seen in Fessenden's (1831):

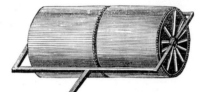

In Fessenden's 1836 edition appeared the "new" implements shown on the opposite page: 1. The Quakers' improved self-governing Cheese Press; 2. Seaver's Cultivator; 3. Grindstone on friction rollers; 4. Harrison's Patent Corn Sheller

Of course, no examination of these old farmer's almanacs would be complete without including several examples of the essays usually printed under the heading. "Farm Calendar." These portions of the almanacs speak not only for themselves, but also for me. They spell out in a few words how these various editors came out of their ivory towers to visit the farmer and his family. They could be crotchety or benign, stern or charitable, ministers or clowns, Addison and Steele at their best, or Dickens at his worst. But most of all they had an integrity and charm about them, little seen before their times and almost never seen today.

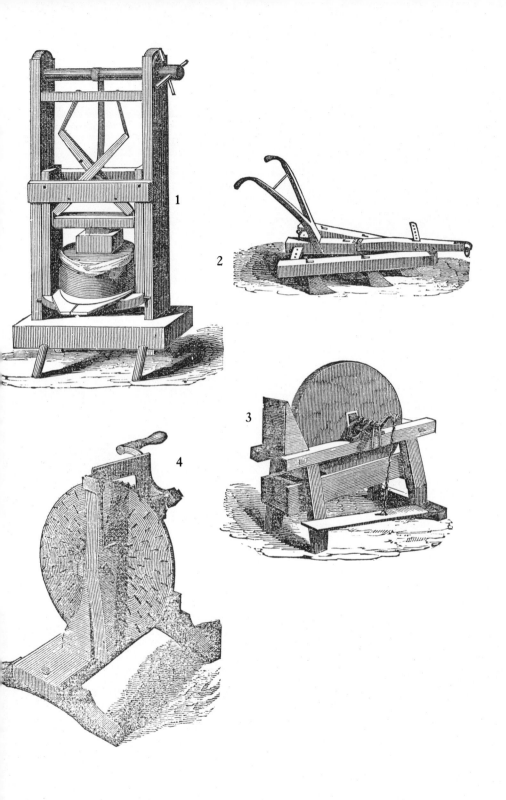

The samples which follow from various almanacs have been chosen almost at random. Some of these were written by Robert B. Thomas.

"Reckon not your chickens before they are hatched"—that is to say, be not too hasty about the enjoyment of those things which are still afar off. Wait patiently until your watermelon is ripe before you eat it. But stop! we have not planted it yet perhaps—spur up, spur up, boys! the garden must not be neglected. Three hundred and twelve years ago, the art of gardening was introduced into England; prior to which, garden produce was imported from the Netherlands. Beets, carrots, turnips, &c. common table vegetables, were imported into a country, which industry has since made one of the most fertile soils.

Plough in your dung as soon as you have spread it—recollect that manure pays great interest—lime is a very excellent material for compost manure. It destroys worms as well as gives strength and body. Your early peas and beans are planted, and you must stir the ground about them. Now turn out your early calves to grass. Do not forget to give your cattle salt when they first go to grass. It is a fine month for business, and we must be as engaged as a hen and her chickens.

May 1821

The season approaches for long evenings, and the girls begin to think of quiltings, frolicks and sweethearts. There is no hurt to be sure in all this, if you only practise temperance.

How is the barn and the woodhouse, and the door-yard, Mr. Snug? Do you keep them in husbandlike order, or is your yard incumbered with brush, old rails, stumps, straw, chips, leached ashes, rotten cabbage, dead cats, old rags, and fleas? And the wood-house filled with broken ploughs dislocated wheel-barrows, hog's nest and skunk skins? And your barn cramm'd with old barrels, sleighs, wheels, useless rakes, forks, gate posts, guide boards, and broken grindstones?

Some will have it that a slovenly farmer gets as much profit from his farm as a neat one. Now this I do not believe, for if a man depends on raising and selling butter and cheese, he is sure to meet a quick market, if he is known to be neat and trim about his husbandry. I can name some whose butter and cheese I would no sooner eat than I would the very filth of a jakes.

September 1812

This little merry and pleasant songster always appears about this time. We consider him a friend to the farmer, though some are disposed to charge him with committing depredations upon the corn-fields. At any rate, his trespasses cannot amount to much, as there are, comparatively, but few of his kind. He is called by some the New England mockbird, and certainly has a singular drollery in his note, unlike any other of the feathered race hereabouts. The boys will often give a sort of translation of it, thus: *Here I come! here I come. Charly, Charly, Charly! What, what, what? Going to plant? going to plant? Scratchem, Scratchem, scratchem! Whew! hah, hah!* Then away he flies to some other field, and, perching upon a tree-top, entertains the laborers there with his innocent melodies. This is the planting month, and there is much to do. We must be busy whenever the weather gives us a chance. It is presumed that your hay holds out for your laboring cattle. Working on green grass feed now will be but too short nibbling, and they will move "faint and wearily." "A merciful man," you know, "is merciful to his beast."

May 1853

"Heigh-ho-hum! Here John, take the jug and run down to 'Squire Plunket's and get a quart of new rum. Tell him to put it down with the rest and I'll pay him in rye, as I told him. Come, Eunice, hang on the tea-kettle and let us have some sling when John gets back.—Wife, how long before breakfast?" "Alas, husband, where is this to end? Our farm is mortgaged, you know; the mare and colt both attached, last week the oxen were sold, and yesterday the blue heifer was driven away; next goes our grain and at last, I suppose, I must give up my wedding suit, and all for sling! A plague on the shopkeepers—I wish there was not a glass of rum in the universe! Now, husband, if you will only spruce round a little, like other men, and attend to business, I have no doubt but we can get along. See Capt. Sprightly, he is up early and late, engaged in business. He lets no moment pass unimproved. See even now, while we are but just out of bed he has been for this hour with his boys in the field! Why can't we be as earnest, and as cheerful, and as prosperous as they. Come, come, hus, let's make an effort."

April 1812

In limiting this overall sketch of the farmer's almanacs to one short chapter, I realize I have omitted a trunkful of material which many seasoned readers will wish I had included. For those who hunger for more meat from these old almanac pages, then, I have included another whole plateful in Chapter VIII. But there is so much more that could be said about the personalities of such editors as Ames, Houghton, Munsell, Leavitt, the two Thomases, Robinson, Fessenden, Beers, Young, Sharp and all the rest. Full-length books have already been written about Ames, Fessenden, Munsell, Stearns, Robert B. Thomas, and Isaiah Thomas. There's little doubt an interesting book could be written about some of the others. However, as at a feast where enough food for ten men is spread out before a single guest, I can only enjoy what I can digest and then move on to the next course. In this case, our next bill of fare is that which farmers, mariners, innkeepers, tradesmen or, in short, all almanac readers, past and present, find themselves most interested in, fascinated with, or amused by: the farmer's almanac long-range weather forecasts.

The farmer, unlike
a city resident
lives by the season.
Here is one
sowing his oats,
wild and otherwise,
in the 18th century

What did they say?

*This section concerns itself with
the actual contents of these early almanacs,
their poetry, humor, forecasts and
whatever else the old time editors*

chapter six

HOW GOOD WERE THEIR FORECASTS?

It is said that most of the five hundred farmer's almanacs of the early 1800's existed as long as they did due in no small part to the continuous reader curiosity as to how accurate their long-range weather forecasts might be.

The natural question of "Well, how did these old almanac weather forecasters do their forecasts?" now comes to the fore.

Quite a few stories have come down to us about the weather forecasting of the almanac makers in 17th century England. There is the one, for example, about John Partridge, England's famous almanac maker of the 18th century, who used to travel from place to place on horseback. One morning as the groom at the inn where he was staying was readying his horse, Partridge asked the lad what he thought the weather was going to be. The boy replied he was certain that by noon the rains would be severe. Partridge laughed —and took off for his next destination. Halfway there he was caught in heavy rain. Feeling that this groom knew something about weather forecasting which he did not, the next time around Partridge asked the groom for his secret.

"It's a simple secret, sir," was his reply. "I am a faithful reader of Partridge's Almanac, and when I want to know what the weather is going to be, I go just the opposite of what it says."

I have already mentioned that Benjamin Franklin, when he was queried about his weather forecasts in his *Poor Richard's Almanac*, replied that when he saw Venus hide herself behind a cloud he could easily guess the reason and would expect rain. The occlusion of stars, sun, or moon by fog, mist, or clouds has long been held a sign of rain or snow. But this, of course, is a short- and not a long-range prediction method.

The key(s) to the "secret formulas" used by Dr. Ames in his almanacs (1726–96) for his weather and other predictions are for the most part astrological and usually found in the astronomical hieroglyphics which accompany each. For the week of January 22nd through 28th, 1749, Ames notes on his right hand calendar page:

```
22    Give me this Week for el-
23        bow Room to Guess in,
24            and I'll promise
25    you High Tides, Stor-
26    my Winds, plenty
27        of Rain or Snow.
```

The inclusion of the quadrature (90 deg. angle) between Jupiter and Mercury on the 26th indicates for Dr. Ames and his readers that a storm of some importance will accompany it. Other quadratures, conjunctions, etc. will bring different kinds of weather throughout the year; different, depending on the season.

Ames, Franklin, and others were not the only Almanack editors who went by the planets. We find Stearns in his North-American Almanac for February 1773 states outright "The planets denote foul weather." Parkhurst's New England Diary and Almanack for 1808 reveals that weather may be "gossiped from the stars," and/or "read from the breastbone of the goose."

One may wonder, in studying these indications, whether or not the weather prophecies ascribed to these different astronomical aspects had any scientific basis in fact or observation; that is, would Dr. Ames' quadrature given above have enjoyed a 50-year record of having brought with it that kind of weather six times out of seven, or three times out of four, or even once in a blue moon. This we do not know. We are aware, however, that the modern Radio Corporation of America in its scientific studies of these same aspects has proved almost conclusively there is a direct relationship between these astronomical aspects and the strength of short wave wireless transmission signals.

In his edition of 1739, Dr. Ames filled the first half of his calendar page for April almost completely with these aspects. In between these, on the 7th, 8th, and 9th, he has allowed himself room to comment

At this Convocation the
Planets all meet and
Vote, Nemine Contradicente
for Peace among the Nations.

Superstitious nonsense? Perhaps, but, in February of 1962 when a similar convocation occurred, the world press, television, radio, and thousands of so-called sensible, educated people believed that it would be accompanied, at the very least, by another world war and perhaps, the end of human existence.

Dudley Leavitt, editor of the farmer's almanac bearing his name for New Hampshire, was one of the more learned of the 19th century editors; a scholar, astronomer, professor, and historian. In his edition for 1888 he fails to predict the famous blizzard of March of that year, but he does sound forth over his Farmer's Calendar each month with what the planets are telling him about the weather. In March, for example,

The planets, in congress this month, hold sessions most every day, and their agreement is not very complex. The state of the weather will be very fluctuating, jumping from storm to sunshine and from sunshine to storm, rain, snow, and sleet.

In May:

> Mars and Mercury, the wind disturbers, this month play a conspicuous part; hence much windy weather ...

In October:

> It appears that October will be a pretty good month for business, visiting excursions, etc. The average temperature rather high. Jupiter, Mars, and Venus rather take the lead; hence magnetic warmth in the air.

Or consider this earnest argument in support of the theory that the planets affect our weather—from *Physician's Almanac* of 1817:

> *Cold Seasons.*
> Much has been said respecting our cold seasons, as to the cause of them; some suggest one thing and some another; some compute it to the approximation of the moon to the earth, which is found to be a fact, by the ancient lunar tables not answering our purpose in present calculations, and the lunar periods being shorter than they were; but that cannot be sufficient, as it is so small and gradual. Perhaps the superior planets do more in governing the weather through the seasons; two of them formed a conjunction in the year 1812, a very poor season for crops, which cannot take place oftener than once in 43 years, and another will take place this year, which cannot occur oftener than once in 23 years. I am aware some will ridicule this doctrine, as superstition of the ancients; but Mr. Ferguson one of our most cele-

brated modern astronomers, says, "It is found there are disturbances among the planets in their motions, arising from their mutual attractions, when they are in the same quarter of the heavens; and the best modern observers find that our years are not always precisely of the same length." The three superior planets are in one quarter of the heavens; a circumstance which cannot occur much short of a century or two. If one planet has such an effect on another, why not on the atmosphere of the same, and the electric fluid therein contained, which is a powerful agent or rather instrument, when acted upon by the agency of the moon or planets, in changing the weather? But let the cause be what it may, it becomes the farmer to alter his course of business, though not to sow all grain and plant no indian corn, as some have suggested, for perhaps this year corn may do better and grain not so well; but let him plant his corn earlier, whether it be hot or cold, wet or dry, and the probability is, he will have a crop in some degree or other.

• • •

Despite the fact that long-range weather forecasting had been a significant feature of almost every American almanac after 1689, it is not until 1877 that one finds an almanac editor devoting his annual publication almost exclusively to it. Henry G. Vennor, F.R.G.S. of Montreal, Canada, geologist and ornithologist, began his career as a weather forecaster with a letter to the Montreal (Canada) *Witness* in the Fall of 1875 in which he predicted a "green Christmas" and a "rainy New Year's." When these predictions came true, he received wide publicity. He decided to ride its wave with the publication of *Vennor's Weather Almanac* for 1877. By its sixth issue, in 1883, according to A. Vogeler & Co. of Baltimore, Maryland, which that year purchased absolute control of this almanac for American and Canadian distribution, it had reached "a sale far exceeding that of any other almanac." One must discount such a boast— for this almanac was given away by druggists or sent free for a 3¢ stamp. But there is no denying, free distribution or not, the *Vennor Weather Almanac* exploited long-range forecasting on a greater scale than any other almanac before or since its day.

On page 13 of his 1883 edition, Vennor reveals that inasmuch as "weather repeats its self" he sees no reason "why we should not be able from one central point to give accurate forecasts of the general weather conditions for the whole Northern Hemisphere." He points out how his predictions for gales and snowstorms in New York for the last week of January 1882 were successful.

In explaining his method further, Vennor adds that although the weather repeats itself, it does so at irregular periods.

I find that seven, or some multiple of this mumber is a very safe base to work upon . . .We find closely corresponding weather periods have frequently occurred in seven, fourteen, and twenty-one year divisions of time, and most of us are familiar with the every seventh storm day of our Winter and Summer months . . . Stormy Saturdays (in 1881) lasted through a period of just about seven weeks.

Henry G. Vennor, F.R.G.S.

VENNOR'S GENERAL FORECAST.

THE AUTUMN AND WINTER OF 1882-1883.

In attempting the forecast of this period, I labor under the great disadvantage of not having yet experienced the Summer weather of this year,—writing as I am from the tenth of June only. The cool, wet, and generally backward character of the Spring, however, has been closely observed, and as it is largely from this I deduce the general characters of the Autumn months, I must be content, since my book is demanded early.

SEPTEMBER.—Beautiful September is hardly, correctly speaking, an Autumn month, but it is in the month of passage to the Autumn, and its behavior, as regards the weather, is of interest to all, particularly to our tourists and travelers. It is in this month, in Northern sections, the forests first give indications of the approach of Winter. "Old Boreas," whose chilling breath begins to be felt in the evenings and nights, causes wraps, shawls and such-like to be very comfortable; yet the days are warm and brilliant; yes, and even hot, with mercury up again to very respectable readings (*vide* last September) over a large part of the United States and Canada. Such heat, however, in September, does not often occur,—it is exceptional.

This year I anticipate a glorious month for the *ninth* in the year. A brilliant dry month in the majority of sections, perhaps more particularly so in Northern sections,—but in general, fine. There will, however, be some sharp frosts experienced during the first and last week of the month; the latter, probably, immediately followed by wet weather—the commencement of the October rainy period. The month, on the whole, will be a favorable one, alike to the farmer planter, and general traveler.

Mr. Vennor is quoted at some length here because his experience illustrates what every honest meteorologist knows; namely, that when and if one has arrived at what seems to be a workable formula for the forecasting of weather, the weather pattern somehow learns of this and, forthwith, like Mary, Mary Quite Contrary, changes itself so that the discovered formula does not work.

After selling out to Vogeler, Mr. Vennor apparently branched out on his own to a weekly magazine weather forecasting venture. But his experience evidently ended the same as that of the famous Mr. Murphy of London, England. The latter, after five successful years of predicting English frosts, found himself with over a million pounds of profits. However, in his sixth year he was unsuccessful, and he lost them all.

Vennor, however, was not the inventor of "weather theories." Almanac history abounds with these. Leavitt, for example, was satisfied with an unusual number of sunspots as the explanation for the year 1816—the year without any summer. Abbot Godfrey in his almanac published at Keene, New Hampshire, in 1843 had this to say about "the Philosophy of Storms."

THE PHILOSOPHY OF STORMS.

This subject, which, but a few years ago, presented to the inquirer but a mass of chaotic observations and contradictory conclusions, is rapidly attaining the clearness and precision of the exact sciences. It has been examined with the square and compass of strict observation and minute detail, and in proportion to the extent of these observations, has success been wonderful and certain.

William C. Redfield, of New-York city, began his investigation a few years ago, by inducing interested observers from all parts of the United States, to communicate to him at New York, whenever they should notice a storm of unusual extent or severity—the time of its beginning and ending, the direction of the wind, its changes and time of continuance. These observers, together with the log-books of vessels off the coast, and other similar sources of information, formed, as it were, a chain of posts from the equator to the extreme North; whence were regularly telegraphed to him at head quarters, the ever varying phenomena of the wind and the sky.

In this way, Redfield has observed the rise, progress and final dissipation of a large number of our Atlantic storms; accounts of which have from time to time been published in our scientific journals.

From these, it appears that storms travel great distances in nearly straight lines. All the storms which Redfield has observed, appear to have moved very nearly *in one and the same direction;* always from a southerly to a northerly direction, and nearly in a line parallel with the general course of the Atlantic coast.

A great storm, in 1830, began in the Tropics, near the Island of St Thomas, on the 13th of August; on the 14th, it reached the Bahamas—Florida, the 15th—South Carolina, the 16th—Virginia, the 17th—Boston, the 18th—Nova Scotia, the 19th—travelling, in about six days, more than three thousand miles, and from seventeen to twenty miles an hour.

This storm, in New England, moved *towards* the North-east, and yet it blew a gale *from* the North-east the whole distance. The direction of the wind, then, does not necessarily coincide with the direction of the progress of the storm. In fact, it is settled almost beyond doubt, that all our large storms come to us from southern latitudes, and pass over towards the North, and that too, whether the wind *blow from the South or from the North, from the East or from the West,* or in whatever direction.

To account satisfactorily for these remarkable facts, and many others not herein contained, it follows, almost of necessity, that storms, besides this northerly progress, have also a whirlwind motion; in fact, are immense whirlwinds, and turn always in the same way, contrary to the hands of a watch.

This theory prevails extensively in this country, in England, and among navigators; and in striking conformation with it, is the recent publication, by an English writer, of an independent series of observations, made in the East Indies. This writer thinks it established. almost beyond doubt, that storms in the southern hemisphere originate near the equator, and move towards the *South Pole;* have also a whirlwind motion, but in an opposite direction from those observed by Redfield, North of the equator.

Whether this theory be true in all its parts, remains for our constant observers of the weather to decide; and to such we leave it, adding only the following hints, which we believe will be found in accordance both with the theory and actual observation.

All storms, of course, appear in the South and Southwest; they may be first noticed in that quarter by a haze, or dark line of clouds which appears from 10 to 24 hours in advance of the storm, according to the distance of the view, or the rapidity of its approach. In winter, these lines of clouds may be seen retaining the same shape for hours; presenting along its whole front of one hundred miles and more, a regular curve, *with the convexity always towards the observer.*

Storms beginning with the wind from the East or Southeast, are generally our longest and severest storms; and invariably terminate with a wind of equal length and strength from a point nearly North-west; because in those cases we pass through the centre of the whirlwind; and such an event requires exactly opposite winds at the beginning and ending of a storm. The strong North-west winds which terminate three-fourths of our storms, "clearing up winds" though they are, are yet as much a portion of the preceding storm as the rain or the snow.

In fact, according to our theory, a North-west wind must necessarily be a final wind in all storms in which it blows from that quarter; and we venture to say, that a storm in our latitude beginning with a wind from the Northwest, is a thing never known or heard of, and is a physical impossibility; unless, as before said, preceded by some opposite wind.

Again, storms beginning with wind from the South-west, are always much the shortest and lightest of our storms; and always terminate with the wind a few points more West than in the preceding cases. In these storms we pass through but a small segment, the South-eastern limb, as it were, of a whirlwind.

But we think we have presented enough to enable the interested to understand Redfield's views on this subject, which we are assured is well worth consideration. .

Should any considerable storms come off the present year, we intend to give them an impartial hearing, and, if advisable, present to our readers, at some future time, the result of our observations.   AUTHOR.

It is difficult now to go back, especially before 1875 when the U.S. Weather Bureau began collecting records and attempt to verify almanac forecasts. There just aren't that many reliable records. Even now, it is impossible or extremely difficult to obtain daily weather records from the various Weather Bureau stations for the years before 1930.

Offhand, with what little spot checking I have been able to do, I find that almost all the almanacs completely missed, for example, the cold summer of 1816, the Blizzard of 1888, as well as various significant hurricanes and tornadoes. Here, before me, as I write this, is an interesting example.

It is a copy of *The (Old) Farmer's Almanac* by Robert B. Thomas for the year 1804. The owner of it, one Joseph Barrell of Boston, has placed interleaves between its left and right hand calendar pages and on these pages he has written what the weather actually was.

In January he mentions that it rained on the first; snowed, rained and "lightninged" on the third; and that there was a violent snow storm on the 8th. His copy of the almanac, however, had not forecast any of these. Again he mentions snow on the 14th, rain changing to snow on the 17th, and a cold snap on the 20th and 21st. Again, the almanac fails to catch any of these. The only forecast the almanac had correct for the entire month of January 1804 was that for snow or rain on the 28th!

In some of these months of 1804 the (Old) Farmer's Almanac did a lot better than its performance for January, but in October it completely missed—and here I quote the words of Joseph Barrell what happened— and those of his son, what happened to Joseph Barrell!

9th began a furious Storm of rain with Severe thunder and lightning and very high Wind NNE wch cont. all day & night when it blew a perfect Hurricane wch blew down the Steple of the North Church, a very high New Brick house of M. Paton's which killed a Woman in the fall, unroof'd partly the Baptize Meeting house, the Ball & Vane of M. Mony Meet'ghouse, the Vane of the Meet'ghouse at Roxbury, the roof of the Tower of the Stone Chapple, many Chimneys, many houses and ?, tore up Trees, hedges. My rain gage blew away in the Storm, after collect'g ... 3000 10th The storm cont'd. The rain 175.

Written by Barrell's Son:

This is the last entry made by my Father, who died on the 13th of the month, caused by the storm now recorded.

George Barrell

Orange, N. Jersey
June 12, 1848

Barrell's Handwriting about the storm of September 10th, 1804 as it appears in his copy of the Old Farmer's Almanac for that year

So frustrating over the years was this weather forecasting that many of the old time almanac editors ceased forecasting altogether.

Thomas G. Fessenden, editor of *The New England Farmer's Almanac,* after years of coming off second best, threw in his admission of defeat this way in 1832:

> In our tabular pages we have omitted those deceptive prognostications relative to the weather . . . Those who prefer almanacs filled up with the guesswork of weather-wise-acres, exhibit notable exemplifications of the truth of
>
> *'T is borne the pleasure is as great*
> *In being cheated as to cheat.*
>
> The time is rapidly approaching when the prognosticators of Calendar-Conjurors will rank with the exploded fooleries and atrocities of witchcraft, palmistry, astrology, etc. etc.
>
> The *wizards* of the Calendar are as truly imposters as the *witches* of Lapland who sell winds for a valuable consideration to superstitious sailors.

Again, one finds Samuel Hart Wright, in the 1873 edition of the *Long Island Farmer's Almanac,* making this statement—

> Now that the United States Government has established a Signal Office which gives the public through the newspapers the probability of the weather every day in the year, the usual prognostications heretofore given in this almanac are discontinued.

Five years later this same Wright was still trying to defend his action by pointing out that almanac predictions "should be regarded as mere guesswork entitled to no confidence and as likely to fail as be true."

However much one may agree with the honesty of such a position, no almanac maker has ever been able to climb up on such a rock—and still remain in business. Fessenden came down from it in a few years. It took Wright (and his successor) some twenty-five years to do so, but they finally did.

Upset as Fessenden and Wright were about their failures, one Samuel Wood of No. 278 Pearl Street, New York City, apparently, as early as 1812, had avoided including any weather forecast at all.

> The Publisher, while he returns his acknowledgments to the many who have approved and encouraged the sale of his Almanac, has regret, that amongst an enlightened people, an age of increasing knowledge, there are some who object to it, because it does not contain the vague and ridiculous predictions on the weather so common to publications of this kind: and although he has been advised to insert it (or something of no harm) yet, notwithstanding his wish to please all, he would rather relinquish the publication, than to insert matter so preposterous, and in his opinion, so unwarrantable. One great object in view is to be of some small service by circulating an Almanac which shall contain nothing that will encourage vice or immorality.

Crotchety, wasn't he? He paid for it, eventually, in "relinquishment." But Nathan Wild, who addressed his almanac to "farmers, mechanics and gentlemen," included in his edition of 1834 a contribution about the weather from the then celebrated Dr. Adam Clarke. Here, at long last, was the "definite rule" for which so many almanac makers and meteorologists had been casting about. The "rule" which accompanies Dr.

Clarke's remarks has had as wide a circulation over the years as perhaps any other single sheet of printed matter. Further, in Dr. Clarke's relation of his weather studies is probably a perfect example of how, before the days of instruments and weather bureau services, the "weather man" found his way around.

.Spiders make larger webs
as rain approaches

Swallows fly low when
rain is coming

Insects bite more severely
when rain is near

The following article is from the pen of the celebrated Dr. ADAM CLARKE. It is not unworthy
of attention.

THE WEATHER

From my earliest childhood I was bred up on a
little farm, which I was taught to care for and cultivate ever since I was able to spring the rattle, use
the whip, manage the sickle, or handle the spade;
and as I found that much of our success depended
on a proper knowledge and management of the
weather, I was led to study it ever since I was eight
years of age. I believe meteorology is a natural
science, and one of the first that is studied; and
that every child in country makes, untaught, some
progress in it; at least so it was with me. I had actually learned, by silent observation, to form good
conjectures concerning the coming weather, and,
on this head, to teach wisdom among those who
were perfect, especially among such as had not
been obliged, like me, to watch earnestly, that
what was so necessary to the *family support* should
not be spoiled by the weather before it was housed.
Many a time, even in tender youth, have I watched
the heavens with anxiety, examined the different
appearances of the morning and evening sun, the
phases of the moon, the scintillation of the stars,
the course and color of the clouds, the flight of
the crow and the swallow, the gambols of the colt,
the fluttering of the ducks, and the loud screams of
the sea-mew—not forgetting the hue and croak-
ing of the frog. From the little knowledge I had
derived from close observation, I often ventured
to direct our agricultural operations in reference
to the coming days, and was seldom much mis-
taken in my reckoning.

About twenty years ago, a Table purporting to be the work of the late Dr. Herschel, was variously published, professing to form prognostics of the weather, by the times of change, full and quarters of the moon. I have carefully consulted this table, for several years, and was amazed at its general accuracy; for though long, as you have seen, es-gaged in the study of the weather, I never thought that any rules could be devised liable to so few exceptions. I have made a little alteration in the arrangements, illustrated it with further obser-vations, and have sent it that you may insert it, as it has hitherto been confined generally to a few al-manacs.

Witness the hand of the Commentator

Adam Clarke

With the Herschel table available, anyone—including an almanac editor—at last had a "scientific system" (providing he could determine in advance the times of the phases of the moon) whereby he could tell his readers what the weather was going to be. It didn't matter, apparently, what one's location upon this earth was, the timing of the moon's phase would bring to that location the rain or snow such timing called for.

However, once these editors "got with the moon," we find men like Arago and others looking hard at these phases in a different way. Some felt, for example, that precipitation in any given month was most likely at or near the full of the moon and, to a lesser degree, at the new. Almost 150 years later meteorologists are again "with the moon" in exactly the same fashion.

How many of the editors used Herschel, or other methods or averages, I have no way of knowing. All I can point out is that Robert B. Thomas never, in all his fifty-six years of editing, failed to include a weather forecast—nor has his almanac since then failed to include one either. In 1936, unfortunately, it was just a presentation of the averages—and the sale that year fell to its lowest point.

• • •

With respect to events other than weather, the American almanac editors were not as prone to forecast these as their English, French, and German predecessors had been. One or two exceptions, however, are worth noting.

Nathaniel Ames is credited by *The New York Mirror* of 1836, in his almanac printed in 1745, with "anticipating the growth of our country for a century to come. It is a miraculous calculation. The only error in it is that the fulfillment of all his forecasts came in seventy-five years instead of one hundred. The people con-

55

MOON WEATHER TABLE,
For foretelling the Weather through all the lunations of each year, forever.

This table, and the accompanying remarks, are the result of many years' actual observation, the whole being constructed on a due consideration of the attraction of the sun and moon, in their several positions respecting the earth, and will, by simple inspection, show the observer what kind of weather will most probably follow the entrance of the moon into any of its quarters, and that so near the truth as to be seldom or never found to fail.

This weather table will answer very well for anywhere in the United States. It is taken from the 1860 issue of The Old Farmer's Almanac and was widely used before the advent of the Weather Bureau. Do not be surprised if the forecasts arrived at by this table do not agree with those on other pages. THE OFA goes by many factors besides the moon.

WEATHER TABLE FOR ANYWHERE

Time of Change	In Summer	In Winter
From Midnight to 2 A.M.	Fair	Hard frost, unless wind be S. or W.
From 2 A.M. to 4 A.M.	Cold, with frequent showers	Snow and stormy
From 4 A.M. to 6 A.M.	Rain	Rain
From 6 A.M. to 8 A.M.	Wind and Rain	Stormy
From 8 A.M. to 10 A.M.	Changeable	Cold Rain if wind be W.; Snow if E.
From 10 A.M. to Noon	Frequent Showers	Cold & high wind.
From Noon to 2 P.M.	Very rainy	Snow or rain.
From 2 P.M. to 4 P.M.	Changeable	Fair & mild.
From 4 P.M. to 6 P.M.	Fair	Fair.
From 6 P.M. to 8 P.M.	Fair — if wind N.W. Rain — if S. or S.W.	Fair & frosty if wind N. or N.E.; Rain or snow if wind S. or S.W.
From 8 P.M. to 10 P.M.	Same as from 6 P.M. to 8 P.M.	
From 10 P.M. to Midnight	Fair	Fair & frosty.

Observations. — 1. The nearer the moon's change, first quarter, full, and last quarter are to midnight, the fairer will it be during the next seven days. 2. The space for this calculation occupies from ten at night till two next morning. 3. The nearer to midday, or noon, the phases of the moon happen, the more foul or wet weather may be expected during the next seven days. 4. The space for this calculation occupies from ten in the forenoon to two in the afternoon. These observations refer principally to the summer, though they affect spring and autumn nearly in the same ratio. 5. The moon's change, first quarter, full and last quarter, happening during six of the afternoon hours, i.e., from four to ten, may be followed by fair weather; but this is mostly dependent on the wind, as is noted in the table. 6. Though the weather, from a variety of irregular causes, is more uncertain in the latter part of autumn, the whole of winter, and the beginning of spring, yet, in the main, the above observations will apply to those periods also. 7. To prognosticate correctly, especially in those cases where the wind is concerned, the observer should be within sight of a good vane, where the four cardinal points of the heavens are correctly placed.

The above table was originally formed by Dr. Herschell, and is now published with some alterations founded on the experience of Dr. Adam Clarke.

sidered the great almanac maker as a conjuror. Thus it is that sane minds, on the basis of the past, call up visions of the future, and deserve the name of seers." In this prophecy, Mr. Ames was some twelve years ahead of Jonathan Ludeman of Amsterdam, Holland, whose similar prediction made in 1756 is still viewed with wonder. This was quoted by Low in his edition of 1800.

The New England Farmer's Almanac, 1843, by Truman Abell, included a three-page discourse on "The Resurrection and End of the World." One William Miller, founder of the Second Adventists, had become convinced through his Biblical studies that the second coming of Christ and the Day of Judgment would occur between the vernal equinoxes of the years 1843 and 1844. Mr. Abell does not dignify Miller's prophecy by naming the actual day (October 22, 1844) but had the Miller prophecy come true Mr. Abell would have been the only almanac maker who might have been said to have predicted correctly by quoting Miller, the end of the world. I sometimes wonder about this. With no world, who would be around to make Mr. Abell famous? Or Mr. Miller?

• • •

In conclusion, some of my associates have urged that I include some of my own experiences and thoughts about the weather. They seemed amused, for example, by my forecast for the week in March, 1952, when Robert Taft was campaigning against Mr. Eisenhower in the New Hampshire primary. It read "blizzard up to your Gizzard." When it snowed only a few inches, the scoffers were quick to point out how wrong the almanac had been. On the contrary, they came to learn that only a chicken has a gizzard so the forecast was reasonably correct.

Again, returning from Spain in 1954 the Captain of the *Constitution* kept asking me what the weather would be into New York from the Azores. I kept telling him it would be awful. He kept cabling Washington for confirmation of the Weather Bureau's "fair weather" forecasts. It turned out that I, that is, the Almanac, was right. It had to be. There has always been a Northeast storm on the East Coast of America in November and on this voyage, late in November, it had not yet arrived.

Another time, I had the last chuckle on Harvard University, where it was my privilege to serve for three years as an Alumni Director. Every June Harvard holds its Commencement out-of-doors in the Harvard Yard. Each year, while I was a Director, the Marshal in charge of the occasion asked me for the Almanac forecast. The first year the Almanac declared it would be clear, and it was. The second year of my term the same thing happened. In the third year, however, the Almanac called for rain. The Marshal was no believer.

Harvard Yard Circa 1800

He went ahead just as if no rain would fall. When the rain did come the Marshal stood at the microphone in a steady downpour and announced that, despite the Almanac forecast, it had never rained for a Harvard Commencement and, forsooth, it was not raining then!

I could go on at some length with these personal experiences. The fact that I correctly predicted the Worcester tornado in 1953, for instance, has quite a story behind it. However, I really do not wish to give the impression that I believe in my own or other predictions. "Man," as the Almanac has said in its *Note to Patrons* for years and years "proposes, God disposes."

At the present writing, anyone who has studied meteorology and worked with it for any length of time will tell you that successful weather forecasting over 48 hours ahead is not as yet possible. *The Old Farmer's Almanac* and its venerable Old "Abe Weatherwise," in its ten new regional forecasts for all of the U.S.A., knows this to be true. Yet it has found that by means of different long-range cycles (ocean temperatures, sunspots, storm tracks, etc.) it can call, in some months, the weather correctly (100%). In some other months, however, it will as likely as not, do poorly (0). Its average for the year runs between 60% and 80% and has done so for many years.

After weather forecasts, the subject people most often want to discuss with me is whether or not our climate is changing. People who should know better are always sounding off about palm trees coming to Labrador and icebergs to Palm Beach. My answer is often simply to refer to a table in the Isaiah Thomas edition of 1796 which does give us some basis of comparison between the now and the then.

In Charleston, South Carolina, for the five years 1738–42, the mean temperature for the year was 66 degrees, the coldest day was 18 degrees, and the warmest was 101.

At Cambridge, Massachusetts, for the five years 1784 −8, the mean for the year was 47 degrees, the coldest day −12, and the warmest 93. At Rutland, Vermont, 1780 averaged 43.6 degrees, its coldest day was −21, and its warmest 92.

The "now" seemingly is not too different from the "then"?

In any event, it would seem that if there is any change in continental or world climate, it takes place at such a slow rate that no one generation actually becomes aware of it. Which is not to say one year or series of years does not differ from another year or series of years. There is a remarkable difference, for example, between the winters of the 1950's and those of the 1960's. In the '50s we had many solemn proclamations that the climate was growing warmer; now it is just the other way around. It seems to be growing colder!

Finally, we have "the bomb" questions. During the 50's in particular, we had a good deal of discussion as to the effect of the H bomb explosions on the weather. The Atomic Energy Commission did not release until recently its findings in this regard and then only in a desultory way. Inasmuch as volcanic dust has been known, through sun ray occlusion, to lower temperatures in Florida and on the French Riviera by as much as ten degrees over a period of a year, it seems obvious to me that the bomb *did* affect our climate as well as leave layers of strontium all over the world, including Antarctica.

Casting about in 1954 to try to learn for *The Old Farmer's Almanac* about the effects of the Bomb, I wrote to Albert Einstein. He, I felt, would know if anybody did.

His reply , dated March 25, 1954 was to the effect that if man were damaged by such experiments, he deserved to be.

chapter seven

ESSAYISTS ON WOOD

Of the many good almanacs which were to flourish in the 19th century none would seem so interesting were it not for the illustrations and decorations which were brought to them as the 18th century closed. There was very little illustrating in the 1600's and 1700's. In 1686, Samuel Atkins, in his *Kalendarium Pennsilvaniense,* explained why this was so.

I had thought to have inserted a figure of the Moon's eclipse, a small Draught of the form of this city and a Table to find the hour of the day by the Shadow of the Staff; but we, having not Tools to carve them in that form that I would have them, I pass it for this year.

There were, of course, exceptions. One was the Bicker-staff Almanack for 1784 in which the first farm calendar page illustrations on this side of the Atlantic were to appear. Others, as the late Clarence Brigham has pointed out, were the Sauer almanacs in Pennsylvania of 1739, 1762, and 1763, and the title page woodcut of Queen Anne in Whittemore's Almanac for 1714.

Also, it is interesting to note that Isaiah Thomas in his *Almanack* (1795) was using a tripartite decoration, one part of which contained the Zodiacal sign of the month.

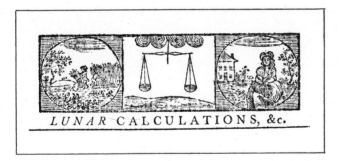

Isaiah Thomas' tripartite decoration for the month of October

Another exception was Robert B. Thomas who, in developing his competitive *The Farmer's Almanac* (k) of the 1790's, at first used a kind of, shall we say polite, adaptation of Isaiah's closed-in-box. Later he switched to the odd blend of sign and scenic which is seen in his edition of 1806.

After the edition of 1809 his emphasis was strictly on the sign rather than the scenic—this way, with the crab for June 1810.

After about forty years of continuous use, the crab plate became worn. Boston engraver Hammatt Billings made it over in the 1850s. Thus, it has appeared as Billings' version, except for the years it was printed upside down, in every year since. But we're getting ahead of our story.

• • •

Exactly two days after the Battle of Lexington and Concord, a son was born to one John Anderson in an "humble abode near Beekman's Slip in New York City." The father, then a printer and outspoken publisher of the patriotic *Constitutional Gazette,* was soon to realize that the then "reigning power" of the city, not too happy about having this rebel thorn in his Tory side, was making plans to have it extracted. Wishing to live a few years longer, rebel Anderson succeeded in reaching Washington Heights with all his family and possessions. There he was dispossessed of his wagons and everything else he could not personally carry. Undaunted, he managed to reach Greenwich, Connecticut, where he found asylum with friends, and a reasonably safe place for the upbringing of his family. Later, he returned to New York, not as a printer, but as an auctioneer.

However, it was in Greenwich that young Alexander Anderson, his youngest son, acquired his lifelong interest in drawing, design, and engraving. It was there he was allowed "an occasional peep . . . at Hogarth's illustrations of the careers of the *Idle and Industrious*

Apprentices . . . These prints determined my destiny."
At this age also, after learning from *Chambers' Encyclopedia* how engravings were made, he took some of his large copper pennies to a silversmith and had them rolled into thin copper plates. From these with his pocket-knife he made not only his first engraving (a head of Paul Jones) but also printed it on a home-made roller press in red oil paint.

Inasmuch as engravers were few and far between in America at this time, and there was no prospect of engraving as an industry or profession, Alexander's father was loath to encourage him in this, his first and only love. Instead, he apprenticed him to a doctor.

For those who would follow Anderson's career as a doctor, there is Frederic M. Burr's excellent Limited Edition of *The Life and Works of Alexander Anderson, M.D.* In one of its opening chapters, we are told how he always carried his engraving tool in one trouser pocket and blocks of wood in the other.

Eventually, Anderson abandoned his medical career and, greatly influenced by the work of England's Thomas Bewick, became not only America's first wood engraver but, in the opinion of many, her greatest.

Before viewing the illustrations of Alexander Anderson's work and discussing some of his contemporaries, it would be well perhaps, to describe the mechanics of wood engraving in specific relation to Thomas Bewick, the Englishman from whom all the early engravers derived so much.

• • •

Woodcuts are made by cutting with the grain of the wood. However, wood engravings (worked on the face of the block across the grain) were better adapted. Thomas Bewick decided early in his career, "to express the ease, the freedom, and spirit which ought to characterize portraits of animated beings."

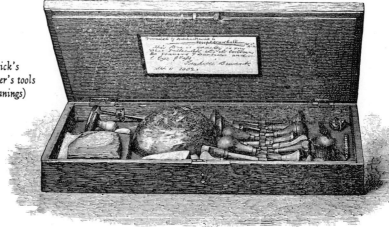

The block of wood may have been boxwood, cherry, apple or rosewood; whatever was used, the important artists or "essayists on wood" began on metal and then gained some experience, as did both Bewick and Anderson, working with the grain. In the end the best artists turned to the upended block with their gougers, scribes, knives, and other tools.

One must remember, also, that the description of these men as "artists" is correct. They not only prepared the blocks of wood (now a lost art) and engraved them, but they also fashioned the picture in their own style and with their own ingenuity. It was not until well into the 19th century that wood engravers or cutters executed or copied only the design, drawing, or painting some other artist had first created.

By 1790 Thomas Bewick, through the revolutionary use of his wood engraving technique, had brought about a virtual renaissance in the art of book and pamphlet illustration. His English *History of Quadrupeds* and *History of Birds* are outstanding examples of his work. No small part of the explanation of Bewick's

success, as in the case of Anderson's later on, is found in Bewick's love of the farm scene, of animals, of country people, and (as with Wordsworth) his romantic interpretations of rural life.

R. Hunter Middleton of the Ludlow Typograph Company of Chicago has a collection of some 170 of the original Bewick blocks. In 1945 he established a private press, named "Cherryburn," after Bewick's birthplace, and produced a portfolio of 24 prints using blocks from Bewick's *Quadrupeds* and *British Birds*. At this writing, he is printing a portfolio of 100 prints in an edition of 150 portfolios for the Newberry Library which will produce and print it.

Let's now look at some of these Bewick wood engravings—certainly the American engravers did!—and then compare them with the equally exquisite work of Alexander Anderson.

Winter hunting of the hare

The superstitious dog

The frightened mother

The solitary Cormorant

The sheep storm

The irreverent cat

For purposes of further comparison, there are reproduced here three other Bewick engravings, followed by three from Anderson's later work.

This first one is unique because it appeared only in the first copy of Bewick's first edition (bound in with *Poems* by the Rev. Joseph Relp) of his *History of British Birds* (1798).

BEWICK'S

Anderson's engraving
of himself in
his 81st year.

In reviewing the next four of Bewick's cuts, one notices
a seasonal quality about each one, that very quality
which the American wood engravers imitated.

Alexander Anderson was hired by
G. R. Waite and Company to
do the Wood engravings for a book
called "A General History of Quadrupeds"
copied chiefly from the original
of T. Bewick. In comparing the
original with Anderson's copy we find
these two "Barbary" squirrels. The
lower one is Anderson's, the other
is Bewick's. Note how Anderson
has reversed the original

Of some importance in studying almanac illustration,
along with Bewick's and Anderson's original works,
are those of Anderson's pupils and followers. There
was, for example, Garret Lansing, who, after studying
with Anderson, went to Albany, then to Boston, back
to Albany, and finally returned to his master in New
York. During his travels in 1806 he illustrated Seneca's
Morals at Keene, New Hampshire. John Hall, Edward
B. Purcell, Tompkins H. Matteson, and Anderson's
daughter, Ann, are other pupil names one runs across
in illustrations of the period. Some of the fun in collecting examples of the work of this period, by the
way, is finding the initials and signatures of the various

artists on the engravings and thereby relating the works to the correct artist.

William Mason became the leader in Philadelphia. At first apprenticed in 1808 to Abner Reed of Hartford, Connecticut, a copperplate engraver, he was inspired by Anderson to his first essays on wood. He apparently moved to Philadelphia to carry on his work there. In 1822 he relinquished his trade to one George Gilbert.

In Boston, Abel Bowen (1790–1850) is said to have been New England's first wood engraver (Anderson, you'll remember, was a New Yorker). Whether or not Bowen actually studied with Anderson, or just copied him, or copied Bewick, history does not state. Our guess is that he followed Bewick directly, as had Anderson. Bowen began his work in Boston in 1805 at the early age of fifteen. By 1812 he had opened his own shop on Court Street with orders from the principal Boston publishers. His first important work was illustrating the Naval Monument in 1816, but perhaps his most significant were Snow's *History of Boston,* 1825, and his own *Picture of Boston,* 1829.

From these dates it will be seen that Bowen was a few years later than Anderson. The list of his pupils— Alonzo Hartwell, George Loring Brown, George T. and Nicholson B. Devereux, Richard P. Mallory—as well as of his followers—William Greenough, John C.

Abel Bowen and one of his engravings

Crossman, Samuel S. Kilburn, Benjamin F. Childs, William Croome—is long and impressive.

Nathaniel Dearborn, whose signature is often seen in these early illustrations, also opened a shop in Boston shortly after Bowen. The peak of Dearborn's art was not reached until about the year 1840 when his Webster vases, maps of Mt. Auburn Cemetery, and the state of Maine, and depiction of Colonel Johnson's Battle with Indians during the War of 1812 were widely advertised.

Slightly later than the period with which we are concerned appeared John Warner Barber of New Haven, Connecticut. Later, too, are Branston, who had studied under Bewick in England, and thence removed to Connecticut; E. S. Peters of Harrisburg, Pennsylvania; William Williams of Utica, New York, James Akin of Philadelphia, Thomas Wightman, John T. Young, Abraham J. Mason, Alfred A. Lansing, Joseph W. Morse, Samuel Hill, and George Emmons.

Around these artists on wood grew what even now would be considered a large publishing industry. Samuel Griswold Goodrich, for example, born in 1793 in Ridgefield, Connecticut, was to publish under the pseudonym of Peter Parley, some one hundred and seventy juveniles and to become the "Father of the American Juvenile."

• • •

Esquimaux dog by
Abraham Mason, 1824

With this preamble, we are now ready to examine the little calendar heads of the almanacs themselves. A fair amount of detective work on my part reveals that some wood (or steel) engravers made a good business of copying (without credit) Bewick, Anderson, Bowen, and others. These copies they then sold to any printer or almanac publisher who cared to buy them. Thus it is seen, more than occasionally, that competitive almanacs might bear almost exactly similar cuts. Herewith, I include samples of these little heads and brief notes on their origins as well as the almanacs in which they appeared.

There are undoubtedly examples of Bewick cuts which English or American engravers copied directly for use in 19th century almanacs. My research, however, has not turned up any of them. The one below nevertheless does have the boy and hoop which will reappear in the American cuts which follow this one of Bewick's.

The first American use of this particular kind of Bewick rural scene as calendar heads appears in *Low's Almanac* for 1819. A good close look at the bottom of the print, just to the left of the larger boy's hoop, will reveal "A. Bowen. Sc."

Now follow two cuts, identical with the one above, except for the omission of Bowen's signature, both of which appeared at the top of July farm calendar pages in, respectively, Daniel Robinson's *Maine Farmer's Almanac* for 1820 and Bancroft's *Agricultural Almanac* of 1826.

Here the same cut appears again, but many years later, in Truman Abell's *The New England Farmer's Almanac* of 1843.

Again there is no signature or other identification of the wood engraver. In the 19th century almanacs there are literally hundreds of examples of woodcuts, similar in style to the foregoing, very few of which will be identifiable either as to artist or origin.

• • •

In concluding this chapter on illustration, I must point out that although, in general, the so-called farmer's almanacs of the 19th century had the editorial tone of the Bewick illustrations, they also contained some of America's early attempts to give their readers illustrated, factual accounts of historical events as they happened. They were the newspapers, magazines, radio and television of their day.

The following examples of this sort of reporting are from Low's of 1820.

Melancholy Fate

of

MADAME BLANCHARD,

The Celebrated Aeronaute.

Paris, July 6, 1819.—The extraordinary fete which had been for some time announced to take place this evening at the Tivoli gardens, has been signalized by a shocking catastrophe. Among the numerous spectacles, which had been announced to the public, was the ascension of Madame Blanchard in a luminous balloon furnished with fireworks. Accordingly, at half-past 10 at night, this intrepid aeronaute clothed in white, with a hat and plumes of the same colour, mounted her car. At a given signal, the balloon rose, but so slowly that part of the fireworks came in contact with the surrounding trees. However, by throwing out some ballast, Madame Blanchard soon rose rapidly. The ascension was illuminated by Bengal lights; the aeronaute waved her flag, and the air resounded with acclamations. On a sudden the balloon entered a slight cloud, which completely obscured the Bengal lights. Madame Blanchard then set the match to the fireworks, in order that they might produce the expected effect; when it

was perceived that some rockets took a perpendicular direction to the balloon and set fire to it. Immediately a dreadful blaze struck terror into the hearts of the spectators, leaving them in but little doubt as to the deplorable fate of the unfortunate aeronaute. It is impossible to describe the scene which Tivoli now presented. Cries of lamentation burst from all sides; numbers of females fell into convulsions, consternation was depicted in every face! Some spectators rode at full gallop towards where it was supposed the fall might take place; and in about a quarter of an hour returned with the lifeless body of Madame Blanchard. She fell in the Street de Provence; she was in her car, enveloped in the network that had attached it to the balloon. This unfortunate lady was about 45.

Interesting to Farmers.—The summer of 1816, having been remarkably cold and unfavourable, the harvest was very late, and much of the grain, especially oats, was green in October. In the beginning of October the cold was so great, that in one night it produced on ponds, ice, 3 quarters of an inch thick. It was apprehended that such a degree of cold would effectually prevent the further filling and ripening of their corn. In order to ascertain this point, Dr. Rockbuck selected several stocks of oats, of nearly equal fulness, and immediately cut those, which on the most attentive comparison appeared the best, and marked the others but allowed them to remain in the field fourteen days longer; at the end of which they too were cut, and kept in a dry room for ten days. The grains of each parcel were then weighed; when eleven of the grains that had been left standing in the field were found to be equal in weight to thirty of the grains which had been cut a fortnight sooner, though some of the grains were far from being ripe. During that fortnight (from the 7th Oct. to 21st) the average heat, according to Farenheit's thermometer, was little above 43. Dr. Rockbuck observes, that the ripening and filling of grain in so low a temperature should be the less surprising, when we reflect that the seed grain will vegetate in the same degree of heat; and he draws an important inference from his observations, viz: that farmers should be cautious of cutting down their unripe grain, on the supposition that in a cold autumn it could fill no more.

THE GREAT MARINE SERPENT
As seen at Nahant and Gloucester in Aug. 1819, from a sketch by James Prince, Esq.
As we have recorded the visit of this animal in 1817 in a former Almanack, we should not mention his appearance at various times during the month of Aug. 1819, at Nahant, & c. we have se-

lected the letter of one gentleman, whose situation enabled him to view the Serpent to advantage; to which is annexed Marshal Prince's Sketch of his appearance and attitude when seen by him. All the accounts agree in substance.

Extract of a letter from CHEEVER FELCH, Esq. of the U.S. Navy, dated Gloucester, August 26, 1819.

"Dear Sir,—Forasmuch as others have taken in hand to give some account of the Sea Serpent, I know not why I should not have the same liberty. Being on this station, in the U.S. Sch. Science, for the purpose of surveying this harbor, we were proceeding this morning down the harbor, in the schooner's boat; when abreast of Dolliver's Neck, Wm. T. Malbone, esq., commander of the sch. seeing some appearance on the water, said, 'there is your Sea Serpent.'—The animal was then between 30 and 40 yards distance from us. Mr. Malbone, Midshipman Blake, myself, and our

four boatmen had a distinct view of him. He soon
sunk: but not so deep but we could trace his course.
He rose again within 20 yards of us, and lay
some time on the water. He then turned, and
steered for Ten Pound Island; we pulled after
him; but finding that he was not pleased with our
oars, they were laid in, and the boat skulled. We
again approached very near him. He continued
some length of time, plying between Ten Pound Island and Stage Point.—From my knowledge of
aquatic animals, and habits of intimacy with
marine appearances, I could not be deceived. We
had a good view of him, except the very short
time he was under water, for half an hour. His
colour is a dark brown, with white under the
throat. His size we could not accurately ascertain, but his head is about 3 feet in circumference,
flat and much smaller than his body. We did not
see his tail; but from the end of the head to the
farthest protuberance, was not far from 100
feet. I speak with a degree of certainty, from being
much accustomed to measure and estimate distances and length. I counted 14 bunches on his
back, the first one say 10 or 12 feet from his head,
and the others about 7 feet apart. They decreased
in size towards the tail. These bunches were seen
sometimes with, and sometimes without a glass.
His motion was sometimes very rapid, and at
other times he lay nearly still. He turned slowly,
and took up considerable room in doing it. He
sometimes darted under water, with the greatest
velocity, as if seizing prey. The protuberances
were not from his motion, as they were the same
whether in slow or rapid movement. His motion
was partly vertical and partly horizontal, like
that of fresh water snakes. I have been much ac-

quainted with the snakes in our interior waters. His motion was the same. I have given in round numbers 100 feet, for his length; that is what we saw; but I should say he must be 130 feet in length, allowing for his tail. There were a considerable number of birds about the Sea Serpent, as I have seen them about a snake on shore.—The sketch or picture by Marshal Prince is perfectly correct. C. Felch."

The annexed cut is a reduced copy of the Serpens Marinus Magnus, as it is represented in Pontippidan's *History of Norway,* published in 1747.

The account accompanying this representation is as follows:—

The Serpens Marinus Magnus is a wonderful and terrible Sea Monster, which deserves to be noticed by those who are curious to look into the works of the great Creator. It is usually in July and Aug. he appears, and when it is calm. . . . His head was more than 2 feet above the surface of the water, and resembled that of a horse. Beside the head and neck, 7 or 8 folds or coils of the animal were distinctly seen, & were about a fathom apart.

This is the statement of a Capt. DeFerry and others. The historian adds, "that many other persons on the coast of Norway had seen the Sea Serpent—and thought it a strange question when seriously asked whether there were such an animal in existence; being as fully persuaded of the fact, as of the existence of an eel or a cod."

• • •

We've now covered a great deal of the sort of material from which these early almanacs were made— The Farm Calendar Essays, the weather forecasts, the fascinating illustrations etc. etc. So what's left? The answer is "plenty" as the next chapter amply demonstrates—

chapter eight

QUIPS and QUOTES on WRY

One can describe the American almanac for hundreds of pages, but this isn't really enough for the true student of American history. Reading the actual words of these old-time farmer's almanac editors is the only way to see into their hearts—and, in my opinion, into the heart of Colonial America. Therefore, for those who do not have the time to visit all the libraries where many of the old almanacs are housed (as discussed in Chapter XI), I propose to devote this chapter to the contents of the old almanacs themselves —particularly in those categories which we have not heretofore fully discussed.

Discriptions of
HISTORICAL OR EVERY-DAY EVENTS

Somehow it is only after things get better that we look back and recount how awful they were "then." Thus we have to wait until *Houghton's Almanac* of 1810 for an actual account of how passengers in a 1776 stage coach found that the roll of ship in a rough sea was not too different from the roll of the coach over the bumps and humps of ye olde post roads. And, from an unidentified almanac of 1783 we learn how it was at the day's end of one of these rollicking, rolling journeys.

A Description of a Tavern

A Tavern is a little *Sodom,* where as many vices are practised as ever were known in the great one. Thither Libertines repair to drink away their brains, and piss away their estates; *Aldermen* to talk treason, and bewail the loss of trade; *Saints* to elevate the spirit, hatch calumnies, coin false news, and reproach the Church; *Gamesters* to shake their elbows, and pick the pockets of such cullies who have no more wit than to play with them; *Rakes* with their *Whores,* that by the help of wine they may be more impudent and more wicked, and do those things in their cups, that would be a scandal to sobriety; *Lovers* with their

The Stage to Concord, New Hampshire from
Boston (Trufant's Family Almanac, 1810)

Mistresses, in hopes to wash away that modesty with the soothing juice, which had been a hindrance to their happiness, so that they may fall to without grace, and give a pleasing earnest to each other of their future affections. Thither *Sober Knaves* walk with *Drunken Fools,* to make cunning bargains, and overreach them in their dealings, where cloaking their mental reservations with a grave countenance, they will tell more lies about a hogshead of tobacco, than *Tavernier* in his travels does about Mount *Etna.* Thither *Young Quality* retire to spend their tradesmen's money, and to delight themselves with the impudence of lewd harlots, free from the reflections or remarks of their own servants, whilst their Ladies at home are doing themselves justice after the like manner, and perhaps, for want of better opportunity, are glad to break a commandment with their own footmen. Thither *Bullies* coach it to kick drawers, and invent new oaths and curses, and in feasting, rattling and blustering, to lavish away that scandalous income called a petticoat-pension, though doomed the next day to a three-penny ordinary. Thither run *Sots* purely to be drunk, that they may either wash away the reflections of their own past follies, or forget the treachery of their friends, the falsehood of their wives, the disobedience of their children, the roguery of their lawyers, the bitchery of their paramours, or the ingratitude of the world, that they may drown the remembrance of past evils in the enjoyment of the present.

• • •

Of Indian troubles, in the "J. Weatherwise" almanac
of 1803, printed for L. Trumbull in Norwich, Connecticut, there is "An Affecting Account of the Death of
Miss Polly and Hannah Watts who were taken Pris-
oners and Murdered by the Indians on the 5th of April,
1802." This is a letter from a gentleman in Chete-
ville, Pennsylvania to his friend in Philadelphia. One
Mrs. Watts, captured along with her two daughters,
after witnessing the tortures and subsequent burning at
the stake of her daughters, managed to escape "providing herself at first with about a pound of Bear flesh"
and lived to tell the tale.

Here we pause, also, to take another look at the revolutionary War career of Isaiah Thomas. Here is his *New-England Almanack or the Massachusetts Calendar* for the year 1775, "containing Every Thing Necessary and Useful in an Almanac, to which is added, The Life and Adventures of a Female Soldier." Besides the fact that she was born in Worcester, England, what prompted Isaiah to include Hannah Snell, we aren't likely to find out. Hannah is seen to have married a Dutchman by whom she bore a daughter. Seven months gone, he left her not exactly flat. The child lived for only a few months after she was born and Hannah then took off in pursuit of her husband. Posing as a soldier, later as a sailor, she was not only flogged but also wounded. This edition leaves her at London, her sex still undiscovered, lodging with her brother.

Hannah Snell

Fleet's Pocket Almanac of 1783 tells us about the vast network of signs and signals which gave meaning to the word "Alarm" in the minds of the patriots of that day.

Signals at Nantasket Fort, the Castle, etc.

Signals in the Day

For a Ship in Sight . . . A blue Flag hoisted on the upper Staff.

For a Snow . . . . A Union Flag.˙

For a Brigantine . . . . . A Pendant.

No Signals are made for Schooners or Sloops.

If three Topsail Vessels appear . . . The blue Flag, Union and Pendant, the Pendant uppermost . . . If two Topsail Vessels, two Flags . . . If more than three Topsail Vessels appear, and under twenty, then a Gun is to be fired, and the two Flags and Pendant hoisted, the Pendant lowermost; the firing to be repeated every four minutes till the Signals are answered at the Castle . . . If Twenty or more Topsail Vessels appear, the large blue Flag is to be hoisted uppermost, the Pendant next, and the Union lowermost, and two Guns fired at one Minute's distance, and if the Signals are not answered at the Castle in five Minutes, then three Cannon are to be fired, at one Minute's distance, till they are; and when answered, the Colours are to be haul'd down . . . If they are discovered to be French Vessels, St. George's Ensign is to be hoisted, and kept flying till the same Signal is answered at the Castle.

Signals in the Night

Upon discovering the Enemy in the Night, the Alarm is to be given at Nantasket by firing one Cannon and three Rockets successively; and if the same Signal is not repeated at the Castle in six Minutes, the firing and throwing of Rockets are to be repeated every six Minutes.

The Castle is to answer the Signals given at Nantasket in every respect, and repeat them till they are answered at Boston by the Fort on Fort-Hill, and they are not to salute any Vessels coming in, except Men of War, Frigates, and armed Vessels belonging to our Allies, and none of them with more than 13 Guns, and always to discharge two less then the Vessel discharges.

If an Alarm is to be general in the Night, then the Beacon is to be fired at Boston, and Expresses sent into the Country to fire the other Beacons there.

If a Fleet of Topsail Vessels is discovered from Cape Ann, Marblehead, Plymouth, Barnstable, etc. Expresses are immediately to be sent to Boston.

• • •

The valuation for tax purposes on homes, according to *Poor Robin's,* 1799, included in those days the house, "and out houses," and not over two acres of the land on which the house stood. The rate was 20¢ per every hundred dollar valuation, but lowered as the valuation increased until at $50,000 valuation (the peak) it was ten cents per hundred.

In a *Beer's* edition of 800 one finds another list of valuations. If anyone today had any one of these items in his house or barn, it would certainly bring this valuation and then some.

Each Chariot and Post Chaise at 700 dollars.
Each Phaeton on Steel Springs at 300 dollars.
Every other four wheel Pleasure Carriage at 100 Dollars.
Every Brass and Steel Clock at 40 Dollars.
Every Gold Watch at 50 Dollars.
All other watches at 12 Dollars each.
Every able bodied slave held for life from twelve to
 fifty years old at 100 Dollars.
All river sloops and vessels above 30 tons at 500
 Dollars each.

• • •

A now curious refinement with regard to tide times is found in Leavitt's *Farmer's Almanac* for 1869. Here the information is addressed to "those who are engaged in Cutting Salt Hay"—an industry by now almost forgotten but certainly widespread before, during and after the Revolution. Salt Hay, formerly harvested from many seacoast meadows along the Atlantic Seaboard, was known as a valuable livestock feed. Growing, as it did, on land at times inundated by the salt water tides, it contained iodine and other ingredients beneficial to both man and beast. The cutting of this hay was dependent on the certainty with which the seacoast farmers could depend on the almanac tide tables at the time of the Harvest Moon . . . a time which would afford not only the lowest tides but also the most light.

• • •

As early as 1797 the *Maine Farmer's Almanac* by Thomas Baxter Wait carried an essay on the American Buffalo. Its author, strangely prescient, concluded: "The hunters are too apt to destroy them wantonly, a circumstance much to be regretted." In this same almanac, Mr. Wait urges his readers to pay more "Attention to Observation, Experiment, and Reading." He recommends "Dr. Deane's Dictionary" in its new edition—a veritable farmer's Bible.

That a lively interest was being maintained in education and learning is seen in the fact that many an almanac publisher, either as a printer or bookseller, was connected with the bookselling trade. Munroe and Francis, one of the largest of the early Boston days, had this to say about themselves on the back cover of Low's edition of 1820:

Munroe & Francis,
AT THEIR BIBLE, SCHOOL-BOOK, AND
MISCELLANEOUS BOOKSTORE,
No. 4, CORNHILL, BOSTON,
KEEP for sale an extensive assortment of BOOKS and STATIONERY; particularly for Schools, Bible Societies, Social Libraries, and Country Traders; with perhaps the largest variety of CHILDREN'S BOOKS in any store in America; Cummings's, Morse's and Adams's Geog-

raphies, &c; Webster's, Pike's, Perry's, Juvenile; Alden's, and every other kind of Spelling-Books, Dictionaries, Readers, Grammars, Arithmetics, &c. &c.; Playing Cards, Blanks; Marking instruments; warranted Durable Ink; School Rewards; Village Harmony, Bridgwater Collection, Hymn Books, &c.—One gratis for every 5.

They have just published the 3d edition of the Militia Instructor, by Col. House; the Artillery Discipline: Sword and Pike Exercise, &c.

The Atheneum, or Spirit of the English Magazines (an interesting periodical work) is published by them every fortnight, price 5 dis. per ann. • • •

Early Industry

Catching our eyes as we thumb through the almanacs we have set aside for reason of their early industry content, is this sketch and description of Making Maple Sugar.

MAKING MAPLE SUGAR.—The sugar-maple is a beautiful tree, reaching the height of seventy or eighty feet, the body straight, for a long distance free from limbs, and three or four feet in diameter at the base. It grows in colder climates, between latitude 42 and 48, and on the Alleghenies to their southern termination, extending westward beyond Lake Superior. The wood is nearly equal to hickory for fuel, and is used for building, for ships, and various manufactures. When tapped as the winter gives place to spring, a tree, in a few weeks, will produce five or six pailfuls of sap, which is sweet and pleasant as a drink, and when boiled down will make about half as many pounds of sugar. The manufacturer, selecting a spot central among his trees, erects a temporary shelter, sus-

pends his kettles over a smart fire, and at the close
of a day or two will have fifty or a hundred pounds
of sugar, which is equal to the common West India
sugar, and when refined equals the finest in flavor
and in beauty. When the sap has been boiled to a
syrup and is turning to molasses, then to candy,
and then graining into sugar, its flavor is delight-
ful, especially when the candy is cooled on the
snow. On this occasion the manufacturer expects
his wife, children, and friends, if near, to enjoy the
scene.

There is this fine set of directions, adopted by the Shakers at Canterbury, New Hampshire, for making cider. It appeared first in the Massachusetts Agricultural Journal and was later picked up by some almanac of which I have only a fragment.

We shall not hesitate to give it as our decided opinion that cool climates are much more favorable to cider than warm. However, what greatly contributes to the goodness and delicacy of cider, is the cleanliness of the casks which contain it. In fine, all utensils used in making cider should be kept clean, and not suffered to get sour through the whole process: even the press should be frequently rinsed down, during the time of making cider, to prevent sourness or a change in the cider.

To clean casks which have been used for cider, we take them from the cellar as soon as convenient after the cider is out, (reserving the lees for stilling) and rinse each clean, first with a pailfull of scalding water, then with cold, leaving the casks

with the bungs down for a day or two, or till dry.
Then we bung them tight, and return them to the
cellar, or some convenient place (not too dry) for
their reception. Previous to filling these casks with
cider, the ensuing season, we scald and rinse them
as above. Foul, musty casks ought to be committed
to the fire. Hogsheads or large casks are the best

for cider, especially those that have been recently
used for rum or other spirits.

Apples that drop early, we make into cider for stilling, as being unfit for table use; the spirit of
which, together with that of the lees, we return
back to our store cider at the time of racking,
which is generally about the 1st of January. Cider
made of apples before they are fully ripe, we deem
unfit for drinking; and even when ripe, if they are
made into cider during warm weather, so as to produce a sudden, rapid fermentation, the cider will be
unavoidably hard and unpleasant. The fact is, the
slower cider is in fermenting, the better it will be
at any age; consequently, the later in the season it
is made, and the cooler the weather, (if the business can be conveniently performed), the better,
especially for long keeping. However, this is a cold
work for the fingers, unless pressed in a rack,
which is the best method.

About the first of November, we think a suitable season, if the weather be dry, to gather and put under cover, apples for store-cider. After lying in this situation till mellow, (not rotten,) we commence grinding.

Doubtless good cider for early use, or perhaps for the first year's drinking, may be made previous to this time; but cool, serene weather should be chosen for the business.

The grinding trough should be spacious enough to contain a cheese, in order to admit the pomace (if the weather is cool) to lie over one night before pressing. This method contributes much, both to the colour and quantity of the cider.

In the morning, press it out gradually, and put it up into the casks through straw, or rather a coarse sieve fitted and placed within the tunnel; after which we convey it immediately to a cool cellar, leaving out the bungs till the fermentation chiefly subsides which may be ascertained by the froth settling back at the bung-hole. We then drive in the bungs tight, leaving a small spigot vent awhile longer, if need require, to check the pressure, which must finally be made air tight.

About the first of January, we rack it off free from the lees into clean casks. Those that have been recently used for spirit are to be preferred. But otherwise; having drawn off one cask, we turn out the lees, scald and rinse out the cask as above; add three or four pails full of cider; then burn in the cask, a match of brimstone attached by a hook, to the end of a large wire fixed in the end of a long tapering bung fitting any hole. When the match is burnt out, take off the remnant; apply the bung again, and shake the cask in order to impregnate the cider with the fume. Add more cider and burn another match. Then add from one to three gallons of spirit, (obtained from the lees as above) to one hogshead; fill up the cask with cider, and bung it down air tight, and let it remain till it becomes of mature age.

Cider managed in this way will keep pleasant for years. We would not be understood to suggest a notion, that good cider cannot be obtained without the addition of spirit; especially for immediate use, or the first year's drinking; but the contrary. Yet spirit will give it a new and vigorous body, and insure its preservation.

To make matches for stumming casks, take strips of linen or cotton rags about 1½ inches wide, and 3 or 4 inches long, dip the end of each in melted brimstone, to the extent of one inch.

FRANCIS WINCKLEY

As the century progresses and the great industrial revolution was transforming the country from an agricultural to an industrial economy, I like this illustration from Frank Leslie's *Illustrated Almanac,* 1867.

America's first automated hair brusher

HUMOR

The oldest continuous joke in America was first printed in *Ming's Hutchins Improved Almanac* of 1819. It was entitled "How to Break Ill News."

Mr. G.:   Ha, Jarvis, how are you my old boy? How do things go on at home?

Steward: Bad enough, your honor, the magpie's dead.

Mr. G.:   Poor Mag, so he is gone. How came he to die?

Steward: Over-eat himself, sir.

Mr. G.:   Did he, in faith, a greedy dog! Why, what did he get that he liked so well?

Steward: Horse flesh, sir! He died eating horseflesh.

Mr. G.:   How come he came to get so much horseflesh?

Steward: All your father's horses sir.

Mr. G.:   What, are they dead, too?

Steward: Aye sir, they died of overwork.

Mr. G.:   And pray, why were they overworked?

Steward: To carry water, sir.

Mr. G.:   To carry water! And what were they carrying water for?

Steward: Sure, sir, to put out the fire.

Mr. G.:   Fire, what fire?

Steward: O Sir, your father's house is burnt to the ground.

Mr. G.:   My father's house burnt down? And were it set on fire?

Steward: I think it must have been the torches.

Mr. G.:   Torches, what torches?

Steward: At your mother's funeral.

Mr. G.:   My mother dead!

Steward: Ah, poor lady! She never looked up after it.

Mr. G.:   After what?

Steward: The loss of your father.

Mr. G.:   My father gone, too?

Steward: Yes, poor gentleman! He took to his bed as soon as he heard of it.

Mr. G.:   Heard of what?

Steward: The bad news, Sir, an' please your honor.

Mr. G.:   What! more miseries? more bad news?

Steward: Yes, sir, your bank has failed and your credit is lost, and you are not worth a shilling in the world. I made bold, sir, to tell you about it, for I thought you would like to hear the news.

Almanac humor is not as bad or as good as the fore-going. For those who like this sort of thing, I include here some ten examples:

A Stretcher: The Portlander says that the reason the Vermont and New Hampshire boys are so tall is because they are in the habit of drawing themselves up so as to peep over the mountains to see the sun rise. It's dreadful stretching work.

Leavitt, 1845

A facetious Hibernian once had a bell hung in his lodging room with a string so annexed that he could ring the bell while in bed. "And what use is that?" said one of his neighbors. "Oh, it is mighty convenient," he replied, "for when I have slept long enough, I can ring the bell and wake myself up."

Wild 1837

Rapid Travelling—A traveller on a miserably lean steed was hailed by a yankee who was hoeing his pumpkins by the road side. "Hello, friend, where are you bound?" asked the farmer. "I'm going to the Western Country," replied the other. "Then git off and straddle this 'ere pumpkin vine; it will grow and carry you faster than that there beast."

A lady who made pretensions to the most refined feelings, went to her butcher to remonstrate with him on his cruel practices. "How," she asked, "can you be so barbarous as to put innocent little lambs to death?" "Why not, madam," said he, "would you eat them alive?"

Wild, 1836

An Account of a late Marriage.
A short time since a couple were married in a neighboring town. The ceremony was performed at 8 o'clock in the evening, the Company supped at nine, the Bride danced until twelve, and at two in the morning was delivered of a son. This circumstance did not interrupt the jollity of the occasion as the Bride and her little one were in a fair way to do well.

Low, 1774

A Poser: "Daddy, I want to ask you a question." "Well, my son, what is it?" "Why is neighbor Smith's bar room like a counterfeit dollar?" "I can't tell, my son." "Because you can't pass it," said the boy and he was sent right to bed.

Munsell, 1855

215

"I shall be at home next Sunday night," a young lady said when she followed her beau to the door who seemed to be wavering in his attachment. "So shall I," was his reply.

Thomas, 1842

A self-conceited coxcomb was introducing an acquaintance to a large company, whose physiognomy was not very pre-possessing. Thinking to be extremely witty, he thus ad-dressed the company who rose at his entrance. "I have the honor to introduce Mr.———, who is not so great a fool as he looks to be." The young man immediately replied to this introduction. "Therein consists of the difference between my friend and me."

Thomas, 1824

A Swap—Mr. Snooks was asked the other day how he could account for nature's making him so ugly. "Nature was not to blame," said he, "for when I was two months old I was considered the handsomest child in the neighbor-hood, but my nurse, the slut, one day swapped me away for another boy just to please a friend of hers, whose child was plain looking."

Signs of a Good Cow

She's long in her face, she's fine in her horn,
She'll quickly get fat without cake or corn,
She's clean in her jaws, and full in her chine,
She's heavy in flank, and wide in her loin.

She's broad in her ribs, and long in her rump,
A straight and flat back, without e'er a hump.
She's wide in her hips, and calm in her eyes,
She's fine in her shoulders, and thin in her thighs.

She's light in her neck, and small in her tail,
She's wide in her breast, and good at the pail;
She's fine in her bone, an silky of shin,
She's a grazier's without, and a butcher's within.

Leavitt's, 1862

• • •

In a slightly different category from the humor of the old almanacs are their so-called "Anecdotes." From the rush and hurry of modern living, these little anecdotes are a good means of setting back the clock.

John Dudley, of Deerfield in New-Hampshire, was a captain in the militia. He was an old bachelor, had an old maid for a house-keeper, and tilled his ground like an honest man. He was acquainted with Gov. Wentworth and frequently called upon him when at Portsmouth, that he might tell his rustic neighbours how thick he was with His Excellency. To add to his importance he once invited the Governor to call upon him at Deerfield, on his way into the country; and the Governor promised to do so. The captain expected the visit some time in a certain week, and kept near his house busily employed as usual. One very warm day his housekeeper came puffing into the field to inform him that a grand carriage, which must be the Governor's, was at a little distance. The captain ran into the house and hardly had time to slip on his military red coat, and cocked hat, ere His Excellency drove up. With his trusty sword in hand, Dudley ran into the street, and assuming a true captain-like strut, paid a martial salute to His Excellency, who on beholding him, burst out into a hearty laugh. This rather discomposed the man of the sword; but he was put to immediate flight by the following speech of the Governor. "Captain Dudley, I am glad to see you, but think your appearance as a militaryman would be improved, if you were to add to your uniform a pair of breeches!"—an article which the good captain, in his haste to pay his respects, had entirely forgotten.

Nathan Wild, 1830

Breeches

217

SLEIGH-RIDING WITH A WIDOW.—Snow had fallen; the young of the village got up a grand sleighing party to a country tavern at some distance, and the interesting widow Lambkin sat in the same sleigh, under the same buffalo as myself. "Oh! Oh! don't!" she exclaimed, as we came up to the first bridge, catching me by the arm and turning her veiled face towards me while her eyes twinkled in the moonlight. "Don't what?" I asked; "I am not doing anything." "Well, but I thought you were going to take toll!" replied Mrs. Lambkin. I rejoined, "What's that?" "Don't you know that gentlemen, when they go on a sleighing party, claim a kiss as toll when they cross a bridge! Well, I never!" When next we came to a bridge and claimed toll, the struggles of the widow to hold the veil were not sufficient to tear it, and somehow when the veil was removed her face turned directly towards my own, and in the glittering of the moonlight the horse trotted on himself; toll was taken for the first time in his life by Dr. Meadows. Soon we came to a long bridge, but the widow said it was no use to resist, and she paid up as we reached it, without a struggle. "But you won't take toll for every arch, will you, doctor?" To which the only reply was a practical affirmative to the question. Did you ever, reader, sleigh ride with a widow, and take toll at the bridge?

Munsell, 1855

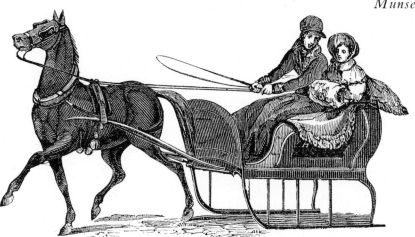

A Vermont Snow-Storm.

The storm was very severe on the mountains. A
stage driver was compelled, in consequence of the
vast quantity of snow to detach one of the horses
from the stage, and attempt to carry the mail on it.
He got along very comfortably, all things considered, until the horse stumbed and pitched him,
neck and heels into the snow. On recovering himself, and looking around to discover the cause of
the accident, he found the horse had stepped one
foot into—the chimney of a *two story house*.

Godfrey, 1843

• • •

Although by 1753 New York was requiring that physicians be licensed, it was perhaps just as well, even
twenty-three years later, to put up with one's ailment
as best one could rather than subject one's self to the
cures.

The recipe Doctor Stearns or anyone else would have
used against catching a disorder of any kind, as well as
for curing the headache, read this way:

Take rue, sage, wormwood and lavender, a handful of each and infuse them into a gallon of white
vinegar in a stone pot and set on warm wood ashes
for four days . . . strain and put in well corked
bottles . . . with a quarter ounce of camphire . . . in
each bottle . . . When you go anywhere infection
is, rub temples, nose, mouth, and palms of the
hands with this mixture.

For chills, cold, and sweating, known then as the ague
(a gu), one made tiny balls from whatever cobwebs
one could find around the house and mixed these with
the syrup of elder or any other syrup to be rolled into
pills, one of which was to be taken an hour or so before

the "fit comes on." A half pint of warm ale was to be taken after the pill—and then "walk for an hour as fast as possible without settling down." A smaller pill, half the quantity of ale, and half an hour's walk would do for children but "If the child cannot walk, it must be kept in motion."

If the fever were constant, accompanied by a cough, a more drastic treatment was called for: an ounce of powdered salt-petre divided into sixteen half-drachm parts, one part to be taken every three and a half hours dissolved in sage tea. Twenty drops of balsam capivi (derived from an African tree of the senna family) with powdered sugar, were added for the cough.

• • •

PUZZLES In our 1963 edition of the Old Farmer's Almanac, we published the following puzzle:

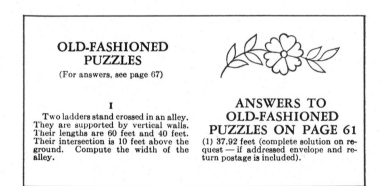

OLD-FASHIONED PUZZLES

(For answers, see page 67)

I

Two ladders stand crossed in an alley. They are supported by vertical walls. Their lengths are 60 feet and 40 feet. Their intersection is 10 feet above the ground. Compute the width of the alley.

ANSWERS TO OLD-FASHIONED PUZZLES ON PAGE 61

(1) 37.92 feet (complete solution on request — if addressed envelope and return postage is included).

This one little puzzle brought more comment and mail than anything else in the issue. Puzzles have been a popular feature of almanacs for as far back as most casual fans will care too look. Accompanying them, usually, were the familiar rebuses, conundrums, charades, etc. Here (at right) are a few more samples:

CHARADES, REBUSES, CONUNDRUMS, ENIGMAS, etc.

(For answers, see page 120)

I

II

I am composed of 25 letters.
My 12, 4, 1, 18, 20, is a word meaning empty.
My 11, 3, 22, 9, 12, 13, 10 is a kind of monk.
My 2, 24, 17, 5, 19 is a piece of money.
My 6, 16, 8, 22 is a division of time.
My 25, 3, 10, 25, 7 are sometimes bad.
My 17, 21, 5 are thought after dinner.
My 13, 3, 14 is large.
My whole is an old saying.

III

What bird is that whose name represents nothing, twice yourself and fifty?

IV

My first in cities is well known,
And by me many live,
Obtain their freedom in the town
And then a vote can give;
My second we can never see,
Whether on the land or sea;
My whole the sailor ofter braves,
When he plows the briny waves.

V

VI

Why does a man in paving the streets correct the public morals?

VII

Entire, I am a companion; beheaded, a verb; replace my head, curtail me, and I am found in nearly every house; curtail again, I am a nickname; reversed, a verb.

VIII

My 1-2-3 designates abbreviations of three states. The whole these states would be before the Revolution. See?

IX

There is a word of five syllables —take away the first and no syllable will remain.

X

I am found in a jail; I belong to a fire;
And am seen in a gutter abounding in mire;
Put my last letter third, and then 'twill be found; I belong to a King, without changing my sound.

XI

My first is irrational, my second is rational, my third is mechanical, and my whole is scientifical.

XII

What word is that to which if you add a syllable, it will make it shorter?

XIII

XIV

What is that which is lengthened by being cut at both ends?

ANSWERS TO CHARADES, ETC. ON PAGE 85

(1) A man cannot gather grapes from thistles. (2) A penny saved is a penny earned. (3) Owl (O + UU + L). (4) Tradewinds. (5) W HAIR over each eye (i) n gander or a bound will p over t and v ice beef hound. (Where over-reaching and error abound, will poverty be found.) (6) He is amending the public ways. (7) Mate, ate, mat, ma, am. (8) Colony. (9) Monosyllable. (10) Grate. (11) Horsemanship. (12) Short. (13) Hew hop lace S C on F I dents in awl purse on swill short L y C on F I D E in no body. (He who places confidents in all persons will shortly confide in nobody.) (14) A ditch.

There was one development in the puzzle line which is not seen very much today. This is the Picture Puzzle. The one below is from Vennor's *Weather Almanac* of 1883 and, as you will note from the caption, you are supposed to find some nineteen different animals.

THE GREAT ANIMAL PUZZLE
A CAREFUL inspection of the hidden beauties of the above weird landscape will show illustrations

of the following named animals: LION, TIGER, RHINOCEROS, ELEPHANT, MULE, ALLIGATOR, WOLF, FOX, PORCUPINE, BULL, BEAVER, MONKEY, DOG, GIRAFFE, CAMEL, EAGLE, OWL, PARROT, DEER, SNAKE, and DUCK. The venerable monk, St. Jacob, is also seen, calmly seated among the foliage, meditating upon the immense benefit brought to man and beast by his wonderful discovery—ST. JACOBS OIL—the Great German Remedy.

• • •

RECIPES

One does not find too many recipes in almanacs before 1850. In fact the title RECEIPTS on an almanac page in those days was followed only by remedies. Advice on food was more concerned with how to preserve it or, as with wine, cyder, etc., how to make it. In the *New England Almanac* for 1809 by Isaac Bickerstaff, for example, appears this

METHOD OF PICKLING

The following mode of pickling may be applied for preserving a great variety of vegetable buds, pods, seeds and fruits, in vinegar, upon a principle little practiced or understood among housewives, but which on trial will be found superior to the old mode now in use.

Pickles are a grateful condiment to the stomach, particularly when joined with animal food; and are in general use in this country: therefore any improvement in the art of pickling, must be valuable and worthy of adoption. Every person of observation knows that the watery juices of succulent fruits and other vegetable matters, such as cucumbers, melons, beets, etc. weaken and neutralize the vinegar in which they are pickled, and consequently bring it into a state of putrid fermentation, which in a short time spoils and destroys them.

The method we advise, and have tried with success, is to take out the watery juices, not by steeping them in a strong pickle of salt and water till they are half rotten (as is usual) which process not only partially decomposes the texture of the article, but extracts and draws out its flavour; but by dissipating it by evaporation, which takes out all the superfluous moisture, and at the same time leaves the true flavour behind.

Take young cucumbers four or five inches long, musk-melons or mangoes of the size of a large goose egg, etc.—Make a longitudinal incision of about half their length, and sufficiently deep; spread them in an open airy place well secured from the sun. Let them remain till they have wilted and grown considerably soft, in which state they are fit for pickling.

Lay them in your pot with the spices, etc. you approve, stratum superstratum, till it is about three parts full. Pour the best and strongest vinegar with a little salt over them cold, so as to stand about three fingers breadth upon them, lay a clean board on the pickles, and a stone on it, to prevent them from rising to the top.

In twelve or fourteen days you will find a frothy scum rise to the top, which must be carefully taken off, then pour out the vinegar, and strain it through a cloth. If the pickles are for immediate use, the same vinegar will do; but if they are intended for long keeping, fresh vinegar must be used, and the pot closely covered.

Cabbages should be quartered before they are put out to wilt. But kidney beans, sprouts, etc. require no preparation; as they are small and not so full of juice, they easily give out the watery parts. If you made use of aromatic herbs for flavouring your pickles, they should be wilted in the same manner.

With some diligence and patience, of course, in these early almanacs, you will find a few recipes. This one appears   in the Rhode Island Almanac for 1822— sandwiched between "The Chinese Method of Mending China" and "Cure for a Sprain or Bruise."

APPLE BREAD

M. Duduit de Mazieres, a French officer of the King's household, has discovered and practised with great success, a method of making bread of common apples, very superior to potato bread. After having boiled one third of peeled apples, he bruised them while quite warm into two thirds of flour, including the proper quantity of yeast, and kneaded the whole without water, the juice of the fruit being quite sufficient. When this mixture had acquired the consistency of paste, he put it into a vessel, in which he allowed it to rise for about twelve hours. By this process, he obtained a very excellent bread, full of eyes, and extremely palatable and light.

After 1850, there was more interest in recipes, and other matters which concern the housekeeper. As good as an example as any of this interest is to be seen in the *Farmer's Almanac and Housekeeper's Receipt Book* for 1851 published by John Simon of Philadelphia. The first nine pages pertain to raising poultry and duck. Then come the livestock, cows, sheep, etc. Finally, the recipes.

ACORN COFFEE

Take sound ripe acorns, peel them and roast them with a little butter, or fat, then, when cold, grind them with one third their weight of real coffee.

TOMATO CATSUP

To a gallon skinned tomatos add 4 tablespoonsful salt, 4 co. black pepper, half a spoonful alspice, 8 red peppers, and 3 spoonsful of mustard. All these ingredients must be ground fine, and simmered slowly in sharp vinegar for three or four hours. As much vinegar is to be used as to leave half a gallon of liquor when the process is over. Strain through a wire sieve and bottle, and seal from the air. This may be used in two weeks, but improves by age, and will keep several years.

VINEGAR

To make Vinegar with water. Put 30 or 40 pounds of wild pears in a large tub, where you leave them three days to ferment. Then pour some water over them, and repeat this every day for a month; at the end of which it will make very good vinegar; the goodness of which may be increased by the above method.

JUMBLES

Take flour, 1½ pound; sugar, 1 pound; butter, ¾ pound; four yolks and two whites of eggs; rose-water, one wine glassful. Roll thin with fine powdered sugar, and bake on tins.

BLACK CAKE
(That Will Keep A Year)

Sugar, 1 pound; butter, 1 pound; flour, 1 pound; ten eggs; brandy, ¼ pint; raisins, 2 pounds; currants, 2 pounds. Mace, Nutmegs, and Cloves to flavour. Bake it well.

WAFFLES

Milk, 1 quart; eggs, 5; flour, 1¼ pound; butter ½ pound; yeast, 1 spoonful. When baked, sift sugar and powdered cassia on them.

PLUM PUDDING

To make rich plum pudding, take a pound of marrow, or suet well chopped, a pound of fine flour dried, eight or ten eggs beaten well; half a nutmeg grated; as much mace, cinnamon, and ginger, all powdered very fine; a pinch of salt; mix these well together, and beat up into a batter; then add one pound of currants, one pound of raisins, stoned and chopped a little; the currants should be rubbed in a cloth, and well picked, or well wash and dry them; two ounces of candied citron peel, or part lemon, and orange, cut small; and two ounces of sweet almonds, blanched, and cut up in bits; two ounces of loaf-sugar grated; then add these to the batter, and put in a wine-glassful of brandy; well mix them together. It may be boiled in a buttered basin or mould; if the batter should be too stiff, put a glass of white wine in it. It will take four or five hours' boiling. Strew over it powdered loaf-sugar, garnish with sliced lemon - Sauce containing half a glass of best brandy, a little rind of lemon grated, and a little powdered cinnamon, half an ounce of grated loaf-sugar, mixed with an equal quantity of very thick melted butter. It is a good plan to make and keep by you a little of this sauce, and then it is ready at any time. In a bottle containing a pint of sherry, and half a pint of best brandy, add two ounces of loaf sugar, a quarter of an ounce of mace, half an ounce of shaved lemon rind, with kernels of apricots, peaches, and nectarines, and steep in a little white wine; when steeped, pour it off clear, and put to the wine and brandy: and add half a quarter of a pint of capillaire. Two tablespoonfuls of this sauce will flavor a boatful of thick melted butter.

RASPBERRY JAM

Take 1 pound loaf-sugar to every pound of fruit; bruise them together in your preserving-pan with a silver spoon, and let them simmer gently for an hour. When cold, put them into glass jars, and lay over them a bit of paper saturated with brandy —then tie them up so as carefully to exclude the air.

CAROLINA CORN CAKES

Mix together in a pan, a pint and a half of sifted corn meal, and a half-pint of wheat flour, adding a heaped salt-spoon of salt. Beat three eggs very light. Have ready a quart of sour milk. (You can turn sweet milk sour by adding a very little vinegar.) Put into a tea-cup a small-tea-spoonful of super-carbonate of soda, and dissolve it in a little lukewarm water, then stir it into the milk. In another tea-cup, melt a full salt-spoon of tartaric acid, and stir that afterwards into the milk. Then add, alternately, the beaten eggs, and the meal, a little of each at a time, stirring them well into the milk. It should be about the consistence of sponge-cake batter. Having beaten the whole very hard, butter square tin pans, into a hot oven and bake them well. They may be baked in muffin rings, pulling them open when brought to table.

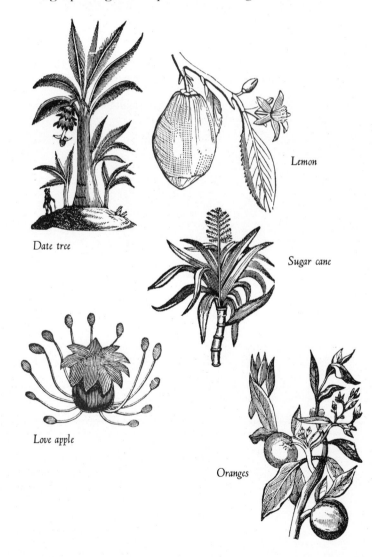

Date tree

Lemon

Sugar cane

Love apple

Oranges

The little verses at the top of the calendar pages were always (and still are as far as I'm concerned) an integral part of the farmer's almanac calendar pages. The following, found in *Houghton's Genuine Almanac* for 1809, is typical:

> April, Fourth Month,
> *"Awaits the sudden rising of the trout*
> *Down slips the feathery lure; the quivering rod*
> *Bends low: in vain the cheated captive strives*
> *To break the yielding line: exhausted soon,*
> *Ashore he's drawn, and, on the mossy bank,*
> *Wettering, he dyes the primrose with his blood."*

One notes, the closing quotation marks on this descriptive and suitable verse. Mr. Houghton, or Mr. Prentiss, or someone connected with this almanac has evidently garnered it from some newspaper, book, or poet—for free or for pay.

The Albany Almanack for 1815 by Andrew Beers includes both a top and a bottom of the page verse. There are no quotes around either. The quality of each is not too much better than a good bright school girl of that year could have written.

Anson Allen, in his *Newtonian Reflector* for 1825:

> *The Sun with sultry Sirius now doth rise*
> *And Jove's red lightning flashes from the skies:*
> *The angry gods heaven's arm'ry open flings,*
> *And whizzing bolts ride forth on burning wings.*
>   August Calendar Page

and Nathan Wild in his almanac for 1831:

Rude Boreas comes in dread array,
And all his boisterous powers display;
The mountain top his pinions sweep,
And wakes with rage the briny deep.

                                    S. S.
                    December Calendar Page

These pretty much show how these early Calendar Page verses were. The latter reveals (at long last) a signature—"S.S." But who was S.S., we wonder? By and large, throughout most of American almanac history, these calendar verses were unsigned or uninitialed. After some there appears only the single word, "Communicated." There is little doubt that many were transcribed from the works of famous English or European authors. In later years, no doubt, Whittier, Holmes, Longfellow, and others were, knowingly or otherwise, included in these pages. However, only a good literary detective could give the answers as to which are by whom. And we doubt if the knowledge thereby gained would be really worth the effort.

Nevertheless, Nature was ever a theme of great interest to all poets. There can be little doubt that, for this reason, almanacs (of which a great part have always been given over to the country) may have interested more than one good and mature poet. We know from Celia Thaxter's diary that she was inspired to become a poet solely through annual copies of *The Old Farmer's Almanack*. With this, and other almanacs, entering and remaining for a whole year in as many homes as they did, many future poets and writers must have gained from them an early interest in poetry as well as in many other fields of endeavor. It is not, however, until the 20th century that one begins to find any serious effort on the part of almanac makers to include signed poems by famous writers.

Robert Frost, David Morton, John Holmes, Ogden Nash, Hal Borland, are among those poets found in The Old Farmer's Almanac in recent years. Whether or not such famous names really fit into the Calendar Pages and become integral parts of these pages is what each reader has to decide for himself. Our own view in this is that each Calendar Page, after all else in it was made up, called for a certain kind of poem or verse to make that page complete. If the editor had been able to obtain just that verse or poem from a well-known writer, so much the better. If not, the page was better off as a whole with at least the thought which was required—even if it was written in the worst of doggerel. At least this is the way it seems from the examination of thousands of verses which have appeared on these Calendar Pages. Otherwise, these verses or poems presumably would have been better than they are.

Perhaps the best conclusion of the matter is found in the four pretty verses concerning the Seasons, quoted in *Poor Robin's* of 1808. These came from the cook-maid of the author's uncle.

SPRING

About the seasons of the year;
Astrologers may make a fuss:
But this I know, that Spring is here
When I cut asparagus.

SUMMER

Concerning dates, whate'er they pen
No matter whether true or not
I know it must be summer when
Green peas are in the Pot.

AUTUMN

And Autumn takes his turn to reign
I know as sure as I'm a sinner
When leaves are scattered o'er the plain
And grapes are eaten after dinner.

WINTER

Winter is known by frost and snow,
To all the little girls and boys;
But it's enough for me to know,
I get no greens except savoys.

The specialty almanacs

*As one moves out of the
18th century and into the first
half of the 19th, the nature of the almanac
business is seen to change. Commercialism
has crept in to ride the waves of the
high standards set by the
old time editors. Still
worse, politics, patent medicines—
almost any cause one can
name—take over the
almanac as a tool
for winning the
populace.*

chapter nine

One for every PURPOSE

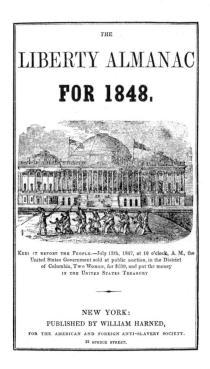

THE

LIBERTY ALMANAC

FOR 1848.

KEEP IT BEFORE THE PEOPLE.—July 13th, 1847, at 10 o'clock, A. M., the United States Government sold at public auction, in the District of Columbia, TWO WOMEN, for $530, and put the money IN THE UNITED STATES TREASURY

NEW YORK:
PUBLISHED BY WILLIAM HARNED,
FOR THE AMERICAN AND FOREIGN ANTI-SLAVERY SOCIETY.
22 SPRUCE STREET.

Although the British had abolished slavery from the British West Indies in 1833, abolitionists in our own country were being regarded by the public in general as visionaries and troublemakers. Men like the poet John Greenleaf Whittier and the orator Wendell Phillips, however, were standing up for these idealists. After the murder of Elijah Lovejoy, Abolitionist editor, a Liberty political party was formed from which the *Liberty Almanac* evolved. This party favored direct political action and became sufficiently powerful to bring about the national defeat of the Whigs and subsequently, the death of that party.

From this same *Liberty Almanac,* one can clearly visualize the initial struggles of a society of these idealists to gain equal rights for the colored people. As early as May, 1840 it owned its own headquarters "with a steam engine, and printing presses" and had established itself in a "commodious building opposite the Patent Office . . . at Washington City."

This particular *Liberty Almanac* is typical of a number of different specialised almanacs which flourished in the United States from about 1840 on. Inasmuch as the good farmer's almanacs had by then become well established and accepted in the home not only as trustworthy but as informative and entertaining, the specialised almanac, trading on the almanac name, was accepted almost automatically—especially since it was generally given away (to advertise some cause or product) free of charge. This led eventually to a demoralization of the almanac business from which it was never fully to recover. In the meanwhile, some of these special purpose almanacs, as the forerunners of America's great public relations industry, are assuredly worthy of attention.

• • •

The victory of the Liberty political party aided and abetted as it was by its *Liberty Almanac,* was not won, apparently, on the issue of slavery alone. The Whigs, actually, had *The Whig Almanac* as their own. In its issue of 1848, it quotes Henry Clay's long speech of November 14, 1847 in which he took a strong position against the annexation of Texas as well as a dim view of the Mexican War. This political stand is said to have lost him not only the support of New York state but to have brought about a crushing defeat for himself and his party. Clay's political fortunes were not to his liking in 1840 either, when Daniel Webster deserted him in favor of William Henry Harrison.

However, we learn nothing of this disappointment in *The Harrison Almanac* of 1841 which is devoted almost entirely to General Harrison's biography. It places special emphasis on his bravery as a soldier, his subduing of Tecumseh, his charity towards the negro, and his love for the poor and underprivileged.

Harrison giving
his horse to
a Methodist Minister.

Before Harrison or Clay there had also been the Whig, David (Davy) Crockett, 1786–1836. The original Davy Crockett almanacs (1835–56) are scarce today. As he gave up his life for his country at the Alamo in 1836, only two of these are perhaps in his own backwoods, boisterous, and amusing idiom. The others were published by his heirs in Nashville, Tennessee. Crockett's "first" had competition, viz, the *Jackson Almanac*, 1835, which was embellished with no less than fifty illustrations.

Colonel Crockett's
encounter with
a bear

In addition to the anti-slavery and political crusades of those times was the one encouraged by the American Temperance Society of Clinton Hall, New York. An example of the extremes to which this Society was willing to go is seen in the 1834 edition of its Almanac.

This particular temperance almanac was by no means the first in the field. In 1834, for example, there had been *The Temperance Almanac* of the New York State Temperance Society in Albany, New York. On page 15 this almanac began a twenty-page illustrated dialogue between a mother and her child on the evils of demon rum.

How the nurse kept the baby quiet

Child. Mother, what is this picture?
Mother. It is the picture of a nurse with a little infant on her lap. And there is a bed on one side; a cradle for the babe on the other; and a table standing near the nurse.
Child. But what is nurse doing to the baby? Is she going to kill it?
Mother. No, my child. She is feeding it with gin and water made sweet with sugar. The decanter stands, you see, on the little table.
Child. But, mother, why does nurse give gin to the baby? I thought only men and women ever used spirit.

In some copies, but not all, of Robert B. Thomas's *Old Farmer's Almanack* of the same year, this same twenty-page illustrated dialogue also appears. As Thomas does not appear as a teetotaller in most of his issues it is likely that, for this particular year at least, some sort of pressure must have been brought to bear upon him. If not, then he may have felt that the idea of borrowing the cuts for his territory would not only serve to keep the *Temperance Almanac* in its New York home but also add to the interest of some of his New England readers.

Why Father
was late

The year 1829 was greeted by *The New England Anti-Masonic Almanac* by Edward Giddins. Its editor, of Rochester, N.Y., explains its appearance on the grounds that it contains his own, much-sought-after account of the alleged confinement and murder of one William Morgan . . . by the Masons. The occasion of this crime was the suppression of a book, unfavorable to the Masonic Order, which Morgan was about to publish. "Remember the fate of Morgan," quoth the paragraph atop the calendar page of this almanac for December, "and shun Masonry as a pestilence."

The unfair trial
of William Morgan

In the Rhode Island Almanack of 1822, by Isaac Bickerstaff, Esq. Philom. (the name, as we have already seen, is fictitious) appears a four-page article on the Peace Societies. It points out how peace is as important a cause as "was" slavery; how one Anthony Benezet, a Philadelphia schoolmaster, was the first in this country to raise an organized cry against war, and how a pamphlet published in Massachusetts about 1818, entitled *A Solemn Review of the Custom of War,* resulted in the establishment of many peace societies here and abroad. The one this particular almanac represents is called The Rhode Island Peace Society. It was established March 20, 1818 and had representatives in every large town of that state. In its edition of 1823 appear Thomas Jefferson's words "that war is an instrument entirely inefficient towards redressing wrong; that it multiplies instead of indemnifying losses."

"A pacific people will naturally insure a pacific government, so long as it shall be elective," this 1823 edition concludes, "and a contentious people will be pretty sure to produce a contentious government or to give a contentious aspect and direction."

• • •

One of the most important and long-lasting of the "crusade-for-religion" almanacs was founded by The American Tract Society and the Religious Tract Society of New York. This was called *The Christian Almanac.* Its edition for 1825 reached the extensive print order of some 150,000 copies and was published by separate individuals or firms in Boston, New York, Rochester, N.Y., Philadelphia, Pittsburgh, Baltimore, and Huntsville, Alabama. By the arithmetic of that day, the editor tells us that every individual who purchased a copy of *The Christian Almanac* of 1824 provided through his or her purchase for the "printing of a Tract for perpetual circulation." He adds that "A respectable Mercantile House last year purchased 10,000 copies from which profit accrued to the Society sufficient to furnish for circulation in our own country 10,000 tracts . . . a donation to the Society of Fifty dollars . . . and, a sum to print 6,000 tracts in the Mahratta language, at Bombay, in India." The editor appears confident that *The Christian Almanac* will eventually be purchased by one million families in our own country, and thus provide a further million Tracts for ourselves, in addition to some 600,000 for the people of India.

On page 37 of the edition for 1822, begins an interesting "General View of the Movements of the Church for the last Thirty Years." It points to the year 1792 as a "new era in the history of the church." After tracing the origins of various missionary societies in England and Scotland, it tells us:

> In 1799 a new institution, *the first of its kind,* was established. Some Christians in England, beholding the success which attended the small tracts circulated by the atheists in France, caught the idea of opposing the enemy with weapons like their own, and formed the *London Religious Tract Society*. This institution has printed and circulated more than 36,000,000 of these tracts . . .

The Tract Society was established in New York in 1812 and at Boston as the *New England Tract Society* the following year. They were the parents of this *Christian Almanac*. The work in this new era of the church is just begun, we read, and all Christians are called upon to "increase their donations, efforts, and prayers, in a ten-fold proportion."

When we realize that the *New England Tract Society* during its first year of existence circulated no less than

2,708,000 tracts, we can understand how it was that these tracts, jointly with the Almanac, became perhaps the most widely distributed kind of reading matter—not even excepting the Bible—in the world.

The American Tract Society is now located in Oradell, New Jersey. It traces its lineage directly from the London original via the Boston Tract Society (1814). This past year it not only distributed some 35 million tracts but also presented each member of the freshman class at West Point with an engraved Bible. Ever hear of "Colparteurs?" We never did until we talked with a member of this Society. These "colparteurs" were men with leather socks who delivered tracts house to house in the early 19th century. No doubt they delivered an almanac or two besides. At the beginning of the 20th century the Society of this name "embraced members of fourteen evangelical denominations" and its constant aim is to "lead men to Christ as the only Savior and then to help them to become like Him and to live for Him." At least so reads *The Family Christian Almanac* for 1899, also known as *The Illustrated Family Christian Almanac,* the title which the Society took for its Almanac of 1849.

There is a wealth of illustration, anecdotes, verse, historical information, humor, statistics, and other material in this long run of *The Christian Almanac*. Students of American 19th century religion will wish to give these little volumes more than a cursory study. They will not wish to neglect, either, some of the other religious almanacs of these years like *The Congregational Almanac* which, beginning in 1846, stressed the importance of that sect and continued to do so for some years.

• • •

Any consideration of the specialised almanacs can be made as broad, detailed, and as extensive as one wishes to make it. For example, with the secession of the Southern States and the outbreak of the Civil War, there appeared *Clarke's Confederate Household Almanac* by H. C. Clarke for, respectively, the first, second, third, and fourth years of the "Independence of the Confederate States of America." Its first three issues were published in Vicksburg; the final one from Mobile. Or, one can study the "Monumental" edition of the *Veterans of the Civil War Almanac,* published in 1869 in the north upon the cessation of hostilities. Here one will find a complete "History of the Rebellion" as well as an illustrated article on the Hottentots and the "Bucku" leaf cure for the wounded soldiers.

Further, one may wish to include some of the industrial applications of the Jayne and Ayer techniques. One of these would be *Bradley's Farmer's Reference Book & Almanac* for 1887. On its cover is an Indian brave. To his left are three sheafs of corn towering high above his head "grown with Bradley's Super-Phosphate of Lime." To his right is one measly spindle, scarcely as high as his shoulder "grown without Bradley's phosphate." On its back cover is a colored lithograph of The Bradley Fertilizer Company's Works at North Weymouth, Mass., "The largest Fertilizer Works in the

World." Within its covers are thirteen almanac calendar pages, thirty-five pages of text relative to the efficacy, with testimonials, of Bradley's fertilizers, and the facsimile of the Company's poster which announces to all that Bradley's pays the highest cash price of all for BONES.

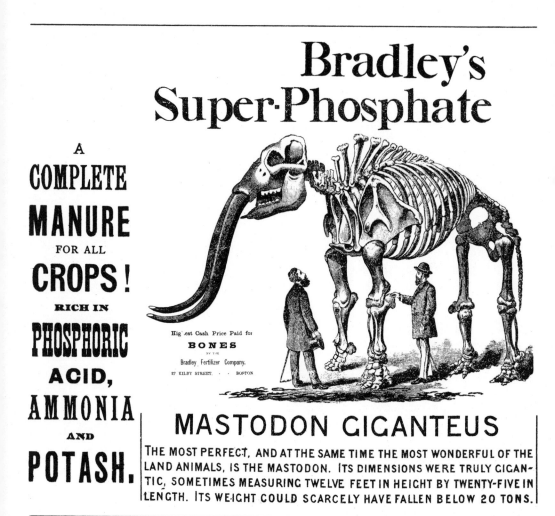

Bradley's Super-Phosphate

A
COMPLETE
MANURE
FOR ALL
CROPS !
RICH IN
PHOSPHORIC
ACID,
AMMONIA
AND
POTASH.

Highest Cash Price Paid for
BONES
BY THE
Bradley Fertilizer Company,
27 KILBY STREET. · · BOSTON

MASTODON GIGANTEUS

THE MOST PERFECT, AND AT THE SAME TIME THE MOST WONDERFUL OF THE LAND ANIMALS, IS THE MASTODON. ITS DIMENSIONS WERE TRULY GIGANTIC, SOMETIMES MEASURING TWELVE FEET IN HEIGHT BY TWENTY-FIVE IN LENGTH. ITS WEIGHT COULD SCARCELY HAVE FALLEN BELOW 20 TONS.

In the same category are the Castoria page from *The New York Almanac,* of 1890, and Dr. Hall's Balsam heading for one of A. L. Scovill & Company's testimonials in its *Farmers' and Mechanics' Almanac* for 1862.

The list of these industry-sponsored almanacs is long and varied. The Ford Motor Company has carried one along in various different styles for many years. Miles Laboratories, Rexall, and Plough, Inc. have all used these and wall almanac-calendars as sales aids for their drugstore customers. Today, many banks, insurance companies, and oil companies, etc. are using almanacs as part of their sales promotion programs.

Grier's (These are not industry-sponsored.) and *Blum's* are well established in the South. *Baer's Agricultural* is just now coming into national distribution as are *American Farm & Home* and the American version of Britain's *Old Moore's. Gruber's* is a Maryland standby.

Today, at Lewiston, Maine, the genial president of the Geiger Bros. Company out of Newark, New Jersey, using the Farmer's Almanac title said by him to have been used by one David Young in 1818 and continued ever since, has built up a large give-away business (3,5000,000 copies).

Profitable publication of this kind of almanac also permitted the issuance of more than one edition of just plain fun. The first of these was *The American Comic Almanac,* 1831, by Charles Ellms of Boston.

The illustration and caption shown here are from Page 31 of that edition.

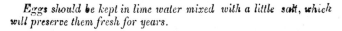

Eggs should be kept in lime water mixed with a little salt, which will preserve them fresh for years.

Elton's, which made its first, and last, appearance in New York in the year 1847, included a feature on "The Go-Ahead Quadrilles, or *Sailor's Instruction in Dancing.*"

Almanac readers of the 1870s were to find (as have many since then) *Josh Billings' Farmer's Allminax* good for chuckles if not for outright laughs. From the editions which ran between 1870 and 1874, I have chosen Billings' calendar page for December 1872 as one which gives the best idea of the approach the famous humorist used throughout.

Henry W. Shaw
"Josh Billings".

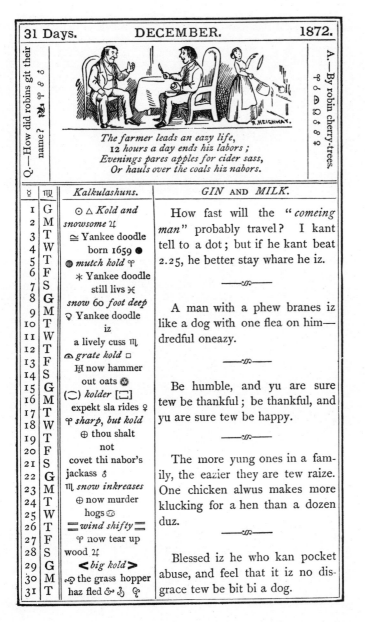

Q.—How did robins git their name? ♍ ♈ ♉ ♂

A.—By robin cherry-trees. ♂ ♉ ♈ ♐ ♑ ♒ ♓

The farmer leads an eazy life,
12 hours a day ends hiz labors ;
Evenings pares apples for cider sass,
Or hauls over the coals hiz nabors.

R. HEIGHWAY.

☿	♍	*Kalkulashuns.*
1	G	☉ △ *Kold and*
2	M	*snowsome* ♃
3	T	≏ Yankee doodle
4	W	born 1659 ●
5	T	◑ *mutch kold* ♈
6	F	✳ Yankee doodle
7	S	still livs ♓
8	G	*snow 60 foot deep*
9	M	♀ Yankee doodle
10	T	iz
11	W	a lively cuss ♏
12	T	♋ *grate kold* □
13	F	♅ now hammer
14	S	out oats ◉
15	G	(◡) *kolder* [□]
16	M	expekt sla rides ♀
17	T	♈ *sharp, but kold*
18	W	⊕ thou shalt
19	T	not
20	F	covet thi nabor's
21	S	jackass ♂
22	G	♏ *snow inkreases*
23	M	⊕ now murder
24	T	hogs ♋
25	W	☰ *wind shifty* ☰
26	T	♈ now tear up
27	F	wood ♃
28	S	‹ *big kold* ›
29	G	♋ the grass hopper
30	M	haz fled ⅋ ☊ ♈
31	T	

GIN and MILK.

How fast will the "*comeing man*" probably travel? I kant tell to a dot; but if he kant beat 2.25, he better stay whare he iz.

———〰———

A man with a phew branes iz like a dog with one flea on him—dredful oneazy.

———〰———

Be humble, and yu are sure tew be thankful; be thankful, and yu are sure tew be happy.

———〰———

The more yung ones in a family, the eazier they are tew raize. One chicken alwus makes more klucking for a hen than a dozen duz.

———〰———

Blessed iz he who kan pocket abuse, and feel that it iz no disgrace tew be bit bi a dog.

December 1872 calendar page
from Josh Billings' Farmer's Allminax

249

Nast's Almanac for 1871 is more complex than Billings'. Some seventy-two pages long, it carries Nast's drawings on almost every page as well as, in the front and back, pages of advertising for such items as Thomson's new style Glove Fitting Corset. This item, we may add, appears to be more the shape of a western saddle than of a glove.

Perhaps as amusing as any of Nast's pages are those on which appear his paraphrases of "Mary Had a Little Lamb."

Illustrations accompanying Mary's Funny "Little Lamb" were drawn by Thomas Nast

MARY'S FUNNY "LITTLE LAMB."

LITTLE MARY had a Lamb,
Its fleece was snowy white,
That followed her around all day,
And slept by her at night.
Once Mary's little lamb was small,
But now it is not so,
For Mary's pretty little pet
Has had a chance to grow.

One day it went with her to school;
They tried to put it out,
Which made the little girls all laugh
The boys all raised a shout.
The teacher was a little man;
His face was cross and red;
And had but little hair upon
His bald and shiny head.

The scholars all enjoyed the sport,
And thought it jolly fun
To see the teacher jump about—
He wasn't built to run.
He wiped his forehead, shook his cane,
Then roughing up his hair
He mutter'd, and a scholar said
"She thought she heard him swear."
An inkstand at the lamb he threw,
Then a three legged stool;
And such an angry man before
Was never seen in school.

The fleece which once was snowy white,
With ink was covered o'er—
And Mary's lamb was never seen
In such a plight before.
The teacher ran till out of breath,
And then could run no more;
While desks and benches round him lay
Upset upon the floor.

And when he could not catch the lamb,
He called upon the boys,
Who chased it all around the room,
And made a dreadful noise.
And still it ran around the room,
And did not seem to tire,
Until at last the stove upset,
And set the house on fire
The bells then rang, the firemen came
And made a dreadful noise;
They quenched the fire, and saved the girls,
And nearly all the boys.
When Mary missed her little lamb,
She raised a dreadful wail;
Just then a fireman pulled it out,
And saved it by the tail.

There's no doubt that the farmer's almanac editors viewed the onslaught of the specialty almanacs with some alarm—and with good reason.

Nathan Wild, observing the growing zeal of the various crusaders of his day and their almanacs, announced to his Patrons, Correspondents, etc., of 1833 that—

> It is and ever has been our design, since commencing the first number of our publication, to publish nothing in regard to different opinions to *Religion,* to *Politics,* to *Masonry,* or *Antimasonry*—but Morality we have ventured to touch upon, and in making up our matter for publication, we have endeavored as much as might be to embrace such as would tend to promote this worthy Principle, and to furnish nothing which would offend the most devout in Religion, the most tenacious in Politics, the most zealous in Masonry, or the most delicate in Chastity.

But poor Nathan. If he felt that such a policy on his part would persuade readers of the specialised almanacs back into the general farmer's almanac fold, he was to be disappointed. It was too late for that. A new type of almanac, that had been coming on strong since the first one appeared in 1817, was now in full flood. This phenomenon now deserves a chapter of its own.

chapter ten

SARSAPARILLA will cure ANYTHING

The so-called "health almanacs" made their first appearance in 1817 and, by the latter part of the 19th century, had increased to millions and millions of copies each year. Their medical advertisements, outlandish health recommendations and lavish, phony endorsements were a far cry from those passages in the farmer's almanacs which dealt with medicine and health —as we shall soon see. They imprinted an aura of deceit and vulgarity on the almanac industry in America which unfortunately remained to a certain degree even after the Pure Food Laws of 1906 brought these particular publications to an end.

One comparatively innocuous one is *The Physician's Almanac* of 1817. Along with notes on the medical lectures at the Massachusetts Medical College in Boston, sponsored by Harvard University, readers will find a strangely modern note, with cryptic verses, about the evil effects of smoking.

Something else again is *The Health Almanac,* of 1843, by a Vegetable Eater. Quoting Genesis 1:29 as its theme, this Almanac leaves little to be desired for a vegetable eater's diet and adds, for good measure, essays on Mastication, Relations Between Man and Wife, the Stomach, the Head-Ache, and the Formation of Teeth.

Although there seems to be no evidence—at least none that I can find—of the widespread use or sale of quack patent medicines in this country until at least 1830, one must accept the fact (from Nathanael Low's edition of 1809) that the 19th century must have brought them and their purveyors with it. There is a chuckle or two in Low's opinion of this illicit traffick, quoted verbatim.

ADVERTISEMENT.—Dr. Botherum Smokum, having quitted his former profession of chimney-sweeping, now carries on the business of inventing and preparing his much approved mineral, vegetable, and animal go-to-bed-ical get-up-ical go-to-sea-ical and stay-at-home-ical Medicines. His patent cut-and-thrust phlebotomizing emetic, cathartic, and diuretic double distilled and double barrelled fire and brimstone Cordial.—An amiable, interesting, pleasing, and agreeably innocent un-medicinal sudorific, nephritic, great-toe-ic, narcotic, stimulatic, broken-shin-ic, alterant, astringent, stomachic, belly-ache-ic, diaphoretic, aperient, emollient, carminative, sedative, ruby-faceient, antispasmodic, pectoral, crural, back-bone-ical emmenagogue. It is a sovereign specific and instantaneous remedy for distempers acute, chronic, nervous, general, local, real and imaginary, and epidemic disorders for gunshot wounds, simple and compound fractures, casualties of all kinds, and sudden death. It operates equally on the body, mind, estate real and personal, and place of residence of the patient. It is an efficacious and safe cosmetic, rendering the skin clear and smooth to a fault. It clears the bile and gastric juices from the brain, and induces a calm train of ideas. It removes obstructions in the capillary tubes, thoracic duct, esophagus and caecum; and extirpates the spinal marrow, which is the case of such frequent and fatal complaints. It dissipates adipose tumours and premature births, and is an effectual remedy against old age. It assists nature in her attempts at amputation in diseases of the head and pluck. From its styptic qualities it is eminently useful in promoting excessive hemorrhages, by which surgical operations of all kinds become unnecessary. Applied to the eyes it eradicates the optic nerve; and in disorders of the ears it will be found useful in perforating the tympanum. In extreme watchfulness and lay-awake-ible irritability it induces a permanent and neverending uninterrupted sleep. In sudden attacks from an ememy's cavalry it brings on an instantaneous coma which may save the patient's life. From its drying qualities it is useful in cases of drowning; and hanging yields to its elevating stimulus *** Price $10 per bottle.

To prevent counterfeits, every bottle is wrapped in a twenty-dollar bank bill of Detroit bank. By this means a great saving is made by those who purchase by the dozen.

As we have seen in earlier chapters of this book, the old time farm almanack editor came to be looked upon as a friend, counsellor, and man of general wisdom. For the most part he accepted the responsibility of this trust and in the fields of medicine and health was careful to include only such cures and remedies in which the physicians of his day believed. Some of his recommendations, such as the one which follows from Low, 1814, may seem to us ridiculous or quaint. But at least it cannot be said of these men they were foisting all manner of cures and remedies they knew to be of no avail, for profit, on unsuspecting, frightened readers.

HEAD-ACHE

A medical friend informs, that after exercising his utmost skill to cure, or even alleviate, a distressing case of headache in a distinguished character, in which he was unsuccessful; after the use of Bark, Valerian, Steel, Asafoetidae, Magnesia, Volatile Alkali, Mineral Acids, Mercury, and Arsenic; an old woman proposed the use of Milk, by taking a tumbler three times daily, which effected a cure. A head-ache very generally proceeds from a disordered state of licquor of the stomach (gastric juices). Perhaps the Milk may produce its beneficial effects, by neutralising acid.

The same cannot be said for The "health almanac" editors such as David Jayne, M.D. of Philadelphia. The first edition of his *Dr. D. Jayne's Medical Almanac and Guide to Health for Gratuitous Distribution* is said to have been inflicted on our unsuspecting country in 1843. This almanac and *Bristol's Free Almanac,* 1844, (Batavia, New York) seem to be the first of the patent medicine almanacs which discarded conscience altogether for profit. There are at least two excellent books, *The Toadstool Millionaires* by James Harvey Young, and *One For a Man, Two for a Horse* by Gerald Carson, for those who wish to be filled in on the case histories of an host of these cures and almanacs. As Jayne's was one of the first, and had a long run; and as Ayer's had the largest circulation of any almanac ever published, these two will serve as prime examples.

Dr. Jayne, despite his $300,000 mansion and twenty-five page will for the dispersal of his $3,000,000 estate does not seem to have made the 19th century versions of *Who's Who*. However, in the foreword to his edition of 1887 we note that his "Word to All

Factory and warehouse. Dr. Jayne's Medical Almanac and Medical Remedies, 1857. Dr. Jayne also had homes for his employees—almost a complete self-contained and self-supporting economic unit

Readers" is dated December 1865, and that the business is being carried on by Dr. D. Jayne & Son in the huge Jayne building in Philadelphia next door to the Western Union Telegraph office.

In this foreword Dr. Jayne explains that after attending the University of Pennsylvania, "one of the best medical institutions in the United States," he has had some thirty-seven years of experience in the acquisition of a "knowledge of diseases, and the remedies best calculated to remove them." There then follows a statement in italics. This may explain the wide cracks in the faces of his daughters which he had caused to be sculptured in the mantels of his fireplaces.

I can therefore recommend these preparations with the greatest confidence, being fully persuaded from past experience that they will give very GENERAL, if not UNIVERSAL SATISFAC-

TION ; *but at the same time, I do not pretend to assert that they are "CURE-ALLS," nor that they are in all cases, and under all circumstances, absolutely infallible.*

In about an equal division of space in Jayne's Medical almanac, there appear features on Dr. D. Jayne's Expectorant (for coughs, colds, asthma, bronchitis, consumption, hives, and pleurisy) ; Jayne's Tonic Vermifuge (for worms and dyspepsia) ; Jayne's Specific for Tape-Worm (illustrated) ; Jayne's Carminative Balsam (for dysentery, diarrhea, cholera, headache, heartburn, and insomnia) ; Jayne's Alterative (for boils, cancer, dropsy, epilepsy, erysipelas, gout, neuralgia, and rheumatism) ; Jayne's Sanative Pills (for liver complaint) ; Jayne's Hair Tonic; and Catalog of all Known Diseases, their Remedies (Jayne's, of course), and How to Nurse and Care for the Sick. After these appear eight pages of "Certificates" or signed testimonials with regard to the efficacy of each of Dr. Jayne's remarkable patented products.

One such testimonial, from the Rev. W. Thomas, Missionary at Bareilly, India (Jan. 30, 1882), must have brought down at least two hurricanes and one blizzard from above upon those born of Adam's sin.

Your medicines have proved particularly adapted to the prevailing diseases among the poor of this hot country, and with their help I am accumulating constant evidence how effectively I have been able to relieve the sick. These remedies assist us materially also in our proper missionary work, and you have the assurance, therefore, that they are accomplishing here a double office.

Quite a combination—from a swig of Jayne's Alterative you cured the consumption and got religion, too !

• • •

R. R. R. Pills.

PURGATION

MADE PERFECT IN

RADWAY'S PILLS.

UNIFORMITY AND SAFETY OF ACTION SECURED

The Digestive Organs,

showing the course of substances taken into the stomach along the canal.

1. The Mouth.   2. The Trachea.
3. Æsophagus.   4. Inside Stomach.
5. Gall Bladder.   6. Duodenum.
7. The Anus.

PERFECT DIGESTION

will be accomplished by taking one of Radway's Pills every morning about 10 o'clock, as a Dinner-Pill. By so doing, Dyspepsia, Headache, Foul Stomach, Biliousness, will be avoided, and the food that is eaten contribute its nourishing properties for the support of the natural waste and decay of the body.

Imperfect Digestion frequently occurs when the bowels are regular; the constituents of solids that are not absorbed in the circulation, from imperfect digestion, are frequently directed to the kidneys for their escape. In such cases serious damage is done to the kidneys, as the urine secreted from imperfectly digested substances or food, or those constituents not secreted by the liver or gall-duct, establishes a foreign secretion in the form of Albumen, Sugar, Urea, Uric Acid, causing Bright's Disease, Diabetes, Dropsy, Renal Diseases of the Kidneys, Congestion, Degeneration, Ulceration, Gravel Bloody Urine, etc. To prevent these serious and often fatal difficulties. take one of Radway's Pills every morning, two hours before dinner.

Imperfect digestion may be known by a capricious appetite, craving for food, great thirst, dryness in the mouth, dry skin, hot, fetid breath, restlessness, acidity, heartburn, swellings in the abdomen, chest, legs, cold feet, frequent desire to urinate, varied color of urine, etc. Where these symptoms are present the **Sarsaparillian** should be taken three times per day, and the Pills one to six, as the case may require. As soon as digestion becomes perfect, these unfavorable symptoms will disappear.

20

As Lowell was the headquarters of the Ayer Almanac, and associated patent medicine businesses, no doubt the files of the Lowell, Massachusetts *Sun* are revealing with regard to the career of one Dr. J. C. Ayer, "Practical and Analytical Chemist." As was the case with his contemporary, Dr. Jayne, however, I find no mention of him in the books to which one usually refers for 19th century biographical information. Lowell is better known for the rise and fall of its textile industry, and to me as the busy industrial center where P. T. Barnum began his career by enticing, at so much a head, farm girls from the fields of northern New England for employment in the textile mills.

I would assume, nevertheless, that said Dr. Ayer and the Dr. J. C. Ayer & Company, which carried on his business, did alright. Beginning in 1852, Ayer's *American Almanac* maintained an almost uniform content and format for more than sixty continuous years. Distributed gratis through dealers, for whom Ayer imprinted the dealer's name, according to its foreword of 1889, the almanac "varies from thirteen to fourteen millions of copies—more by millions than any other almanac or calendar in the world."

Illustrations for Ayer's various cures

The bound volume in my file for the year 1889 contains Ayer almanacs in thirty different languages and fly leaves for others in nine more. These will run from 32 to 36 pages each as "worthy advertisements of Dr. Ayer's Standard Family Medicines; Ayer's Cherry Pectoral for cough and colds; Ayer's Sarsaparilla for Purifying the Blood; Ayer's Ague Cure for all Malarial Disturbances; Ayer's Hair Vigor for the Toilet; and Ayer's Cathartic Pills for Constipation and Indigestion. The magic which Dr. Ayer carried in his briefcase was such that as early as 1856 he could boast that Ayer's

Cherry Pectoral has been presented by the American embassies at those courts to the Emperors of

263

Russia, China, and Brazil; to the Kings of Norway, Denmark, Portugal, and Siam; to the Shah of Persia, the Sultan of Turkey, the Imaum of Muscat, and to the Presidents of Chili, New Granada and Peru.

From these presentations flowed back "highly Laudatory acknowledgements" such as this one from the ruling Pasha of Trebizond, at Erzurum.

God is Great Forever: I have received your letter of affectionate love with the present of choice essence in bottles, by which your excellent skill teaches to cure the afflictions of my children. As the life of one of my people is dearer than camels and gold we shall pray for you in our heart when they are raised up from the tent of sorrow by this product of your deep learning and beautiful wisdom ..."

Signed, Neschid El Hassan Pasha.

No. 1. The photograph of Jessie Fraser, of Fine, N. Y. She says:

"My hair is nearly 64 inches long, of fine quality, and very thick, as you will see from my photograph which I send you. I am asked many times a week how I preserve its beauty, and I always reply: 'By using Ayer's Hair Vigor.' As a hair preserver and beautifier I recommend it to all."

No. 2. The photograph of Ella Morrison, of Brooklyn, N. Y., who writes:

"I have used Ayer's Hair Vigor to promote the growth of the hair, and I find it very satisfactory. I cheerfully recommend it to all as the best hair tonic with which I am acquainted. I send you my photograph by this mail."

No. 3. The photograph of Mrs. A. Boydston, Atchison, Kansas: She says:

"About a year ago my hair was coming out very fast. I bought a bottle of Ayer's Hair Vigor to stop this. It not only stopped the falling, but made the hair grow very rapidly, until now my hair is 45 inches in length and very thick. I send you one of my photographs, which shows just what your Hair Vigor has done for me."

No. 4. The photograph of Laura Maas, Ridley Park, Pa. She says:

"I send you my photograph in order that you may see what Ayer's Hair Vigor has done for me. From actual experience I can say it is the very best hair tonic on the market, and it gives me great pleasure to testify to its merits. You may use my photograph in anyway you desire."

No. 5. The photograph of the granddaughter of Mrs. Eugenia Thompson, St. Louis, Mo. Mrs. Thompson writes:

"I send you a photograph of my granddaughter, nine years of age. Ayer's Hair Vigor has done such wonderful things for her that I want you and your friends to know about it. When she was two years old she lost all her hair, and was entirely bald for many months. I tried a great many things, but without effect. I then began using Ayer's Hair Vigor, and in a few weeks I could see that the hair was commencing to grow. I still use the Vigor once or twice a week, in order to keep the scalp healthy and that the growth may continue. Her hair is now 37 inches long, is very thick, soft, and glossy."

In this 1856 edition are testimonials also from Henry D. Pierce, brother of the President of the United States, from the Chief Engineer of the U.S. Mint, the President of Mexico, the American Minister to Turkey, and from doctors, newspaper editors, and the Medallion awards from three great American Institutes of Art.

In the edition of 1863 we learn that Dr. Ayer is (as was Dr. Jayne) a graduate of the University of Pennsylvania's School of Medicine, Member of the Society of Arts and Sciences, Chemical Institute, College of Pharmacy, Medical Association, College of Physicians and Surgeons, etc., etc. We may also read in his almanac what must be the testimonial of all testimonials for all time.

TO DOCTOR AYER IN AMERICA, THE GREAT CURING BARBARIAN OF THE OUTSIDE COUNTRY:

Your present of sweet curing seeds (PILLS) and fragrant curing drops (PECTORAL) of the Cherry smell, has been brought to Hug-seu-Tsene —the mighty Emperor (Kwangto) of the terrible, stout Ming dynasty, by grace of Heaven revived after an interval of ages—Prince of Peace (Ta-Ping-Wang) of China—the central flowery land. He directed his powerful Mandarins to give them to the sick, according to what the Interpreters read from your printed papers. (Directions). Be profoundly happy, O wise Barbarian! for I Yang-seu-Tsing, say it. Your curing seeds and sweet curing drops were given to the sick in his army of the Winged-Sword, and have made them well. Be profoundly happy while you live, for this is known to the Mighty Emperor of China, who approves your skill and permits you to send more of your curing Medicines for his fierce armies of myriads of men.

They may be given to Chiang-Lin, chief Mandarin of the Red Button at Shanghai, who will repay you with Tea, or Silk, or Gold.

The high Mandarins of China have heard of your great knowledge, surpassing all other foreigners, even aspiring to equal the divine wisdom of our own healing teachers, who make remedies that cure instantly. We are pleased to know you bow in trembling terror before our Mighty Emperor.

Written by Yang-Seu-Tsing, Minister-in-chief of the restored Imperial Ming dynasty, destined by the heavenly wisdom to rule in China. (translated at the American Consulate of Hong Kong, China, 3rd May, 1855.)

• • •

As time went on (1875) one begins to note in the Ayer almanacs that the Hair Tonic is receiving more emphasis than the other Ayer remedies. The Ayer Company, however, never lost sight of capitalising on the integrity, content, and excellent contemporary almanacs built up and issued by Robert B. Thomas, Dudley Leavitt, Robinson, Munsell, and others. Its opening message *To the Reader* in almost every issue would be like this one of 1883:

In presenting Ayer's Almanac . . . we have faithfully endeavored, as heretofore, to maintain the reputation it has acquired as an established authority, and an acceptable book of reference for daily family use. To accomplish this we have spared neither labor or expense. The calendar tables. . . .

Immediately after this prologue would then follow, with ten times as much space given to them, the "concise descriptions of our medicinal preparations."

In one of the early editions we also note that the Ayer Company had made a contract with the government of Nicaragua for the supply of sarsaparilla roots which had "formerly been purchased by Russia." As for the rest of the ingredients, we note that as the pressures of the new Food and Drug Act were beginning to be felt, the Ayer Company announced in its almanac of 1907, "We Banish Alcohol." Glycerin has taken its place . . . and by 1912 the full formulas of all the Ayer products are there for all to see.

Before reform, however, and the disillusionment of the Ayer company as well as its millions of *Ayer Almanac* readers, it is difficult not to accept the inside front cover of the almanac edition of 1889 as the Ayer epitaph. It is by this we would like to remember, but cannot, those degrading decades of patent medicines and their almanacs which finally so debased the name "almanack" that only a few "legitimate" ones survive today—that is, almanacs for which there is a retail sale.

A MEDICINE SUITABLE FOR ALL SEASONS AND ALL CLIMES.

The Uninterrupted Success of

HOSTETTER'S STOMACH BITTERS

FOR OVER 35 YEARS, COMMENDS ITS USE TO

SUFFERERS FROM ALL DISEASES

That Sap the Vital Powers and Render Life a Torture and a Burden.

THIS CUT REPRESENTS ONE SECTION OF OUR PRINTING OFFICE.

CHECK DISEASE AT ONCE WITH THIS HOUSEHOLD REMEDY.

Almanacs are fun

In this, the concluding
section, I have described some of
my experiences in collecting old almanacs
and in visiting various libraries where
rare editions now impossible to collect
may be seen. Half the fun of it,
of course, is being on your own.
For this reason, I have purposely
omitted much of the detail,
such as the time I visited the
Huntington Library in California
to see one particular almanac
but became so interested
in another, I completely
forgot to look at the
one I came to see.

chapter eleven

I COLLECT OLD ALMANACS

I have collected almanacs for some thirty years—from the old Books of Hours of the 1200 to 1600 period, through the Austrian Alter Bauernkalendar (oldest in the world) to the first editions of the Old Farmer's Almanac and other American Almanacs. I have purchased from individuals, estates, institutions, book stores. I have been given innumerable editions and, in turn, have given away countless early issues.

In short, almanacs have been my avocation as well as vocation. They have taken me to every state of the union and into the offices of the famous, the infamous and everything in between. As I mentioned in the beginning of this book, wherever I went, or whoever I spoke to, whatever almanac I happened to have in my

The house of
the President
of the
United States
in 1820

hand seemed to elicit a smile and good will—i.e. an immediate entree.* The one exception to this rule occurred in a garden of roses!

This little incident had its beginning in the late 1950's when I consulted with the White House Librarian. I wished to know if the White House library had copies of the 18th century editions of the Old Farmer's Almanac. I learned it did not. Inasmuch as the cornerstone of the White House had been laid in the same year that Robert B. Thomas began the Almanac, I believed these 18th century copies should be there.

Several years later, in 1961, as a member of an art group I was invited to the White House and introduced to President Kennedy in the Rose Garden there. I had brought with me for the occasion a small bound volume

---

* I have learned, incidentally, that it does not pay to fool around with almanac lovers. Many is the writer and broadcaster who has attempted to poke fun at The Old Farmer's Almanac and has found himself scorned by the very friends he had been trying to cultivate with his ill-advised humor.

containing the almanacs of 1793 to 1799. I started to present this volume to him—but alas, no! The secret service men around him, suspecting it was a bomb, immediately snatched it—and took me with it to an isolated corner. After I explained what it was all about, the volume did find its way to the library. Afterwards I had a very nice note from Mrs. Jacqueline Kennedy thanking me for it.

Another experience I'm fond of remembering is my visit to the Rosenbach Foundation in Philadelphia. Its headquarters are not in the business district, but on an attractive, restored street in the historic old part of the city. There, in one of the old houses (purchased by the brothers Rosenbach because it had an elevator) I trundled to keep the appointment given me some weeks in advance. My request had been simple; a three-minute perusal of the first edition of *Poor Richard's Almanac* by Richard Saunders. I had expected to find this most expensive almanac in the world, for which the Rosenbachs had paid $50,000, under glass.

The visit stands out, even though it took place in the fifties, clearly and pleasantly. I was conducted up three flights, led into a small library, and asked to wait a few minutes. Then Dr. Rosenbach appeared. He had the almanac in his hand. He sat opposite me, chatting about this, that, and the other—then asked me if I would mind looking at the almanac alone as he had other things to do. Imagine anyone trustful enough to leave a fifty-thousand-dollar piece of paper, only about $2\frac{5}{8}$ inches wide by $5\frac{1}{2}$ inches high, alone in the hands of a complete stranger. I was so overcome I scarcely dared to turn its pages. Upon his return he pointed out to me the fine points which proved it was a "first impression" and then the conversation turned to his and his brother's experiences in collecting. Among them were one or two with a son of President Hoover. I have forgotten the context but I do remember his saying that Herbert Hoover had almost never hand-written a letter to anyone and rarely even signed his name. The legacy his heirs will receive will be for the most part in a number of his signatures—each one of considerable value.

Some of my most rewarding visits were to the American Antiquarian Society in Worcester, Massachusetts, which owns the largest and finest collection of almanacs in the world. Founded by Isaiah Thomas, almanac publisher and printer of that city, it is a veritable goldmine of New Englandiana and Americana. Clifford K. Shipton, Curator during one of my visits, was only one in a long line of distinguished authors in that position. His facility at bringing Revolutionary (and earlier) personalities to life is unequalled anywhere.

Mr. Shipton showed me the Society's portraits of the Thomas family. These were in better condition than the ones I had bought but seemed to be by the same limner, one Belknap (an artist who used about the same bodies for everyone but painted on a new head). He showed me the early Tulley almanacs and the 17th century

Antiquarian Hall
Worcester, Massachusetts,
of the American
Antiquarian Society.
The central part was
dedicated August 24, 1820

Cambridge "Philomaths." One of the latter, through the death of the heir to it, had just come up for bids. He and either the Houghton or Widener Library at Harvard were bidding against each other for it. My memory may not be correct but it seems to me it went to Harvard.

• • •

After the farm calendars with their weather forecasts, current readers seem to be most interested in the value of old almanacs. Just about everybody seems to have a small collection up in the attic or has just bought one at an auction. It is intriguing to think that these little literary gems may be worth money too. However, as in all collecting, it is only the real rare bird (in excellent condition) which brings a high price. A volume one, number one, of Franklin's *Poor Richard,* 1733, will surely bring fifty thousand or more today to its finder. But try and find one! Below I have compiled a list of the prices various almanacs have brought over the years. As some of these go back to the fifties, some will be higher now. If you are selling, you must expect, from any reputable bookseller, approximately 30% less.

Anything that's a book

from
GOODSPEED'S CATALOGUE
18 Beacon St., Boston, Mass.

Poor Richard, 1743. An Almanack. . . . By Richard Saunders, Philom. 12 leaves (about 6-¼″ x 3-¾″), stitched, uncut. Philadelphia: Printed and sold by B. Franklin . . . [1742]. $500.00 a copy at the U. of Penn. No auction record in the entire run of American Book Prices Current. Nice copy.

Same, for 1759. Original embossed green wrappers. Phila. (Franklin & Hall), [1758]. $300.00 Evans 8254. Published with blank inter-leaves, on which, in this copy, are interesting contemporary manuscript notes. Nice copy.

Same, for 1764. Original embossed multi-colored wrappers. Phila. (Franklin & Hall), [1763]. $300.00
Evans 9509. With contemporary MS. notes on the inter-leaves. Fine copy.

A Pocket Almanack for 1750 . . . By R. Saunders, Phil. 12 leaves (about 4″ x 2-⅛″), full red morocco by Stikeman, original marbled wrappers bound in, uncut (a little expert repair on inner margins). Philadelphia: Printed and sold by B. Franklin, and D. Hall [1749]. $350.00

With the Epitaph

[**Franklin**, Benjamin.] An astronomical diary; or almanack, for . . . 1771. . . . By Nathaniel Ames. 16mo, stitched. Boston: Printed & Sold by the Printers & Booksellers . . .[1770]. $60.00
On p. [4] appears Franklin's famous epitaph. Lyman H. Butterfield (The New Colophon, 1950) was unable to find any earlier printing than that in Ames for 1771 (above), of which there are six editions or variants—two with Boston imprints, two with Hartford, & one each with New London & Newport.
The source of Ames's text was probably a manuscript revision in Franklin's handwriting, owned by his sister, Mrs. Jane Mecom, though in the Almanack the word "Cover" (in the MS.) becomes "Covering." The year in which Franklin wrote his epitaph is not known.

99A [**Franklin Imprint.**] The American almanack for . . . 1731. . . . By John Jerman. . . . 16mo, original wrappers, (imperfect as noted below) Philadelphia . . . Printed & Sold by B. Franklin & H. Meredith, at the New Printing-Office near the Market [1731]. $150.00
Rare but priced at a fraction of what a complete copy would bring (about $500) because it lacks the final leaf & part of one other; also a corner is torn from the title page, destroying part of the rule border & the last three letters of the word "American." The missing leaf & the two defective ones are supplied in photostat.

8 [**Almanac.**] Thomas, Robert B. The Farmer's [later the Old Farmer's] Almanack. For the years 1794 through 1959 (lacking only the 1948, 1949, 1952, 1957, & 1958), stitched or in wrappers as issued. Boston & v.p., [1793–1958]. $85.00
A fine long run, beginning with No. 2, of the American almanac second in fame only to Poor Richard's & today probably more widely known than that of Franklin.

9 [**Almanac.**] Webster's calendar: or. The Albany almanack, for 1810. By Andrew Beers. Albany, [1809]. $3.00
10 —— Same for 1813, 1815, 1816, 1819, 1821, 1822, 1823, 1825, 1827, 1829, 1830, 1833, 1840, 1841, 1842, 1846, 1848. By Beers et al.   Each, $2.00

7 [**Almanac.**] The New-Jersey Almanac for . . . 1785. . . . By Timothy Truman, Philom. 16mo, disbound, (ex-lib. stamps on title). Trenton, [1784]. $20.00

8 —— Same, for 1789. Calculations by Wm. Waring. 16mo, disbound. Trenton, [1788]. $20.00

9 [**Almanac.**] Poor Will's Almanack, for . . . 1784. . . . 16mo, stitched. Phila., [1783]. $20.00

10 [**Almanac.**] Travis, Daniel. MDCCXXI. An almanack . . . for . . . 1721. 16mo, stitched, (marginal fragment lacking from first leaf, deleting 3 or 4 letters of imprint). Boston, 1721. $30.00

[**Chicago Imprint.**] No. 2. Prairie Farmer Almanac 1847. Illus. 12mo, stitched, uncut (slight stain; marginal fragments lacking from first page & from upper edge of the rest, with small loss of text), pp. [32]. Prairie Farmer Office, Chicago. W. W. Barlow & Co. . . . [1846]. $125.00
Rare, ephemeral, pre-fire imprint. McMurtrie locates only 2 copies.
Among the illustrated articles are several of agricultural interest & a two page description of a typical Midwestern "House for a Small Farm," with exterior view & floor plans.

3 [**Almanac.**] Hutchins' (revived) almanac, for . . . 1823. . . . By David Young. Stitched, uncut. N.Y., [1822]. $2.50

4 [**Almanac.**] Hutchins' improved almanac for . . . 1824. . . . By David Young. Stitched, uncut. N.Y., [1823]. $2.50

5 —— Same, for 1825. $2.50

6 —— Same, for 1830. $2.50

7 —— Same, for 1836. $2.50

5 **The Farmer's Useful & Entertaining Companion;** or New Hampshire, Massachusetts & Vermont almanack, for . . . 1795. 16mo, stitched. Exeter, [N.H., 1794]. $5.00

[Revere Engraving.] An astronomical diary; or, almanack for the year of Our Lord Christ 1766. 16mo, stitched. Boston, [1765]. $50.00
Contains on the first page of signature C a small metal cut by Paul Revere of the eclipse of the sun. See Paul Revere's Engravings by Clarence S. Brigham, Worcester, 1954, p. 133.

13 **Stearns,** Samuel. The universal calendar, & North-American almanack, for . . . 1791. Stitched, (marginal wear). Boston, [1790]. $10.00

2 **Beers,** Andrew. Beer's almanac for . . . 1798. 16mo, stitched. Hartford, [1797]. $5.00
Contains considerable verse & anecdote.

3 —— Same, for the years 1801 (mended), 1802, 1804, 1805, 1806, 1807, 1809, 1811, 1812, 1814, 1815 (ink-stains), 1819, 1820, 1821, 1822.   Each, $3.00

4 **Carleton,** Osgood. An astronomical diary: or, an almanack, for . . . 1791. Stitched, uncut, (marginal fragment of last leaf lacking, otherwise fine). Boston, [1790]. $5.00
Contains 6 pages of duties on imported goods & ship tonnage, imposed beginning Jan. 1, 1791.
Mr. Carleton instructed Robert B. Thomas on how to make—and supplied the astronomy for—his first (1793) (old) Farmer's Almanac.

6 **Freebetter,** Edmund. The New-England Almanack . . . for . . . 1778. 16mo, stitched. New London, [1777]. $6.00
Contains two poems, on Washington & on Burgoyne.

7 —— Same, for 1779. New London, [1778]. $6.00

With a Life of Washington

8 —— Same, for 1782. New London, [1781]. $10.00
Pp. [17–21] contain a "Sketch of General Washington' [sic]. . . . Wrote by an Inhabitant of . . . Maryland." This seems to be all or part of what has been called the first "attempt" at a life of Washington, written by John Bell & first published at Annapolis, 1779, with "A Poetical Epistle to . . . Washington" by Charles H. Wharton.

9 —— Same, for 1783. New London, [1782]. $7.50
Contains the "Articles of Confederation & Perpetual Union between the States."

9 **[Almanacs.]** Daboll, Nathan & David A. New England Almanack, & Gentlemen and Ladies' Diary; [and] New England Almanack & Diary, enlarged; [and] New England Al-

manac & Farmer's Friend. 1796, 1797, 1800–1936 (consecutive). 139 vols., stitched & wrappers. New London, Norwich, & Hartford, [1795–1935]. $20.00

10 **[Almanac.]** George, Daniel. An almanack, for . . . 1779. Being the third [year] . . . of American independence. 16mo, stitched, uncut. Boston, [1778]. Fine copy. $5.00

11 **[Almanacs.]** Leavitt, Dudley (&) William B. Scholar's Almanack & Farmer's Daily Register; [also] New England Almanack; [also] Farmer's & Scholar's Almanack; [also] Farmer's Almanack. 1808, '10, '12, '15, '16, '17, 1819–1934. 122 vols., stitched & wrappers. Exeter & Concord, 1808–1934. The lot, $20.00

12 **[Almanac.]** Strong, Nehemiah. An astronomical diary, calendar, or almanack, for . . . 1798. 16mo, stitched. Hartford, [1797]. $5.00
Strong was professor of mathematics & science at Yale.

10 **The Maine Almanack,** for . . . 1804. 16mo, stitched. Portland (William Jenks, Jr.), [1803]. $5.00
11 **Phinney's Calendar,** or Western almanac for 1822. Cooperstown, [1821]. $4.00
12 —— Same for 1823, 1825, 1826, 1831, 1832, 1833, 1835, 1836, 1838, & 1841. Each, $3.50

from
CEDRIC L. ROBINSON, Bookseller
597 Palisado Ave., Windsor, Conn.

Probable First Printing of the Jackson Johonnot Captivity
257. BEERS, ANDREW. Beer's Almanac and Ephemeris . . . for the Year of our Lord 1793. 16mo, stitched; (36)pp. Hartford. Hudson and Goodwin. (1792). **$350.00**
Contained on pages (19) to (26) is "The Remarkable Adventures of Jackson Johonnot, of Massachusetts. Who served as a soldier in the western army, in the Massachusetts line, in the expedition under General Harmar, and the unfortunate General St. Clair. Containing an account of his captivity, sufferings and escape from the Kickapoo Indians. Written by himself, and published at the earnest importunity of his friends, for the benefit of American youth."

"Jackson Johonnot, a native of Falmouth, Maine, left home at the age of seventeen, went to Boston, enlisted and was sent to join the Western Army at Fort Washington, Cincinnati, Ohio. On August 4, 1791, with several others, he was captured by a band of Kickapoos on the banks of the Wabash and carried to their village on the Upper Miami, five of his companions having been killed and scalped in the fight . . . On the night of August 30, they killed the small squad of Indians with them and started to escape to Fort Jefferson . . . where they arrived on September 18. He ends his narrative with his first-hand account of St. Clair's defeat . . . This is one of the best true stories of adventure and captivity of this period, if it 'is' a true story and not a later fabrication made from contemporary evidence."—Vail, p. 364.

The first separate printing of the narrative, Providence, 1793, which has been located, refers to a Lexington, Kentucky, edition of 1791. No copy of the Lexington edition has been found; nor has any advertising been found for such a printing in Lexington newspapers of the period; further it has been questioned whether there was sufficient time to get an edition through the press in 1791 because the narrative itself Terminates in November. Consequently, most authorities agree that the first appearance of the narrative was in the Beer's Almanac.

The copy offered here is enclosed in a cloth slipcase.

The Abraham Panther Indian Captivity

258. BICKERSTAFF'S Almanack, for the Year of our Lord, 1788 : . . . to which is Added a surprising account of the Discovery of a Lady who was taken by the Indians in the year 1777, and after making her escape, she retired to a lonely Cave, where she lived nine years. 16mo, stitched, trimmed close—cropping the typographical border at the bottom of the titlepage and some of the ruled border on text pages without affecting text, early name on title; (24)pp. Norwich, Conn. J. Trumbull. (1787).

$300.00

This is the earliest available edition and may be the first printing of this captivity. Evans lists two separate printings for the same year, No. 20615 and No. 20616, but gives no location and no copy can be located today. It is known that one of Evans' entries was taken from a newspaper advertisement and the other is assumed to be a bookseller's catalogue entry; both are probably ghosts.

"One of the rarest of all captivities is that generally known as the Panther narrative. It was written under the pseudonym of Abraham Panther but no one seems to have hazarded a guess as to the real name of the author. A reading of the narrative leads one to suspect that it is a simple and somewhat crude, though interesting, bit of early American fiction, but its long continued popularity seems to prove that its original readers believed it to be true . . . The text states that the beautiful young lady of the narrative was made captive in the year 1777 and that she was restored to her father after 'seeing no human being for the space of nine years.' "—

When Almanacks are offered for sale, they will be listed in various ways. There will be those indicating the actual title of the almanac, or again by the name of the editor. It is always important to know, whatever the title, who is its editor.

The costs and selling prices of various almanacs vary in almost direct proportion to the apparent desire on the part of private collectors, libraries, and institutions for any given copy. A complete set of *The Old Farmer's Almanack* some years ago brought $300. It is doubtful one could find one for that price today. The "Rosenbach" *Poor Richard* brought $50,000. The Ames' editions (early) command anywhere from $5.00 to $30.00. Stray single copies of other almanacs often change hands at anywhere from $1.00 to $10.00 each. Copies dated after 1850 are not worth much more than the cover price. Any American almanac before 1700 has a value of at least one hundred dollars. Some will bring a lot more. Special almanacs such as the *Ellicott* which carried, apparently, George Washington's handwriting in the margins of the front cover, sell from $300 up. Condition is always important.

Some editions of *The Old Farmer's Almanack* by Robert B. Thomas are harder to come by than others. The issue for 1806 was withdrawn from sale because of the inclusion of a long poem called "Jonathan's Courtship." In the edition for 1939 Robert Frost's original poem "October" first appeared. The 1942 edition (150th) was limited by wartime paper restrictions. Prices on old almanacs vary from the price on the cover to as high as four hundred dollars each. There is no real authority on such prices; one can obtain what one is offered, or what one can get. I had to give, for example, $75 to obtain The Farmer's Almanac of 1804.

One final word of caution to almanac buffs (if there are

any, besides myself) may be useful. At some (but not all) of the libraries I have found time to visit over the years, the card catalogs listed the almanacs I wished to see. However, the clerk would often report that several of them were available only from the Rare Book section of the library. I would then find these listed in the Rare Book card file. However, word came back more than once that these particular almanacs were not available there either. In one or two instances I went to the Chief of the Rare Book section with the polite question as to where I might see these almanacs. Both times I received no satisfaction. I would presume, therefore, that because almanacs are small and covenient some libraries no longer have certain almanacs they may have thought they had!

The ten most interesting almanacs in my own collection are as follows:

1. *Book of Hours, Circa 1450.* This is all hand painted on parchment. Paragraph initials, and some ten full page illustrations (Biblical scenes) are in full color—still as brilliant as they were 500 years ago.
2. *1744.* A bound volume of ten different almanacs of that year. One is by Richard Saunders, the pen name used by Benjamin Franklin. One is the Poor Robin Almanac whose title Franklin's brother used for the first almanac printed in Rhode Island.
3. An Almanac by John Tulley, 1693. First U.S. weather forecasts. (The American Antiquarian Society has a complete run of these).
4. An Astronomical Diary or Almanack by Nathanael Ames (and his successors) 1725–1795. This was the first almanac with a really long run.
5. Nathanael Low, 1819, 1820. First signed wood cuts.

6. North American Almanac, 1776 by Samuel Stearns. First hand account Battle of Lexington.
7. Hutchins Almanacs, 1772–1815. The New York side of the Almanac picture.
8. The New England Almanac and Farmer's Friend by Nathan Daboll. 1773 to present. Most popular almanac with the whaling captains in the early days.
9. The Austrian Almanac. 1400, oldest almanac in the world—the one in which Hitler and Goebbels substituted themselves for God and St. Paul during the war years.
10. The Old Farmer's Almanac by Robert B. Thomas, 1793–present.

BOOK OF HOURS
Circa 1450
This is all hand painted
on parchment.
Paragraphs, initials, and some
ten full page illustrations
are in full color—still
as brilliant as they
were 500 years ago

1745.

Apollo Anglicanus:

THE
ENGLISH APOLLO:

Affifting
All Perfons in the Right Underftand-
ing of this YEAR's Revolutions, as alfo of
Things paft, prefent, and to come.

A Twofold *Kalendar*, viz. *Julian* or *Englifh*,
and *Gregorian* or *Foreign* Computations, more
plain and full than any other ; with the Rifing
and Setting of the Sun, the Nightly Rifing and
Setting of the Moon, and alfo her Southing,
exactly calculated for every Day.

Of General USE for moft MEN.
Being the Firft after *Biffextile*, or LEAP-YEAR.

To which is added, the Moon's Application to the
Planets: With the Calculations of the Eclipfes : Alfo
Rules and Tables for the Meafuring of Timber : With
many other Things both pleafant, ufeful, and neceffary.

Calculated according to ART, and fitted to the
Meridian of *Leicefter*, whofe Latitude is 52 Degrees, 41
Minutes, exactly fitting all the middle Counties of *England*,
and, without fenfible Error, the whole Kingdom.

By *RICHARD SAUNDERS*,
Student in the Phyfical *and* Mathematical *Sciences.*

LONDON: Printed by A. WILDE,
for the Company of STATIONERS, 1745.

A bound
volume of ten different
almanacs of that year. One
is by Richard Saunders, the
pen name used by Benjamin Franklin.
One is the Poor Robin Almanac whose
title Franklin's brother used
for the first Almanac
printed in Rhode
Island

An Almanac by John Tulley, 1693.
First United States Weather Forecasts.
(The American Antiquarian Society
has a complete run of these)

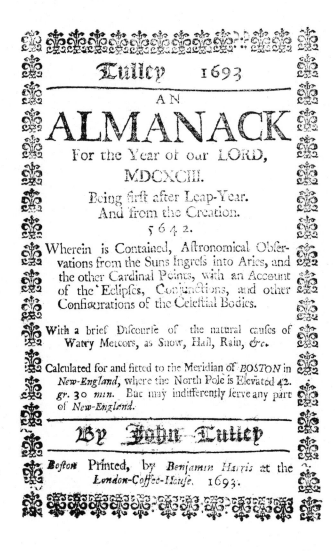

Tulley   1693

AN

ALMANACK

For the Year of our LORD,

MDCXCIII.

Being first after Leap-Year.
And from the Creation.
5642.

Wherein is Contained, Astronomical Observations from the Suns Ingress into Aries, and
the other Cardinal Points, with an Account
of the Eclipses, Conjunctions, and other
Configurations of the Celestial Bodies.

With a brief Discourse of the natural causes of
Watry Meteors, as Snow, Hail, Rain, &c.

Calculated for and fitted to the Meridian of BOSTON in
New-England, where the North Pole is Elevated 42.
gr. 30 min. But may indifferently serve any part
of New-England.

By John Tulley

Boston Printed, by Benjamin Harris at the
London-Coffee-House. 1693.

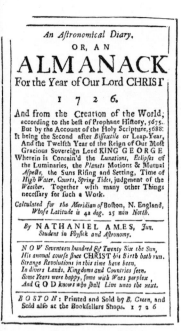

An Astronomical Diary or Almanac by
Nathanael Ames (and his successors) 1725-
1795. This was the first almanac
with a really long run.

These almanac covers and pages are
actually about twice the size shown here.

Nathanael Low, 1819, 1820.
First signed woodcuts.

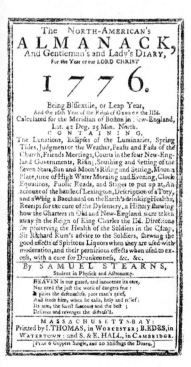

North American Almanac 1776
by Samuel Stearns. Firsthand
account of the Battle
of Lexington.

Hutchins Almanacs 1772-1815.
The New York side of the Almanac picture.

The Connecticut, then the New England
Almanac and Farmer's Friend by Nathan Daboll.
Most popular almanac with the whaling
captains in the early days.

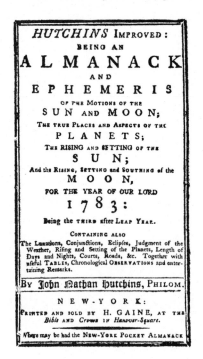

HUTCHINS IMPROVED:
BEING AN
A L M A N A C K
AND
E P H E M E R I S
OF THE MOTIONS OF THE
SUN AND MOON;
THE TRUE PLACES AND ASPECTS OF THE
P L A N E T S;
THE RISING AND SETTING OF THE
S U N;
And the RISING, SETTING and SOUTHING of the
M O O N,
FOR THE YEAR OF OUR LORD
1 7 8 3:
Being the THIRD after LEAP YEAR.

CONTAINING ALSO
The Lunations, Conjunctions, Eclipses, Judgment of the
Weather, Rising and Setting of the Planets, Length of
Days and Nights, Courts, Roads, &c. Together with
useful TABLES, Chronological OBSERVATIONS and enter-
taining Remarks.

By John Nathan Hutchins, PHILOM.

N E W - Y O R K:
PRINTED AND SOLD BY H. GAINE, AT THE
Bible AND *Crown* IN *Hanover-Square*.

Where may be had the NEW-YORK POCKET ALMANACK

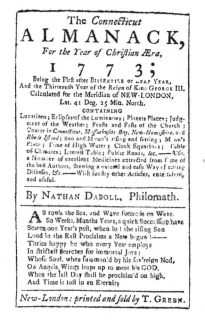

The *Connecticut*
A L M A N A C K,
For the Year of Christian Æra,
1 7 7 3;
Being the First after BISSEXTILE or LEAP YEAR,
And the Thirteenth Year of the Reign of King GEORGE III.
Calculated for the Meridian of NEW-LONDON,
Lat. 41 Deg. 25 Min. North.
CONTAINING
Lunations; Eclipses of the Luminaries; Planets Places; Judg-
ment of the Weather; Feasts and Fasts of the Church;
Courts in *Connecticut, Massachusets-Bay, New-Hampshire,* and
Rhode Island; Sun and Moon's rising and setting; Moon's
Place; Time of High Water; Clock Equations; Table
of Climates; Interest Table; Public Roads, &c.——Also,
a Number of excellent Medicines extracted from some of
the best Authors, shewing a natural and easy Way of curing
Diseases, &c.——With sundry other Articles, entertaining
and useful.

By NATHAN DABOLL, Philomath.

AS rouls the Sea, and Wave succeeds on Wave,
So Weeks, Months Years, a quick Succession have
Scarce one Year's past, when lo! the rising Sun
Loud in the East Proclaims a New begun!——
Thrice happy he who every Year employs
In strictest Searches for immortal Joys;
Whose Soul, when summon'd by his sov'reign Nod,
On Angels Wings leaps up to meet his GOD.
When the last Day shall be proclaim'd on high,
And Time is lost in an Eternity

New-London: printed and sold by T. GREEN.

The Austrian Neuer Bauernkalendar, 1300, oldest
almanac in the world—the one in which
Hitler and Goebbels substituted themselves
for God and St. Paul during the war years.

Neuer Bauernkalender
für das Schaltjahr
1944
Mit Privilegium, bei Strafe 10 Mark lötigen
Goldes keinen in Steiermark einzuführen.

Verlegt bei Leykam in Graz, Stempfergasse 3.

Preis **25** Pfennig.

The new year opens—old is past,
Stern winter comes with its rough blast :
See the farmer shivering with cold,
Driving his flocks and herds to fold.

Days of the Month.

Tuesday	1	8	15	22	29
Wednesday	2	9	16	23	30
Thursday	3	10	17	24	31
Friday	4	11	18	25	
Saturday	5	12	19	26	
SUNDAY	6	13	20	27	
Monday	7	14	21	28	

D M	Calendar, Courts, Aspects, Weather, &c.	FARMER'S CALENDAR.
1	Circumcision. CP. Boston.	Look to your barns and see that
2	Cold [Newglouc. Lenox	your cattle are well served.
3	Lions H. rises 8,6 *and frosty*	See that your fattening cattle
4	Sir I. Newt. b. 1643. *weather*	have not too much given them
5	Low tides. *Cold winds.*	at once.
6	2d past Christmas. Epiph.	Cut timber, if you wish to have
7	*Looks like*	it last long, it being the best
8	Lucin. CP. Hallowell.	time in the year.
9	*snow.*	Improve sledding, while it is
10	*Blustering weather.*	good, and get your supply of
11	High tides.	wood for the summer, for it is a
12	*Moderate* ☿ Stat. ☽ Perigee.	chance if you have a better time
13	1st past Epiph. *weather.*	this winter.
14	Peace ratif. by Con. 1784.	Visit your corn barns and gra-
15	CP. Springf. ✳ ☉ ♃ ☐ ♄	neries ; see that rats and mice
16	*Cold but pleasant.*	don't destroy your grain.
17	Dr. Frankl. b. in Bost. 1706.	Look well to your cattle, and
18	Low tides. ✳ ♄ ☋	see that they are kept clean.
19	*Cold and clear.*	Remember your bees, and if
20	2d past Epi. K. Spain b. 1716	weak, feed them with cakes made
21	*Windy*	of malt flour, mixed up with
22	*weather*	sweet wort ; or give them brown
23	*Clear*	sugar ; and once and a while salt
24	Middling tides. *and cold.*	and water, to keep them from
25	Conversion of St. Paul.	scouring.
26	*Now* ☽ Apogee.	Kill your winter pork and beef,
27	Septuag. *expect*	if you wish to have it swell a
28	Peter the Great died, 1725.	cooking.
29	*snow or rain.*	Feed your doves, and spread
30	K. Charl. I. beheaded, 1648.	ashes among their dung.
31	*Blustering weather.*	Burn or sweep your chimnies.

*The Old Farmer's Almanac
By Robert B. Thomas, 1793-present,
1793 calendar page of.*

Students, collectors, or the just plain curious may find the following list of 54 runs of almanacs useful. However, before you plan to take any trips of considerable distance to see these almanacs, I suggest you first check in *Drake's Almanacs of the United States* to determine if he has found these almanacs at the location given, and also at a location closer to you, then check with the location itself by letter to see if the almanacs are still there. Drake's book will give you other ideas, too, of Almanacs you might wish to see. Don't hesitate to write me, also, if you feel I can be of help.

1. Samuel Danforth Almanacs, printed on the Stephen Daye Press in Cambridge, Massachusetts, 1646, 1647, 1648. Massachusetts Historical Society, American Antiquarian Society, Huntington Library, Los Angeles, California.

2. Philomath Almanacs, American Antiquarian Society, Worcester, Mass.

3. Various Almanacs, 1650–1700, Boston Public Library.

4. Kalendarium Pennsilvaniense by Samuel Atkins, 1685. Historical Society of Pennsylvania, Philadelphia, Pa.

5. Virginia and Maryland Almanack, 1685–1714, Library of Congress, Washington, D.C.

6. The American Almanac by Titan Leeds, 1715. American Antiquarian Society, Worcester, Mass.

7. The Ames Almanacs, 1725–1795, American Antiquarian Society.

8. Poor Richard by Richard Saunders, 1733–56. Library of Congress or Franklin Institute, Philadelphia, or Historical Society of Pennsylvania, or Rosenbach.

9. Astronomical Diary or Almanac by Nathanael Low, 1768–1820. American Antiquarian Society.

10. Samuel Stearns, 1770–93. Harvard College Library or Antiquarian Society.

11. The Hutchins Almanacs. New York Public Library.

12. The New England Almanac and Farmer's Friend by Nathan Daboll, Historical Society, New London, Conn.

13. The New England Farmer's Almanac by Truman Abell, New Hampshire Historical Society, Concord, N.H.

14. Webster's Calendar or The Albany Almanac, 1784–1818, Albany, New York Public Library.

15. Beer's Calendar, 1813–17, by Andrew Beers, Albany, New York Public Library.

16. New England Almanacs by Isaiah Thomas and his son, 1775–1810. American Antiquarian Society.

17. Weatherwise Town and Country Almanac 1781 by Abraham Weatherwise. American Antiquarian Society.

18. Gentlemens' & Ladies' Diary or Almanac 1796–1812, by Asa Houghton. American Antiquarian Society or (perhaps) Keene, N.H. Public Library.

19. The Kentucky Almanac 1801–34. Louisville Free Public Library.

20. Maine Farmer's Almanac by Daniel Robinson, 1818 to present. Public Library at Portland or Augusta, Maine.

21. The Farmer's, Mechanic's and Gentlemen's Almanac, 1815–39, by Nathan Wild. American Antiquarian Society or possibly Hartford, Conn. Public Library.

22. The Rhode Island Almanac, 1821–1830, by Isaac Bickerstaff. Providence, Rhode Island Public Library.

23. Leavitt's Farmer's Almanac by Dudley Leavitt. New Hampshire Historical Society, Concord, New Hampshire.

24. Farmer's Almanack by David Young, 1819. Morristown, New Jersey Public Library.

25. The Christian Almanac, 1827, and similar titles. American Antiquarian Society.

26. The New England Farmer's Almanack by Thomas G. Fessenden, 1827–1836. American Antiquarian Society.

27. The Anti-Masonic Almanack, 1827–36, by Edward Giddins, Albany, New York Public Library.

28. Porter's Health Almanac, 1832, by Henry Porter. Morristown, New Jersey Public Library.

29. American Almanac (1832–61) by Jared Sparks. Chicago Public Library.

30. Temperance Almanac, 1834–1844. American Antiquarian Society or Albany, New York Public Library.

31. Applegate's Whig Almanac, 1835. New York Public Library or Library of Congress, Washington, D.C.

32. American Anti-Slavery Almanac 1836–1844. Boston Public Library or Massachusetts Historical Society.

33. Phinney's Calendar or Western Almanac by George R. Perkins, New York Public Library.

34. Davy Crockett's Almanac, 1835–6, New York Historical Society, New York.

35. Harrison Almanac, 1841–3, by David Young. New York Public Library.

36. The Phrenological Almanac, 1842–50, by L. N. Fowler, New York Public Library.

37. Prophetic Almanac, 1845, by Orson Pratt. Mormon Library, Salt Lake City, Utah.

38. Congregational Almanac, 1846– by C. C. Deane, Boston Public Library.

39. Beckwith's Almanac, 1847–1932, by George Beckwith. New Haven, Conn. Public Library.

40. California Almanac, 1849, by Benjamin Greenleaf. Chicago Public Library, or Library of Congress.

41. Jayne's Medical Almanac by David Jayne. Philadelphia Public Library.

42. Ayer's American Almanac. Lowell, Mass. Public Library or Boston Public Library.

43. Blum's Farmer's & Planter's Almanac, 1860–present, by L. V. Blum, Salem, North Carolina, or Library of Congress.

44. National Calendar or Herrick's Almanac by Dr. Herrick & Bro., Albany, New York Public Library.

45. Western Farmer's Almanac, 1841–61, Louisville, Kentucky Public Library.

46. Clarke's Confederate Household Almanac, 1862–5, Vicksburg, Mississippi and Mobile, Alabama. Library of Congress.

47. Grier's Almanac, 1864–present, by P. T. Ashmore, Americus, Georgia. Library of Congress.

48. Veterans of Civil War Almanac, 1869. Library of Congress.

49. Farmer's Allmenax, 1872–4, by Josh Billings. Morristown, New Jersey Public Library.

50. Hawaiian Almanac, 1875–1901, by Thomas G. Thrum. Library of Congress.

51. Vennor's Weather Almanac, 1877–8, by Henry G. Vennor. Montreal Public Library, or Baltimore, Maryland Public Library.

52. World Almanac, 1886–present. New York Public Library.

53. Baer's Agricultural Almanac, 1821–present, Lancaster, Pennsylvania.

54. Hagers-Town Town and Country Almanac, 1797–present, by John Gruber. Hagerstown, Maryland.

chapter twelve

IT WASN'T ALL That EASY

COPPERPLATE PRINTER

I knew very little about almanacs in 1938. From 1936 on, I had been editing, printing, selling, and publishing YANKEE Magazine. The magazine was not doing too well. In fact, it had been doing so badly in the years since I had founded it in 1935 that I had acquired a reputation for being what is known on Broadway, New York City, as "a foolish angel."

It had, therefore, been only natural for Little, Brown & Company—then publishers of THE OLD FARMER'S ALMANAC in Boston and looking around for an "out"—to call me. After more than one double martini followed by luncheon at the Union Club with Roger Scaife of Little, Brown, I found myself on Boston's Park Street on a blustery, snowy March afternoon the new owner of the publishing rights to the Almanac. I had not agreed to pay anything for them but I did not learn until some days later how much money Little, Brown had been losing each year. This was more money than I had, or at that time could have borrowed. It was not for some weeks either that I learned the reason for the Almanack's poor showing. For one thing, in the 1936 edition, Little, Brown had omitted the usual weather forecast and substituted a United States Weather Bureau average. Readers said this was a worse blunder than T. R.'s omission of "In God we Trust" from the Buffalo nickel. For another, the publication had somehow strayed away from its old time style and was using modern "name" authors in it. To bring it back to its old time popularity and potential profits at once became an almost full-time project.

For one thing, I was now cast in an entirely new role; that of Abe Weatherwise, weather forecaster. For another, there was cast upon me not only the mantle of advertising salesman but also of newsstand sale promoter. As there were only a few months left before my first edition had to go to press, I drew heavily upon the style, colloquialisms, format, etc. of the founder, Robert B. Thomas. I studied each issue he had edited (1793–1856) and took from each what I could transpose to the present.

The change back to the old style was an immediate success. And a good thing it was for after one more issue the guns over Pearl Harbor had sounded.

In my wartime job as consultant to the Office of Censorship, I had to give up my other publishing activities. But I was allowed to hold onto the almanac, and had time to give to it evenings and Sundays. There were few publications in 1942 which Uncle Sam was concerned enough about to care whether they lived or died. But the Almanac was not one of them. Personally, I felt that Hitler would just as soon see America's oldest publication go out of business. But I also realized that if Uncle Sam, in winning the war, tossed overboard most of this country's revered traditions, what was there for his soldiers and sailors to come back to?

In any event, I had a hard time saving it when a copy of the Almanac was found on one of the Nazi saboteurs picked up on the shore of Long Island in 1943. The Army promptly banned further publication saying that its weather forecasts were of aid to the enemy! Fortunately I'd made many friends in the F.B.I., whose agents often would have to be on board new navy ships for final sea trials. Many of these men were from the mid-west and not inclined to rough weather on a destroyer! So they would half-jokingly and half-seriously consult with me about the weather predictions for their sea trial dates. Fortunately I had produced for these men a number of very accurate predictions. At any rate, through these friends I received a hearing on the Army ban of the Almanac and it came off very well. That is, I was told it could remain on sale if the cover subtitle "Weather Forecasts" were changed to read "Weather Indications."

• • •

Another crisis of those early years involved astronomy. Dudley Leavitt, editor of the New Hampshire Farmer's Almanac had been an astronomer. Like many of the early editors, he was able to calculate the times of sunrise, sunset, moonrise, moonset, the planets, the eclipses, well over a year in advance. Robert B. Thomas could not and neither could I. On my part, I was continuing with the man Little, Brown had engaged for this job, Professor Duncan of Wellesley College.

In 1940, still wet behind the ears, I went to Professor Duncan and asked him if his astronomical matter could be readied slightly earlier than he had been delivering it and made, in some way, more interesting. The good professor was not only annoyed but insulted. He promptly told me to go find another astronomer. So I fell into the same predicament faced by just about every old time editor who was unable to make his own calculations.

I especially remembered the problem Isaiah Thomas had had with his astronomer during the war of 1812. At that time this man was residing in Hanover, New Hampshire. But when the day came for him to submit his figures to Isaiah, the latter learned he had taken off to observe the Battle of Lake Erie from a vantage point along the shore of that lake. Thus all that Isaiah received—even weeks after the due date—was this astronomer's desultory account of the battle. Isaiah was furious. He finally nailed him down, however, and almost at pistol point obtained the much needed figures.

However, what Professor Duncan was then unwilling to supply, the Harvard Observatory was—the name of an astronomer who would take on these calculations. His name was Loring B. Andrews. Only once did I have difficulty with him and that was not his fault. This trouble came in 1941 when this country went on war time (double D.S.T.). Loring had already handed in his computations and these had been set in type. But he was no longer available to move up the times an extra hour. He was in North Africa with the troops doing a "softening up" of the enemy with short wave radio. For once I had to take

on a task of this sort myself. It was not as easy as it
sounds . . . especially when, because of my censorship
job, I had to make all the changes during one Sunday!

• • •

After the war was over, I began to concentrate on extending the almanac distribution. The old-time cart
pedlars were no more. They had been replaced with
door-to-door crews of salesmen or motorized specialty
trucks. The bookstores and stationery stores had been
supplemented by newsstands. When I was looking for
Almanac distribution the huge American News Company in New York was at its height. It operated
through a number of branch warehouses and sales offices which distributed magazines and newspapers to
local area shops and stores. Its Boston branch was run
by genial John Tracey. The Old Farmer's Almanac
owes much to John, and his friends, the late John Crow-
ley and John Keogh. The former paved the way for
Almanac displays in all of New England's hotels and
subways; the latter made the South Station look as if
the Almanac lived there.

John Tracey was the one who, for example, helped me
to hire two real pedlars. Both of them were totally
blind—one in Portland, Maine, one in Boston. They
both sold whiskbrooms as well as almanacs. The Boston blind man used to stand by the subway entrance at
Park and Tremont Streets. For as long as he lived, he
sold nearly 15,000 almanacs each year. By visiting
other branch managers and bookstores (there was one
in Worcester called Easton's that used to sell 20,000
copies) and newsstands, I, with John Tracey and the
Maine Branch Manager, Sam Macisso, solved the problem of New England distribution for the Almanac.
National distribution was something else again. This
had to be handled out of New York. "Mike" Morris-
sey, American News Company President and son of a

blacksmith, was the one I had to see and get to know. This I did and, despite a gruff exterior (the trade knew him as the "man with the iron fist"), we became lasting friends.

Joseph Sheeran worked for Mike in those days. Here was an intensely religious Catholic who also drank too much at times for his own good. I sensed, that he took a dim view of sober, Protestant me. I could not get him, despite all of my efforts, to distribute the Almanac anywhere except in New England. Then one day he invited me to visit with him every Catholic Church on the island of Manhattan. Not realizing this meant a stop in a bar before we entered each one, I was quick to accept. After I returned to New Hampshire (it took me a day or two to recuperate) I learned that the American News Company had placed requisitions for Almanacs for each of its branches in all of the United States.

With the friends I had made in the distribution and advertising industry—and I must say they all looked after the Almanac far beyond any call of duty—I had more time to spend with some of the other of the Almanac's squeaking wheels, One of these was printing. In the years before I had taken on the Almanac, I had been printing and publishing YANKEE Magazine in our own shop in Marlboro, New Hampshire. My partner was a man named Bennett. He spent quite a lot of his time doubling for Abraham Lincoln at County Fairs. He was a good compositor and had a working knowledge, which I did not, of typesetting, printing, and paper. During these years, YANKEE had gotten off the ground through two not-so-grievous errors. The first was when, irritated at Bennett for leaving his false teeth around the office, I put the following ad in the magazine; "Will swop one pair of false teeth for an office broom." Bennett was furious when the publication appeared and about forty people showed up with brooms. However, YANKEE had discovered the beginnings of its now famous ORIGINAL YANKEE SWOPPERS' COLUMN.

The second mistake was Bennett's. Two Vermont spinsters had sent in an advertisement for their Stowe, Vermont resort. It read "A perfect place for honeymooners to come and play." Bennett in printing that issue had unwittingly broken and dropped the "p" from play . . . and YANKEE has had no advertising problem from that day to this.

The Old Red Mill
in Marlboro, N. H.
in which YANKEE'S
first print shop
was housed.

It was soon to become obvious, however, that the Almanac printing problem could not be handled at this Marlboro plant. For one thing a trucker had arrived there one evening and called me at home to ask where to put his load of paper. I told him where the key to our shop was and to unload it on the floor. How was I to know that this was a huge trailer truck loaded with paper! I didn't know partner Bennett had ordered all that much. As the last of the paper came off the truck, the entire plant crumbled—press, paper, machinery, desks, and the office brooms—down the embankment into the river.

By this time I had begun to worry about the Almanac's production problems. Its print order was about 250,000 copies per year. It was being printed at the Curtiss Way Company in Meriden, Conn. We were buying paper from the St. Regis Paper Company and having our type set by the Machine Composition Company in Boston. This was all a very happy family except for the fact that the Curtiss Way Company wanted its money in advance; St. Regis thirty days after shipment; and Machine Composition Company sixty days after its work was finished.

How different from the early 19th century days when the paper was being made locally from rags brought in by almanac readers. The composition, too, was all done by hand, which was not only difficult but time consuming. An editor would have to ready the copy for his November Almanac early in March. How he or his readers read, or the typesetters managed to set, the four-point type some of the almanacs used is perhaps a forgotten art.

There was no 4 pt. type in the fonts used by Robert B. Thomas; it was all 6 pt. or larger when I purchased The Old Farmer's Almanac from Little, Brown &

Example of 4 pt. type used in
1804 edition The Old Farmer's Almanac.

Company. This is the same type we use today. I would guess it is at least one hundred years of age—perhaps more.

My problems with printing and paper were not as difficult after the war as they had been with Mr. Bennett before the war. I had been corresponding during the war with Angelo J. Simonetta.

• • •

"Sim," a printer by trade, was anxious, now that his Navy duty was over, to live in New Hampshire. He liked it here—and he wanted to be near me—whose publications he felt had great possibilities. As he was almost the only living soul who felt that way, I liked "Sim." I liked him not only for that but as a person,

The late Angelo Simonetta and the author confer at the former's print shop about type faces, the elections and the Red Sox.

and for the fine craftsman that he was. (When Franklin D. Roosevelt and Winston Churchill signed the Atlantic Charter on board the U.S.S. Augusta on August 12, 1941, it was Sim who printed the menu for that day!) Sim took care of all my promotion problems such as brochures and folders, and also helped me on layout and typography.

Whatever Sim did not know, another extremely valuable friend did. This was Arpe Saunders of the Greylock Engraving Company (his own firm) in North Adams, Massachusetts. Just to look at Arpe and Sim together (they were close friends) made one feel good. With their help, there was no problem too hard to solve. As we three were all in comparatively small businesses, we had much in common and, what is more, the time and desire to talk things over. It was Arpe who could tell me how to prepare the little line cuts I used in the almanac. Many, for example, had to be blown up and repaired.

• • •

Arpiar Saunders,
engraver, of North Adams,
Massachusetts

During this period, as I went about learning, learning, learning about these old almanac makers, I began to realize that in the days of Colonial America everything was country rather than city. Providence, Springfield, Hartford, Newport (Rhode Island), Boston, Portland (Maine), Concord (New Hampshire), Ipswich, Newburyport, Exeter; all these—even New York, Washington and Philadelphia—were where the almanacs at their peaks of popularity had been edited. None of these places was really any more than what today we would call a town. The material which these editors were using, I realized, had to come either from books or from local farmers. In editing The Old Farmer's Almanac I realized then that, besides my trips to museums and purchases from bookstores, I needed much more help and advice from actual dirt farmers.

Upon the closing of the Dublin Grange In February 1967, I pencilled some notes of the memories that the occasion aroused. Although I had joined the Grange in 1933, it was not until the 40's that I was calling upon its members for help, not only on my farm but also with the almanac. These notes seem to underscore how, in those early years of my editing this Almanac in Dublin, I enjoyed pretty much the same sort of environment as the early almanac makers. They also point out how it is this is not true today.

At this final meeting of the Grange (on its 100th Anniversary!) there were present the Secretary, the Treasurer, the Assistant Steward, myself, and one lady who left, almost as soon as she arrived, in a huff because the Secretary was late. Snow whirled around outside. The Secretary reported a cash balance of $43.01. The business of the meeting consisted in the transfer of this $43.01, penny by penny, to the Clerk. There was then a vote that this balance and a Hundred dollar Liberty Bond be donated to the New Hampshire Charitable Fund and administered by the Dublin Foundation. Various seals, a Bible, badges, straw hats, and records were placed at the disposal of the Peterborough Grange. "Demits" would be issued to the handful of Dublin Grangers who might wish to join the Peterborough Grange. I took one for myself and Mrs. Sagendorph. Nobody else did.

This was a sad occasion. With the exception of the Master (the late Mrs. Ethel Adams) who on that evening was seriously ill in the hospital, and the late Mr. and Mrs. Henry Gowing (also in trouble one way or another), Mrs. Sagendorph and I were at this time, the oldest living members. Time (in this case 34 years) is short. It seemed just yesterday that we had joined. The password, then, as in 1967, had been "Determined." It hadn't really mattered. In all of the years of our membership there had never been a meeting which we had attended when either of us had remembered the password.

Cast upcountry from New York by the depression of 1929, I joined the Grange in 1933. I enjoyed talking with the farmers who belonged—Burpee, Gowing, Fiske, Carey, and many others. I admired them, their wives and their way of life.

To these people, a herd of cows, flocks of chickens, teams of horses, clearing stumps, rebuilding walls, haying, planting, plowing, harrowing, slaughtering, were not problems. To me, a city man gone native, they were. I well remember, for example, how I had to milk a balking old red cow outside its stanchion because she refused to go into the stall. Hiram Carey told me at a Grange Meeting to ride her in and if she wouldn't go steer her by her tail from astride the back. At another, Lewis Burpee straightened me out on when

The author and the late
Henry Gowing discuss
the weather

to hatch chicken eggs. "Do it so they hatch on the day
of the Vernal Equinox in March because that's when
the African wild hen—from whom all chickens are
descended—does." I did and my chicks were twice as
healthy and grew twice as fast as those hatched on any
other day.

Slaughtering was something else again. It delighted my
two young daughters when the time came to have our
own bacon, sausage and hams readied for our winter
food supply. Not me. I just stood around and let Joe
Hammond do it—for half the pig. Pigs, by the way, I
found I could raise at a profit. I worked for that
profit though.

No Grange member was ever able to tell me how to
keep them in. For two of them to break out on the day
of the Women's Club meeting at milady's house was as
certain as death or taxes. To get them off the porch
and away from the tea tables was to drive them back
to the barn. Fine, if they had chosen to go in the barn,
which they did not. Instead, it was most of the afternoon driving them in one direction or the other until

at long last pure and utter exhaustion for all concerned brought an end to the running, shouting, beating, and road blocks. At that point, the pigs just went back in as if nothing had ever happened.

Afraid of a cow? Not me, when on its back. But yes, when instead of getting out of my corn it became belligerent and chased me out of it. What I was afraid to do, my daughters did with brooms and the flourishes of pig tails. When they showed up, the cows turned their horns meekly and ran.

From my Grange friends I also learned many a fine art! How to control potato bugs—and how to store vegetables for the winter. My wife learned how to can our surpluses—and lots else.

Today, were I to begin all over again as a city boy who wants to learn to farm, I would not know to whom I could turn.

• • •

Every almanac editor, past or present, has taken great pride in "being right," whether it be about farming, phases of the moon or whatever. In looking over the old editions I have found many slips, perhaps unnoticed by any reader but corrected the following year. With The Old Farmer's up to 1969, I had many a letter questioning our source for this or that date or quotation. Usually I came off fairly well with the retort "What source could there possibly be other than the files of the Almanac itself?"

However, on March 7, 1951 there came the entry apparently penned by myself "Boonville Fiasco 1794." Upon publication the President of the Boonville, N.Y. Historical Society wrote asking "On what authority?" In 1794 there was no Boonville, N.Y.! Ahem, I would look it up and let him know. Seventeen years later on November 19, 1968, to be exact, I was seated beside Walter Edmonds, the noted author of *Drums along the Mohawk,* at a luncheon in Cambridge, Massachusetts. Walter mentioned that he lived in Boonville. I told him about my 1951 entry. He explained that the fiasco was just that—indeed a great tragedy but it had happened at Bonnville, N.Y., and not Boonville! The fiasco, incidentally, was an attempt on the part of Mr. Bonn to manufacture maple syrup on a large scale by running the sap to the sugar house from the trees by means of troughs. The troughs leaked and the whole venture failed. Just think of having to wait all those years before I could tell that Historical Society President to change one "o" into an "n" and the entry would be correct. Alas, he had passed on before I could do this.

Editing and publishing America's oldest existing periodical, however, is a responsibility about which I feel strongly—even unto getting my O's and N's correct. I must say, too, that this burden of responsibility does not go unrewarded.

In restoring The Old Farmer's Almanac to its original stature (sales are now near two million copies a year) I have realized profits far larger than my original investment. In fact, for many years it was the almanac alone which kept Yankee, Inc. out of the red.

However, there are no foreseeable profits in the other two almanacs which have recently come under my wing. One of these is The Maine Farmers' Almanac, published in Augusta, Maine, with a continuous record from 1815. In 1967, the owners of that publication decided to get out of both the printing and the publishing business. I went to Augusta to interview them. They were happy to have us carry it on, as a separate publication, which we are now doing. The profit therein lies chiefly in keeping up for Maine one of Maine's grand old traditions.

The same thing happened when we acquired the Daboll Almanac in 1968. (This was one which had been in continous publication some said, from 1775—others said only from 1793. There was a Volume Number One in 1775. However, those thereafter; until 1793, seem to have been edited by other than Daboll—and under a different title.)

I incorporated the 1969 Daboll Almanac into the 1969 Old Farmer's Almanac. This historic move (from an almanac buff's point of view, at any rate) seemed to go generally unnoticed by our millions of readers across the country. I did, however, receive one letter from Miss Mary Daboll of Rhode Island, dated November 10, 1968. It read as follows:

Dear Sir: -

The inclusion of excerpts from the Daboll Almanac in the OFA for 1969 is of great interest to me. You are joining in print what my father and my mother combined in marriage 75 years ago. His great great grandfather was the grandfather of the Nathan Daboll who founded that almanac. Her great great grandfather was the grandfather of the Hannah Beaman who married Robert Bailey Thomas. Far-fetched and collateral, you say? Granted, but my sisters and I may be unique in having a "connection" with the founders of both almanacs. Though we knew of its existence it was only in 1965 that we actually obtained a copy of the Daboll Almanac.

Life holds more meaning for me somehow when the past, as it does in Miss Daboll's letter, ties into the present. When this happens, one gains the assurance the present will tie into the future. Without this hope, preservation would hardly be worthwhile.

Any future for American almanacs relates, almost exactly in my opinion, as to how well those who publish these accomplish this. It can be done, if there are those who have the will and energy to do it.

Robb Sagendorph

Photo by Ingeborg Tallerek

Bibliography

Nichols, Charles L., Notes on the Almanacs of Massachusetts, *Proceedings of American Antiquarian Society,* April 10, 1912.

Littlefield, George Emery, "Notes on the Calendar and the Almanac," *Proceedings of the American Antiquarian Society,* Vol. 24, April 8, 1914, Oct. 21, 1914. Worcester, Mass. Pub. by the Society.

Appleton's Boston Almanac.

Rhode Island Almanac, 1855.

Spofford, A. R., "A Brief History of Almanacs," 1878.

Tyler, Moses Coit, History of American Literature, Vol. 2, p. 122.

S. Briggs, Western Reserve Historical Society, 1881.

Buckingham, Joseph T., Personal Memoirs, Boston, 1852.

Stickney, Matthew A., Almanacs and Their Authors, Essex Institute Historical Collections, Vol. XIV, Salem, 1878.

New England Almanac, 1850.

Brigham, Clarence S., An Account of American Almanacs and Their Value for Historical Study, Reprinted from the Proceedings of the American Antiquarian Society, for Oct. 1925, Worcester, Mass. Pub. by the Society 1925.

Perry, Amos, "Some New England Almanacs with special mention of the Almanacs of Rhode Island," Reprint from the Narragansett Historical Register, July 1895, Providence, 1885.

Tourtellot, Arthur B., "The Charles," American Rivers Series, Farrar and Rinehart, 1941.

Greenough, Chester Noyes, New England Almanac 1766–1775 and the American Revolution, American Antiquarian Society, Worcester, 1936.

Briggs, Sam, "The Origin and Development of the Almanack," a paper read before the Western Reserve and Northern Ohio Historical Society, Jan. 12, 1887.

Barry, J. S., "Old Almanacs," Atlantic Monthly, 1872.

Kittredge, George Lyman, "The Old Farmer and His Almanac, Being Some Observations on Life and Manners in New England a Hundred Years Ago," Suggested by Reading the Earlier Numbers of Mr. Robert B. Thomas's Farmer's Almanac, Wm. Ware & Co., Boston, 1904.

American Farmer's Almanac 1836–1859.

Clark, J. C. L., "The Famous Dr. Stearns," American Antiquarian Society, Worcester, Mass.

Edelstein, David, "Joel Munsell," Columbia University Press, New York.

Fisher, Samuel H., "Thomas Collins," Historical Society, Litchfield, Conn.

Hixson, Richard, "Isaac Collins," Rutgers University Press, New Brunswick, New Jersey.

Leavitt's, "Farmer's Almanac," 1896.

Wroth, L. C., "The Colonial Printer," University of Virginia Press, Charlottesville, Virginia.

Flanders, Louis W., "Simeon Ide," Rutland, Vermont.

Perrin, Porter G., "Thomas Green Fessenden," University Press, Orono, Maine.

(other books are also noted in the text)

Sources

New York Public Library, New York, N.Y.

New Hampshire Historical Society, Concord, N.H.

Library of Congress, Washington, D.C.

American Antiquarian Society, Worcester, Mass.

The Boston Athenaeum, Boston, Mass.

New York State Historical Society, Cooperstown, N.Y.

Sinclair Hamilton Collection, Princeton, N.J.

Public Library, Exeter, N.H.

Albany Public Library, Albany, N.Y.

Boston Public Library, Boston, Mass.

Essex Institute, Salem, Mass.

The Morristown Library, Morristown, N.J.

The Free Library of Philadelphia (Rare Book Dept.), Philadelphia, Pa.

Louisville Free Public Library, Louisville, Ky.

St. Louis Public Library, St. Louis, Mo.

The Chicago Public Library, Chicago, Ill.

The Houghton Library, Cambridge, Mass.

The Library of Harvard University, Cambridge, Mass.

Public Library, Newark, N.J.

The Library, Rutgers University, New Brunswick, N.J.

New Orleans Public Library, New Orleans, La.

Massachusetts Historical Society, Boston, Mass.

The Public Library of Cincinnati and Hamilton County, Cincinnati, Ohio

University of Pennsylvania Library, Philadelphia, Pa.

Providence Public Library, Providence, R.I.

Yale University Library, New Haven, Conn.

The Lincoln Library, Springfield, Ill.

Henry E. Huntington Library & Art Gallery, San Marino, Calif.

The City Library Association, Springfield, Mass.

The Franklin Institute, Philadelphia, Pa.

Rosenbach Foundation, Philadelphia, Pa.

Library Company of Philadelphia, Philadelphia, Pa.

The Historical Society of Pennsylvania, Philadelphia, Pa.

Reader's Guide

As an Index to this book would consist mostly in the word "Almanac" followed by indented Almanac titles, I have substituted this Reader's Guide. This will give you a general idea of where to look for any particular subject or item.

CHAPTER I
CALENDAR OF THE HEAVENS
Pages 10–27

What is an almanac? • Ancient origin • The first almanac ever printed • Books of Hours • Sources used by almanac makers • Why a history of American almanacs • The unchanging formats — examples • Early almanac distribution, bookstores, advertisings • Imitating • Geographical boundaries of almanac editing

CHAPTER II
THE EARLY YEARS
Pages 30–67

Great Storm of 1635 • Regiomantus • First Printing Press in New England • The Pierce Almanack, first in America • Samuel Danforth Almanack • The Philomath almanacks • Telling time by almanacks • Earliest examples of secular and elegiac verse • Boston Almanacks by John Foster, Boston's first printer • America's earliest known wood

engraver • Samuel Sewall, Printer • Witchcraft • Benjamin
Harris, first of a new breed of almanac makers • John Tully,
originator of the American "farmer's almanac," as we know it
• First almanac weather forecasts • The Man of Signs
• First weather saws • Samuel Clough and his *The New
England Almanack* • Events of the times • Lesser almanac
makers of the early 18th century • Nathanael Ames, first to
establish an almanac as "a household necessity alongside the
Bible" • Learning about the 18th century through Dr. Ames
• Format of early almanacs • Ames' sources, proverbs, maxims
and poetry • Nathanael Ames, Jr. and samples of his writing

CHAPTER III
BENJAMIN FRANKLIN AND POOR RICHARD
Pages 68–87

The Franklin brothers shake the rope • Franklin's humor
• Franklin's background and sources • Franklin in England
• Jonathan Swift vs. John Partridge • Franklin's first
almanac and his prediction of the death of Titan Leeds
• Passage from Franklin's *Autobiography* • The famous proverbs of Franklin • *Poor Richard's,* "the great comic almanac
of the country" • Reflections on these early almanac makers

CHAPTER IV
THE REVOLUTION AND BEYOND
Pages 88–117

Almanac editors as recorders of history • Samuel Stearns
• Stearns' account of the battle of Lexington • Isaiah Thomas
• "Sheet Almanacs" • Isaiah Thomas' association with David
Carlisle • Nathanael Low and his *An Astronomical Diary:
Or Almanac* • Roger Sherman • *Johnson's Pennsylvania and
New Jersey Almanac* • The first genuine New York almanac
• *Hutchins Improved* and John Nathan Hutchins • Book-
seller Hugh Gaine • David Rittenhouse • Nathan Daboll
and *The Connecticut Almanac* • Benjamin West, alias Isaac
Bickerstaff • Abraham Weatherwise

CHAPTER V

THE "FARMER'S ALMANAC"

Pages 118–147

"Farmer's almanacs" as a category • *The Farmer's Almanac* by Robert B. Thomas • Other "farmer's almanac" editors • Robt. Thomas' July, 1816, forecast • Lunar superstitions • Scientific material used • Household hints • Old cures • Religion and Morality • Rules of long life • Recipes for the ladies • Farm machinery • Samples of the popular "Farm Calendar" essays

CHAPTER VI

HOW GOOD WERE THEIR FORECASTS?

Pages 150–173

Secret Formulas • Planets and the Weather • *Vennor's Weather Almanac,* first almanac devoted exclusively to weather • Weather "theories" • Godfrey's "Philosophy of Storms" • Checking the old records • The Almanac editors who ceased weather forecasting — and the consequences • First "Scientific System" devised for forecasting • Forecasts of things other than weather • The author's personal reflections on his own weathercasting • How good are *The Old Farmer's Almanac* predictions? • Changing climate • Effect of the H-bomb • Opinion of Albert Einstein relative to the bomb

CHAPTER VII

"ESSAYISTS ON WOOD"

Pages 174–197

Some exceptions to the pictorially barren almanacs of the 1600s and 1700s • Alexander Anderson, America's first professional wood engraver • Thomas Bewick, who influenced all early American engravers • How woodcuts were made • Samples

of Bewick's and Anderson's work • Anderson's pupils and
followers — such as Lansing, Hall, Purcell, Matteson, his
daughter Ann, Mason, Nathaniel Dearborn and others • Abel
Bowen and his followers • The small calendar head illustration • Illustrated accounts of historical events — such as "The
Melancholy Fate of Madame Blanchard," July 6, 1819

CHAPTER VIII
QUIPS AND QUOTES ON WRY
Pages 198–233

Historical or every-day events as described in early almanacs
("A Description of a Tavern," "Alarm Signals during the
Revolution," "List of Tax Evaluations," etc.) • Early industry
("How to Make Maple Sugar," "How to Make Cider")
• Samples of almanac humor, anecdotes, cures, puzzles, poetry

CHAPTER IX
ONE FOR EVERY PURPOSE
Pages 236–253

Anti-slavery and *The Liberty Almanac* • *The Whig Almanac*
• *The Harrison Almanac* • *The Davy Crockett Almanacs*
• *Temperance Almanac* and demon rum • *The New England
Anti-Masonic Almanac* • *The Rhode Island Almanack* and
the Peace Societies • The American Tract Society and *The
Christian Almanac* • *The Congregational Almanac* • Clarke's
Confederate *Household Almanac* • *Veterans of the Civil War
Almanac* • *Bradley's Farmer's Reference Book and Almanac*
• *The New York Almanac* • The Giveaways • *The Ameri-
can Comic Almanac* • Sailor's instruction in dancing • Josh
Billings' *Farmer's Allminax* • *Nast's Almanac* and "Mary's
Funny 'Little Lamb' " • The farmer's almanac editors see the
handwriting on the wall

CHAPTER X
"Sarsaparilla Will Cure Anything"
Pages 254–269

Health almanacs and their adverse influence on the almanac industry in America • *The Physician's Almanac* • *The Health Almanac* • Nathanael Low's amusing parody • Dr. D. Jayne's *Medical Almanac and Guide to Health for the Gratuitous* • *Bristol's Free Almanac* — conscience discarded for profit • Phony and outlandish testimonials • The low point in American advertising • Dr. J. C. Ayer's *American Almanac* and examples therefrom

CHAPTER XI
I Collect Old Almanacs
Pages 272–291

My favorite "finds" • Incident at the White House "Rose Garden" • $50,000 edition in my hands • Visit to the American Antiquarian Society • Value of old almanacs (a substantial listing) • Discussion of the value of old almanacs

CHAPTER XII
It Wasn't All That Easy
Pages 292–309

I purchase *The Old Farmer's Almanac* • Taking it back to the old style • The U.S. Army bans publication of the *Almanac* • Needed: one astronomer • Distribution in my early years • Two mistakes make *Yankee* a success • Printing problems • Angelo J. Simonetta and Arpiar Saunders • An almanac editor should know about farming — so I try it • The Dublin Grange • Mistakes • Financial rewards • The *Maine Farmer's Almanac* • The *Daboll Almanac* • Preserving for the future